Fat Fashion

D1592353

Fat Fashion

The Thin Ideal and the Segregation of
Plus-Size Bodies

Paolo Volonté

BLOOMSBURY VISUAL ARTS
LONDON • NEW YORK • OXFORD • NEW DELHI • SYDNEY

BLOOMSBURY VISUAL ARTS
Bloomsbury Publishing Plc
50 Bedford Square, London, WC1B 3DP, UK
1385 Broadway, New York, NY 10018, USA
29 Earlsfort Terrace, Dublin 2, Ireland

BLOOMSBURY, BLOOMSBURY VISUAL ARTS and the Diana logo are trademarks of
Bloomsbury Publishing Plc

First published in Great Britain 2022

Copyright © Paolo Volonté, 2022

Paolo Volonté has asserted his right under the Copyright, Designs and Patents Act, 1988, to
be identified as Author of this work.

All rights reserved. No part of this publication may be reproduced or transmitted in any
form or by any means, electronic or mechanical, including photocopying, recording, or
any information storage or retrieval system, without prior permission in writing from the
publishers.

Bloomsbury Publishing Plc does not have any control over, or responsibility for, any third-
party websites referred to or in this book. All internet addresses given in this book were
correct at the time of going to press. The author and publisher regret any inconvenience
caused if addresses have changed or sites have ceased to exist, but can accept no
responsibility for any such changes.

A catalogue record for this book is available from the British Library.

A catalog record for this book is available from the Library of Congress.

ISBN: HB: 978-1-3501-2692-3
PB: 978-1-3501-2693-0
ePDF: 978-1-3501-2695-4
eBook: 978-1-3501-2691-6

Typeset by Deanta Global Publishing Services, Chennai, India
Printed and bound in Great Britain

To find out more about our authors and books visit www.bloomsbury.com and sign up for
our newsletters.

Contents

Illustrations

Figures

Tables

Preface

I started dealing with fat fashion almost by accident, on the suggestion of a colleague at the Politecnico di Milano. Initially, it seemed to be just one of the many facets of fashion worth investigating. Very soon, however, I realized that this particular subject evinces a series of key features of Western fashion that are otherwise not easy to discern, and constitutes a new and exciting way into the field. Naturally, my enthusiasm got the better of me and I began to address the topic in my university courses. Perhaps I became too fond of it, as my students, who are mostly women, were convinced that I must have a very, very fat wife—as they would later confess to me. Their admission shows why the issue of fat fashion deserves investigation. If you are interested in such a topic, apparently something strange must have happened in your life, such as the *inconvenience* of having a fat wife. The topic in itself would not deserve attention, because fashion, in itself, should not be fat. If you care, it is because you must have some personal reason to do so.

Paradoxically, something that does not exist—fat fashion—brings out with particular clarity what fashion actually is. It does not simply emphasize that Western fashion is now intrinsically thin. We already knew that. It highlights less visible aspects, those that disappear against the background of cultural habits, just as certain stains blend into the pattern of a used tablecloth: discourses which are legitimized by fashion and guide the thoughts, sayings, and preconceptions of those who make or follow fashion; practices, which people perform because fashion itself performs those practices through them; constraints that fashion has undergone by incorporating them into manufacturing technologies; the politics of distinction that the fashion system enacts toward the "other" who does not conform. In short, that which is more distant from the creativity of designers and the business of brands, but which is the only framework within which creativity and business can unfold.

Discourses and practices, technologies, and policies are social phenomena that dominate the choices, actions, and wills of the individual, and derive from the social life of a community of individuals. Humans are strange. They do not always do what they want. They do not always pursue their true interests. It is as if dark forces were acting within them, forcing them to behave in certain ways. I mean psychological and psychoanalytic forces, of course, but also social mechanisms. I deal with the latter in this book. For example, there is no reason for the apparently obvious assumption underlying my students' confession—that one must be thin to be beautiful—to be entertained, except the fact that it is shared by a community. Yet, it has the power to constrain our thoughts and behaviors, a power deriving precisely from the fact that we believe it to be obvious, unquestionable. Slim people think it is so, fat people do too. Lazy thinking.

While I was researching and writing this book, I repeatedly wondered if its time had already passed. Indeed, what makes the news today, unlike twenty years ago, is no longer anorexic models but curvy models parading in the main fashion weeks. However, I am convinced that the social phenomena that should spark the sociologist's interest are not those that make the news and are there for all to see, which are easily accessible to the layman and make sociology appear to be the science of the obvious, as it is sometimes considered. The most interesting social phenomena are those hidden in the folds of everyday obviousness and, therefore, invisible to the uncritical eye. It is not what makes the headlines, but the fact that it makes the headlines, that is interesting. Thus, the frequent reports of curvy models or testimonials treading the catwalk or being photographed in a fashion editorial are relevant because, while they signal the inception of a new trend regarding the female body ideal cultivated by fashion, they also make it clear that the thin ideal is still dominant and what should be considered normal—the presence of fat female bodies in the space of fashion—continues to appear strange. The issue of nonexistent fat fashion has undergone various transformations over the last 100 years or so, but it has never ceased to be a fundamental aspect of Western fashion, and continues to be so in the current cultural landscape. Dealing with this issue is valuable not just for the history of fashion, but also for current social life.

This book is only marginally based on independent empirical research. My aim has rather been to bring a degree of order to the literature on the subject and develop a theoretical framework that might account for this phenomenon. The existing literature on the subject is vast, sprawling, sometimes unreliable, and split between highly theoretical sociological and philosophical interpretative approaches and highly specific quantitative empirical research in the fields of psychology, marketing, and business. The few exceptions that have been capable of linking both approaches are represented by a number of ethnographies produced by fashion studies in the last two decades. Building on these materials as a whole, I have tried to encompass within a single theoretical framework the main features of this phenomenon considered both from the proactive side, which implies acceptance of a thin body ideal, and from the negative side, which involves the segregation of fat bodies. I hope that this interpretative framework can serve as a starting point for renewed empirical investigations of the phenomenon in the future.

This book is an original work, not a collection of previously published contributions. However, since fat fashion is a subject I have been dealing with for some years, I have had the occasion to address it in various publications over time. It goes without saying that some of the considerations set out in this book have already been addressed by previous publications, from which I have occasionally borrowed some passages. Nevertheless, none of those contributions has been used as a substantial part of any chapter of the book. I have rather aimed at giving an order to considerations that were distributed in publications that sometimes are not easily available. Three of these publications examine the topics dealt with in this book at greater length and in greater detail:

1. "The thin ideal and the practice of fashion," *Journal of Consumer Culture*, 19 (2), 2019: 252–70.
2. "Modelling practice: The inertia of body ideals in the fashion system," *Sociologica*, 13 (3), 2019: 11–26.
3. "Segregation of the plus size in contemporary Italian fashion," in A. Mascio, R. Menarini, S. Segre Reinach and I. Tolic (eds.), *The Size Effect*, 109–20, Sesto San Giovanni: Mimesis International, 2019.

I owe a debt of gratitude to many people for helping and supporting me during the book writing process. Laura Bovone, Emanuela Mora, and Marco Pedroni have read and commented on various chapters. Their comments were fundamental for me in identifying and addressing errors and inaccuracies. I have received encouragement, suggestions, and food for thought from many other colleagues that have been fundamental for the development of my work at various stages along the way. Some may not be even aware of this. I would like to thank in particular Marita Canina, Chiara Colombi, Joanne Entwistle, Melanie Haller, Sanda Miller, Lauren Downing Peters, Agnès Rocamora, and Raffaella Trocchianesi. Finally, special thanks go to Ludovica Casali, Mauro Davico, Angelo Sabbioni, and Martino Volonté for the material help they gave me throughout the various phases of the work.

Size Conversion Table

Since this book addresses the issue of clothes and body sizes, it necessarily refers to size measurements. Clothing sizes are the simplest measuring parameter we have to put clothing and the body in relation and to compare clothes-body complexes with each other. As I shall explain in Chapter 5, there is no universal sizing system, and even national systems are followed with great freedom by manufacturers and retailers. However, it is not possible to do without sizes. The following table, which compares sizing systems commonly used in countries with a high concentration of fashion companies, is derived from a series of tables available on e-commerce platforms and major fashion brands' websites. Since the body measurements underlying each size in the various national systems are not homogeneous, the equivalence established by such tables is very approximate, and can sometimes differ between one table and another. Accordingly, this summary table is purely indicative.

US	0	2	4	6	8	10	12	14	16
UK (= US + 4)	4	6	8	10	12	14	16	18	20
Japan (= US + 5)	5	7	9	11	13	15	17	19	21
France (= US + 32)	32	34	36	38	40	42	44	46	48
Italy (= US + 36)	36	38	40	42	44	46	48	50	52

The Paradox of Nonexistent Fat Fashion

An Introduction to the Topic and the Book

"Fat fashion" is not just a metaphor, it is an oxymoron. An oxymoron is a figure of speech in which two words that have (or seem to have) contradictory meanings are used together. Fat and fashion have apparently contradictory meanings: if something (such as a body, a garment) is fat, it is not fashionable. And what the fashion system considers fashionable is not fat. Of course, there have been several episodes that have combined fatness with fashion recently. New York has been hosting the Full Figured Fashion Week for twelve years. The Italian company Miroglio markets the plus-size brand Elena Mirò, which showed at Milan Fashion Week from 2005 to 2012 and featured in mainstream magazines like *Elle UK* (see Figure 1). Several top modeling agencies have a plus division, and a few model agencies, such as Bridge in London and Curve Model Management in Hamburg, have specialized in plus-size models. Overweight influencers such as Leah Vernon, to whom *Vogue Italia* dedicated an entire page of the "Beauty" section in its June 2019 issue, have gained great popularity on social media. Several similar episodes could be mentioned. However, even though many of them exist (and, truth be told, there are not so many), they do not challenge but rather confirm that a fundamental characteristic of fashion is that it concerns lean bodies. As long as plus-size clothing is sealed off into containers that are separate from regular fashion, such as the Full Figured Fashion Week, its marginal position within the fashion system is consolidated rather than called into question.

Yet, there is nothing in fatness that is inherently unfashionable, just as nothing in fashion is thin by nature. One might naively think that fat bodies are not fashionable because they are "ugly," but this would require us to overlook the fact that beauty and ugliness are themselves a product of fashion and other cultural constraints. Fat bodies are not unfashionable because they are ugly; rather, they are perceived as ugly because fashionable bodies are thin.

Figure 1 Elena Mirò advertisement, *Elle UK* 2008. Courtesy of Miroglio Fashion.

To be sure, fat fashion is nonexistent. The question that needs asking is why it does not exist, since there is nothing that inherently prevents it from existing. As this book will show in detail, fat bodies are marginalized by the fashion system and plus-size clothing is mostly unfashionable. This has been an enduring condition for many decades now, and a key issue to investigate is what has made it so stable and resistant to change. In recent years, there have been some signs that things are changing. For example, a growing number of plus-size models parade during the main world fashion weeks or appear in the advertisements of major brands published in mainstream magazines. However, they remain isolated or marginal cases within a fashion system that continues to be strongly geared toward the ideal of thinness. In Chapter 7, I shall explain why I feel pessimistic about the real meaning of these signs.

To begin with, we must adequately formulate the question this book seeks to answer. To do so, we need to frame some basic concepts regarding fashion, the body, beauty, fatness, and thinness, and read the topic of fat fashion in the context of the discussion that scholars have long devoted to the tyranny of slenderness. Accordingly, this chapter is intended as a sort of introduction to the topic. I will outline the research question, provide some introductory information, and circumscribe the scope of my argument. In the following chapters, I will return to most of what is anticipated here and discuss it in more detail.

Fashion and the Body

All too often, scholarly works addressing fashion focus on clothing: garments and accessories. This, however, is the effect of an error of perspective caused by the fact that without garments and accessories fashion would not exist. However, fashion is much more than mere garments and accessories. It is, first and foremost, a *practice* that employs garments and accessories. A practice that bestows certain meanings on clothing, places it in a specific context, thereby making it "act" and produce effects (Breward 2004: 11). In short: it makes clothing *live*. In other words, in fashion, the use of objects is always framed by behavior, a situation, social relations, and, especially, a body to which those objects relate. Fashion is all of this, and clothing becomes an empty, lifeless shell if it is detached from a body that wears it and from a situation in which it is worn.

At the same time, it is almost impossible not to discuss clothing when dealing with fashion. Indeed, clothing is the topic of this book. Yet, I will attempt to avoid the "materialist" thinking trap described above and instead concentrate on lived fashion, that is, fashion as a form of social action that uses clothing to manage interactions. Fashion is an instance of social action in that it is a kind of behavior that adapts to other people's expected behavior.[1] More specifically, it is a kind of behavior which, in order to adapt to the expected behavior of other people, uses the technical tool of clothing (garments, accessories, even body modifications). People choose to wear certain styles or items of clothing (e.g., a suit and tie) because they expect a certain kind of reaction from others (e.g., respect).

Furthermore, fashion is a social action that is often (but not necessarily) modeled on a particular *form* of social action, which we also equivocally call "fashion," although it does not apply exclusively to clothing. It consists of acting according to a temporary social norm. I dress like this because I know that others expect me to dress this way, even though I already know that others' expectations will soon change, and my clothing style will also change accordingly.

Fashion, therefore, is not just about clothes. The point I am making here goes a little further than the idea—which first emerged in the context of costume history toward the end of the last century—that clothing artifacts must always be analyzed in relation to the sociohistorical context in which they appeared.[2] Such a perspective, in fact, essentially regards clothing as an expression or evidence of the social and cultural context in which it was created, produced, and used. The garment is still seen as an artifact, an inert thing, and not the extension of a living body, an inseparable part of the clothes-body complex. Despite its importance for fashion history, the concept is still bound to a materialistic conception of clothing, as it continues to consider clothing something separate and *added* to the body according to its needs, and not a constituent part of the human body as a "socially exposed" body. By contrast, a considerable portion of the subsequent literature, starting in particular with the seminal work of Joanne Entwistle ([2000] 2015), has recognized that the human body is essentially dressed and that its presence in the social context cannot be understood without referring to clothing (see, e.g., Haller 2015 and Hansen 2004). I concur. As socially exposed human bodies are normally dressed, the function of clothing cannot be understood in isolation from the behavior of the body that wears it. Fashion is a matter of the human body that acts.

At the same time, fashion is of course a feature of industrial capitalism: mass production, the communication society, and consumerism. Although the meaning of the term "fashion" has already been discussed countless times, I feel that a clarification is needed here to explain what kind of fashion is addressed in this book, and particularly why I am focusing especially on the Western fashion system. In the field of fashion studies, a thirty-year-old debate has developed around the relationship between fashion and Western modernity. I think this debate is based on a fundamental misunderstanding.

The debate initially took shape when Jennifer Craik, taking issue with certain "classic" texts on the sociology of fashion,[3] spoke of the need to reject "the assumption that fashion is unique to the culture of capitalism" (Craik 1993: 3). Craik challenged the simplistic idea that contrasts fashion, which is changeable and meaningful, with traditional costume, commonly considered static and merely functional. Indeed, transformation and innovation are not absent from non-Western local clothing. Yet Craik did not dispute the specific nature of Western fashion, that is, of what has been called the "fashion system" (Kawamura 2005; Leopold 1992). She did not deny that the fashion system has introduced a new, disruptive element, namely the logic of capitalism and consumer culture, into the processes of creating and circulating clothing. However, many protagonists of the ensuing debate took her thesis to mean that the specific nature of Western fashion should no longer be acknowledged, leading to a tendency for fashion phenomena to be considered in exactly the same way wherever they arise. While this movement has been useful in terms of the history of ideas, since it has helped to legitimize interest in non-Western fashion, it has also hindered our understanding of the peculiarity of the Western fashion system. This complex, global system of clothing innovation, which takes in manufacturing companies, designers, fashion weeks, store chains, mass marketing, and specialized media, is a strictly Western phenomenon, originating in Europe in the modern era and based on the industrialization of clothing manufacture. This is not to deny that multiple modernities exist (Eisenstadt 2000). However, we must acknowledge that today's global fashion system has its roots in modern European society, subsequently extending its influence over large portions of the globe on the back of industrial capitalism, as well as Western colonial and post-colonial political power, and well-understood dynamics of cultural imperialism. In its expansion, it continues to be an expression of Western culture, which retains its hold over the creation and control of "pseudo-globalized" fashion, meaning fashion that merely *appears* to be a global phenomenon.

This book does not deal with fashion in general (*à la* Craik), but rather with the fashion *system*, that is the apparatus for creating, manufacturing, retailing, and communicating clothing possibilities, whose headquarters are in the traditional fashion capitals (Paris, London, Milan, and New York), whose concepts are deeply rooted in Western culture, and whose tentacles extend around the globe (Emberly 1987). I have, therefore, decided to restrict my discussion to Western fashion. This choice, besides having the additional advantage of not taking me on a journey into uncharted territory, is based on substantive reasons that I will discuss at the end of this chapter. The nonexistence of fat fashion, the marginalization of fat bodies, the tyranny of slenderness, and all of the key issues that I will discuss throughout, have their origin in the fashion system and are nourished by Western culture. It is the fashion industry that exported them to the rest of the world. As we shall see, the thin ideal that rules the fashion system today did not arise in Africa, South America, or Asia, but in Europe and North America at the beginning of the twentieth century. From there, it went on to contaminate former socialist Central and Eastern European countries (Rathner 2001), Arab countries (Khaled et al. 2018), and almost every other local culture exposed to the fashion system.

Clearly, the limitation of this approach is that I will not be able to talk about the *reception* and *effects* of the marginalization of fat fashion in non-Western countries. Although I am analyzing fat fashion as an overarching feature of the (pseudo-)globalized fashion system, that is, a characteristic relevant for

Western and non-Western clothing cultures, I am not qualified to consider the unpredictable effects produced by the thin ideal—and the marginalization of fat bodies—when it meets non-Western cultures that did not engender it. This is a vast topic, both from the sociological and costume history perspectives. Yet, it is one that I shall leave for others to discuss.

Size and Look

To return to my starting point—namely, fashion as a practice that employs garments and accessories to manage interaction—if we see fashion as a social practice, the body is immediately implicated. The body, in fact, is a fundamental tool of social interaction. Indeed, it is the only tool that is always necessary for human communication.[4] If we acknowledge that fashion is a social practice, we need to recognize clothing as essentially tied to a particular body and situation. A Chanel evening dress is an abstraction; it does not exist by itself in a vacuum. What actually exists is the Chanel evening dress worn by the model in the advertisement in *Vogue*, or by the actress on the red carpet. Or, perhaps, it exists as the Chanel evening dress that my wife tries on in the department store dressing room. The model with her body, her face, her hair, and the studio setting. The actress with her body, her face, her hair, and the context of her professional performance. My wife with her body, her face, her hair, and the life context in which she imagines wearing that dress.

To clarify this idea, I shall use the concept of "the look." The individual look, in fact, goes far beyond the mere sum of the garments that a consumer buys, owns, and uses. It refers to our overall appearance as a tool for social interaction. In addition to clothing, it includes make-up, hair care, body shape manipulation (diets, gymnastics, cosmetic surgery), body adornment (tattoos, piercing), and body discipline (posture, movements, mimicry). Furthermore, our look is something that each of us curates every day, rearranging our body in relation to the life situations and practices in which we are involved. Our look is the appearance we care about. As the term itself implies, it is the appearance that everybody "stages" in view of the "look" of others (Goffman 1959). It feeds on the presence of the other and the anticipation of the judgment of the other. A judgment that is not only aesthetic, but existential and relational: who is this person I am meeting? What do you want from me? What can I expect from you? Should I trust you or not? Do I let myself get emotionally involved or hold back?

Compared to the concept of body image, which is widespread in psychology and in the literature on eating disorders,[5] the concept of the look allows us not to neglect the variability of clothing as it depends on the variability of life contexts. The look is, one might say, relational: it originates from the encounter with the other and takes shape through the anticipation that we produce of that encounter. Entwistle and Slater (2012: 17) describe the look of models as "an object of calculation, something continuously worked upon, molded, contested, performed, something that is [...] constantly de- and re-stabilized in new forms." The same is true for ordinary people, that is ourselves, as through the look we can navigate a situation, the day, and, ultimately, life in a direction that we may or may not like. This is what makes caring about appearance so important. Chapter 2 will address in more detail this clothes-body complex and the role it plays in social life.

The look is therefore a multilayered concept arising from the encounter between the body, clothing, situation, and others. Each of these terms refers, in turn, to a multiplicity of elements. Some of them (such as hair, shape, or shoe color) can easily be modified by the subject, while others (such as skin color, the range of products available in stores, and socially recognized status symbols) are more resistant and, consequently, binding. Among all these elements, body size occupies an important place.

Because of its immediate visibility, size is a fundamental determinant of a person's look. Along with height, sex, age, and skin color, it is one of the first things we mention when we describe a stranger. Size belongs to us whether we like it or not. Although it varies seamlessly across ever-changing three-dimensional shapes, Western cultures classify size into three broad categories: fat, thin, or "regular," with the extremes provided by the obese body and the anorexic body. As often happens, classification brings with it descriptive, value, and normative distinctions. It is not without consequences to be considered fat or thin, although the distinction between fatness and thinness is not objective but hierarchical and relative: we are fatter or thinner than others, and there is always someone thinner than us (Wann 2009: xv). *In contemporary Western societies, a widespread value judgment places thinness, when it is not excessive, among the positive, beautiful, desirable attributes, and fatness, even if not excessive, among the negative, ugly, inappropriate attributes.* A great deal of research has stressed this asymmetry of attitude toward body sizes, an asymmetry that is frequently encountered in everyday life experiences (Bordo 1993: 191–8; Goodman 1995). This asymmetry often leads to social discrimination, for example in terms of job opportunities and social mobility (Conley and Glauber 2007; Fredrickson and Roberts 1997: 178). It is not just employers who practice weight discrimination; research has shown that educators, health personnel, and even family members are not immune (Puhl et al. 2008). In short, being overweight or obese is a highly stigmatizing condition in Western societies, and may adversely affect vocational and educational opportunities (Cash 1990: 63–4; Cogan 1999: 240; Degher and Hughes 1999: 12). This is especially true for female fat bodies (Kaiser 1997: 135–6). Sometimes the stigma is linked to value judgments of the person, as happens for example in American society, in which, probably due to deep-rooted puritan attitudes (Stearns 1997: 243), fatness is often considered an expression of laziness, excessive indulgence, lack of discipline and self-control (Millman 1980: 98). But very often such attitudes may have intrinsic justifications: fat is wrong, period (Bordo 1993: 55; Gilman 2011; Walden 1985: 335).

Body size is an inescapable element of social interaction. As a bearer of a certain body size, everyone is inevitably embedded in the system of values that each culture attributes to the human body. That value system is a fundamental aspect of the context in which our individual look takes shape. Through our physical body, it affects our appearance and our relationship with fashion.

Beauty is a (Feminine) Myth

We need to broaden the framework. The same variety of attitudes that people show in relation to body size are often displayed in relation to many other body characteristics. In contemporary Western cultures, for example, a toned body is "better" than a flabby one, and a tall body (within certain limits) is "better" than a small one. The body as a whole, and the dressed body in particular (i.e., the look), is not neutral. It is the subject of value judgments (right/wrong, good/bad, beautiful/ugly, etc.) that a community explicitly shares or implicitly shows through shared behavior, and that individuals express about themselves, partly by internalizing social judgments.

As positive value judgments regarding a specific body are unlikely, a gap almost inevitably arises between people's actual bodies and the body ideal to which they aspire. People rarely perceive themselves as perfectly toned, tall enough, truly beautiful. Every time we get a haircut, go on a diet, apply make-up, go to the gym, or get dressed, we are modifying our miserable body, which is poor and inadequate because it is real, to tune it to the ideal body we have in mind. As we work to make our body "acceptable," we inherently confirm the existence and power of a body ideal, since the gap between that ideal and real bodies influences the attitude of individuals toward their own body and other bodies. Furthermore, the body ideal is never a purely individual standard of perfection. As people cultivate ideals, social life often ends up producing shared ideals, that is, cultural standards. The alignment of experiences among people, through the sharing of life experiences and through communication, generates a substantial alignment of the meanings they give to situations, of the values to which they conform, and of the ideals they pursue (Hannerz 1992). The alignment of experiences produces what we call culture. Yet culture is not just the effect of behavior. It also forces people to adjust their behavior to social norms.

More concretely: it is normal for a community to develop a shared body ideal that is an expression of its culture, and that also exerts a normative power over the members of the community and possible newcomers. A number of popular outstanding cases help to grasp this coercive character of body culture: the ideal of the wasp waist in nineteenth-century Europe, of small feet in certain traditional Chinese communities, and the long neck in the Kayan culture (Burma), took hold despite putting people's physical well-being at risk (Figure 2).[6] To put it in more precise terms, in many societies, and particularly in contemporary Western societies, we are not dealing with a single body ideal, but with a multiplicity of ideals that vary according to the social groups and practices that we are considering. For example, there is a body ideal in the world of sport (Brady 2005) which is shared by many sportspeople, and a body ideal in medicine (Shah et al. 2006) which is cultivated by doctors, physiotherapists, pharmaceutical companies, and health enthusiasts. Studies of the body ideal have sometimes overlooked such differences.

Since fat fashion is the subject of this book, I shall focus here on the ideal of body *appearance*, which is different from the body ideals mentioned above and particularly sight- and clothing-oriented. Muscle tone, for example, which is considered desirable in sports, may appear unaesthetic, especially for women, when interacting in daily life situations. It then becomes an aspect that the look aims to conceal (Shilling and Bunsell 2009). The construction of the look in situations of everyday life interaction, during both work and leisure time, usually prioritizes *the value of beauty* over values such as health and physical strength.

Beauty, however, is a highly unstable, precarious value, especially if we focus on the ideal of female beauty, which has its own peculiarities. Although in the last few decades male body ideals have also attracted attention (Karazsia et al. 2017), studies suggest that significant differences between the two sexes in terms

Figure 2 Portrait of a long-necked woman of the Kayan Hill Tribe in Myanmar. Photo by olyniteowl, courtesy of Getty Images.

of body image persist (Voges et al. 2019). Women place more emphasis on the aesthetic values and less emphasis on the functional values of their bodies compared to men; they suffer from more pronounced body dissatisfaction, and are more conscious of how their weight affects their appearance (Ålgars et al. 2009).

Feminist theories have long shown that beauty as a value is inherently temporary. Naomi Wolf, in particular, who has called it the "myth of beauty," considers it "a political weapon against women's advancement" (Wolf 1991: 10). She deems the ideal of female beauty a myth because it establishes a false narrative while being used as a tool to subjugate women in patriarchal societies. The story told by the myth of beauty is based on three implicit assumptions that Wolf considers to be false. The first assumption is that objective beauty exists and human beings only need to learn how to recognize it. Although this assumption is contradicted by centuries of aesthetic theories on the subjectivity of beauty judgments, common sense struggles to be rid of it. Wolf's theory, however, is more subtle: to the extent that it establishes standards in order to place people in a hierarchy, the idea of beauty is a tool of political power, a means of controlling individuals without resorting to violence. Since meeting the ideal of beauty involves labor, commitment, and self-denial, patriarchal society embraces the myth of beauty in order to keep women subjugated. The second assumption underlying the myth of beauty holds that beauty is universal, that is, that the ideal of female beauty remains constant throughout time and space, independently of societal and cultural change. This assumption, too, is contradicted by numerous studies and only persists within a perspective based on common sense. The identification of beauty with thinness and youth, for example, is typical of contemporary Western culture and has no equivalent in many non-Western cultures or in past centuries. I will substantiate this statement below and, more extensively, in Chapter 3. The third assumption is that the adaptation of behavior to the ideal of beauty does not depend on sociocultural factors but originates in nature. Women naturally want to be beautiful, and men naturally want to possess beautiful women; this is written in our genes because it derives from the laws of natural selection (Buss 1989). Wolf (1991: 13) challenges this third assumption by citing examples of matriarchal societies obsessed with the myth of male beauty to show that beauty is not an inherently female quality.

Although beauty is an essential aspect of women's lives in contemporary societies, it is not a natural given. The endless work of adjusting one's physical body to make it more or less acceptable according to the ideal reveals that the myth of beauty is not natural, but naturalizes the bodies of real women by "normalizing them" (Bordo 1993: 25). According to Wykes and Gunter, the continuous "reconstruction" of the body is a fundamental experience of being a woman:

> Women learn to reconstruct themselves. It is second nature to disguise themselves, dress themselves and decorate themselves with a huge range of

materials. Over the past 30 years they have gone further than ever before in this process. They can re-arrange some of the organic material that is their body [...]. As well as fashion and diet there is exercise, rejuvenation, surgical re-modelling and chemical maintenance and it permeates all of our popular culture and much of our purchasing. (Wykes and Gunter 2005: 48)

Women are habituated to constantly adjust their appearance, that is, to becoming "acceptable" with respect to the ideal of femininity and beauty that they have internalized, as it pervades the cultural landscape that surrounds them (see Orbach [1978] 2016: 8–9). However, this ideal is removed from the "naturalness" of the human body, so much so that the women who are "elected" to "represent" it, such as the *Playboy* centerfold models, often have to resort to cosmetic surgery to live up to expectations (Saraceni and Russell-Mayhew 2007). This—it goes without saying—has become increasingly possible with developments in the technological manipulability of the biological body (Shilling [1993] 2012: 40, 222–3).

Ultimately, beauty is a gendered myth. Although nowadays men are confronted with an ideal body that is difficult to achieve and increasingly internalize unattainable body ideals leading to growing body dissatisfaction, recent research demonstrates that appearance norms encountered by women are more rigid and pervasive than those for men (Buote et al. 2011). The beauty myth remains essentially feminine, an imperative that affects women's lives much more deeply and extensively than men's. That is why, for a number of reasons that I will discuss at the end of this chapter, this book focuses on female fashion.

Slenderness Exerts Tyranny

The idea propounded by scholars in the feminist tradition is that the myth of beauty is a tool of social control and a normalizing discipline in societies that are still fundamentally patriarchal. However, I do not wish to address the issue of gender discrimination here. Rather, the point that I want to stress is that *before getting into the topic of fat fashion we must first get rid of the myth of beauty, and learn to see female beauty as a social construct.* We must reject the idea that the thinness of the female body is *objectively* beautiful.

As I have already said, the asymmetrical attitude toward body size is manifested in contemporary Western societies through the identification of female beauty with a lean body. However, although lean beauty is naturalized through its pervasive media representation, this is by no means a natural character of femininity. The idea that a woman must be thin to be beautiful is relatively recent and localized, and will inevitably fade or change in the future. It is contingent in at least three ways.

First of all, the thin ideal is not common to all human cultures. For example, with regard to sexual attractiveness, anthropologists argue that

> as far as general body build is concerned, the majority of societies whose preferences on this matter are recorded feel that a plump woman is more attractive than a slim one. In addition to being plump, the Chukchee, Hidatsa, Pukapukans, and Thonga believe that a beautiful woman should be relatively tall and powerfully built. There are, however, a few people who prefer slim women. The Dobuans, for instance, regard corpulence as disgusting and Tongan women diet to keep slim since they are thought to be particularly unattractive if their abdomens are large. Most of the societies in our sample prefer women who have a broad pelvis and wide hips. (Ford and Beach [1952] 1970: 91)

Comparative historical and anthropological studies make it clear that the body ideal, in particular with regard to size, is not universal but varies widely from culture to culture.[7] This is the result both of the diversity of morphological features and the heterogeneity of cultural factors (Singh 1993: 298). If the thin ideal has also taken root in non-Western societies, it is because the Western body ideal tends to spread elsewhere, for the reasons mentioned above. It is not a universal value, but is steadily expanding as Western culture colonizes other cultures.[8]

Second, even in Western societies, the ideal of thinness is an exception rather than the norm, given that historically speaking it has imposed itself only in the last hundred years.[9] This has been pointed out both by art historians who have analyzed human figures depicted in paintings and sculptures (Clark 1980; Hollander 1993 and 1994) and by eating disorder experts. The latter have shown that "each epoch has had different tolerances for weight and for fatness," and "since the 1880s, those tolerances have grown especially narrow" (Schwartz 1986: 4). Schwartz describes how weight and body size were never reasons for dieting or fasting in previous eras. In both religious and secular contexts, until the end of the nineteenth century, dieting and fasting were not undertaken to combat excess weight but rather excessive indulgence of the pleasures of life and the consequent weakening of the body and spirit (Schwartz 1986: 9–12, 21, 47). Body weight, size, and shape are not normally mentioned in historical documents as matters of concern. Indeed, the opposite view was often held, namely that the absence of fat in the right places was considered an imperfection; this could lead to behavior that favored obesity. Hilde Bruch (1974: 18–19) quotes a Parisian physician of the early twentieth century on prevailing standards of female beauty at that time in the French fashion capital:

> One must mention here that aesthetic errors of a worldly nature to which all women submit, may make them want to stay obese for reasons of fashionable appearance. It is beyond a doubt that in order to have an impressive décolleté each woman feels herself duty bound to be fat around the neck, over the clavicle and in her breasts. Now it happens that fat accumulates with greatest difficulty in these places [. . .]. As to the treatment, one cannot obtain weight reduction of the abdomen without the woman sacrificing in her spirits the upper part of her body. To her it is a true sacrifice because she gives up what the world considers beautiful. (Heckel 1911)

This passage explicitly mentions the binding effect of the gap between the ideal of beauty and the reality of human bodies. However, oddly enough by our standards, coercion did not favor thinness but rather obesity. As Roberta Seid (1989) and Peter Stearns (1997) have amply demonstrated with particular reference to the United States and France, the turning point in the history of Western body standards lies between the end of the nineteenth century and the First World War. In that short period of time, arguments and actions spread at all levels in support of the preferability of lean bodies over fat ones both from a medical (health) and aesthetic (fashion) point of view. The thin ideal has since spread throughout the entire Western world, and has gradually imposed itself on ethnic minorities in recent decades (Bordo 1993: 100–3; Roberts et al. 2006). All of this, however, only confirms its ephemeral character and expansive power.

Third, not only is the current body ideal generically thin if compared to past centuries, but there has also been a gradual slimming of the ideal over the last seventy years, as shown by several empirical studies carried out since the 1980s by analyzing actual representations of the ideal of female beauty, such as models featured in the media (see, e.g., Gagnard 1986). Two of these studies have been highly influential. Silverstein et al. (1986) showed that the female beauty standard featured in magazines and films in the 1980s was thinner than in previous decades. Garner et al. (1980) showed that between 1960 and 1979 both Miss America competitors and *Playboy* centerfold playmates became progressively thinner. Subsequently, Wiseman et al. (1990) extended the period of Garner and colleagues' survey through to 1988, confirming the results. Voracek and Fisher (2002) and Seifert (2005) conducted similar surveys on the center pages of *Playboy*, obtaining similar findings. Morris et al. (1989) found a trend toward smaller average hip and breast measurements and increasing height among English models. Sypeck et al. (2004) examined the influence of the media on women's behavior, describing the gradual reduction in the size of the bodies of models appearing on the covers of American fashion magazines between 1959 and 1999. Of course, this and other research findings do not conclusively demonstrate that there has been a constant and significant reduction in *all* measurements over time. However, this is not the point. Since we are addressing body ideals, the key point is the effect that body representations have on the perception of the observer. For example, an increase in height coupled with a slight reduction in bust and hip size might lead to an increased perception of thinness (Seifert 2005: 273). What emerges from the empirical research data is that the thin ideal has proved stubbornly resistant over time despite the continuous variation of individual body measurements, and grew to an extreme in the second half of the last century.

Nonetheless, it must also be acknowledged that the current predominance of the thin ideal does not imply a complete standardization of the idea of female beauty. Even among Western societies, significant differences have been observed in the importance that different social groups attach to appearance and the strategies they pursue to lose weight (Bourdieu [1979] 1984: 200–8; Polivy et al. 1986; Wooley and Wooley 1982). There are also counter-hegemonic pockets of conscious and unconscious resistance. The most widely investigated are found in Latin-American and African American subcultures in the United States, where thin-internalization[10] remains less pervasive than it is among Caucasian American women (Brantley et al. 2012). An analysis of so-called fatshion blogs corroborates this observation, as Chapter 6 will show. Alongside blogs that conform to the thin ideal, providing advice on how to conceal body fat, and blogs that actively combat the thin ideal, thus taking a consciously counter-hegemonic attitude (which, as such, implicitly recognizes the hegemony of the thin ideal), many predominantly African American bloggers simply present an ideal of beauty which is more compatible with the actual ethnic traits of most social groups. Nevertheless, their subcultural status confirms the dominant position of the thin ideal in contemporary Western societies.

To conclude, over the course of the twentieth and twenty-first centuries the ideal of female beauty has come to conform to a standard that has been called the "tyranny of slenderness" (Chernin 1981) and the "cult of thinness" (Hesse-Biber 1996 and 2007). These expressions, as well as the concept of thin ideal, are catchphrases for a complex phenomenon in which at least four different but interconnected factors converge: the size of the body, that is its dimensions (larger or smaller); how much fat is present (particularly in certain zones); weight; and body shape (which can be understood both as the relationship between the measurements of different parts of the body and as the silhouette as a whole). Clearly, an in-depth historical or aesthetic inquiry should address these different factors in detail and in relation to each other, and the existing literature on the subject has failed to address these aspects, in my view. However, it is enough for our purposes here to consider the thin ideal an "umbrella" term to refer to women's desire to publicly show a slender body without visible accumulations of fat, one which is lightweight and which "qualifies" to wear small sizes. This desire, which can and does vary continually in terms of individual aspects, has been a constant feature of the last hundred years or so, dictating the prevailing behavior of women with respect to their body: diets, cosmetics, physical exercise, surgery, and—the facet on which I will focus—clothing choices.

Fat Stigma

The tyranny of slenderness has manifold causes, which I will discuss below in this chapter and in Chapter 4. More important, however, are the effects it has, two in particular. First of all, it leads to the fat (female) body being considered ugly and undesirable. It is a complementary effect: the thin ideal implies an "anti-ideal," which is associated with fatness, and determines the social stigmatization and consequent dehumanization of fat individuals. The fat body is an affront to our culture. And, as Joanisse and Synnott (1999: 50) observe, in such circumstances "[i]t is the offending body that must be changed; not the culture that is offended by it." As a result, fat individuals suffer both externally from social discrimination and internally from low self-esteem. The tyranny of slenderness engenders a fat-related stigma. Second, the idealization of thinness has also led many women to identify their own bodies as fat, therefore in need of adjustment. In fact, it is not generic thinness to be idealized, but a degree of thinness that corresponds to very low percentiles of the actual population: the tenth percentile, according to US statistics reported by Ritenbaugh (1982). In other words, 90 percent of the female population are induced to perceive their weight to be greater than the dominant body ideal. Moreover, aspiring to a lean body very often results in an effort to reduce, eliminate, or conceal the fatness of one's body. The negative stereotype associated with being overweight acts as a force that determines the choices of men and women in many contemporary Western societies (Ahern et al. 2008: 295).

Efforts by women to achieve self-regulation and self-discipline, that is, to continually modify their body to satisfy the myth of beauty, thus often take the form of a struggle to shed fat. This struggle is mainly based on dieting and, secondarily, on more demanding tools such as physical exercise, liposuction, and invasive forms of aesthetic surgery. Clothing, too, plays a fundamental role in all of this. Appearance, as I have pointed out, is produced by that indivisible entity which is the clothes-body complex. Clothes always gloss over our body, in particular its shape and size. They can compress, like a corset, or expand, like a push-up bra, enhance, like a neckline or conceal, like a wide sleeve. In fact, they are a tool that we habitually use, at times unconsciously, to pursue our body ideal. Which is—in the current sociocultural context—to conceal fat.

A preliminary observation should also be made about the term "fat." In many languages, this word has a negative connotation that is consistent with the tyranny of slenderness and fat-related stigma (Keist 2018: 27; Peters 2014). As a result, people tend to avoid using this term, which is deemed offensive. The media, for instance, rarely talk about fat bodies. They use euphemisms like "overweight," "curvy," "stout," "plump," "plus-size," and so forth. I do not follow this practice here, but in agreement with other scholars (e.g., Harju and Huovinen 2015) I consistently use the bare adjective "fat" instead, stripped of any offensive connotations. These offensive connotations stem from the preconceived idea that accompanies it, according to which being fat means being ugly (and maybe even lazy and stupid). Such an idea *derives* from the tyranny of slenderness and does not cause it. In this regard it is worth quoting what Marilyn Wann says about the term "overweight":

> "Overweight" is inherently anti-fat. It implies an extreme goal: instead of a bell curve distribution of human weights, it calls for a lone, towering, unlikely bar graph with everyone occupying the same (thin) weights. If a word like "overweight" is acceptable and even preferable, then weight prejudice becomes accepted and preferred. (Wann 2009: xii)

In other words, the very existence of the concept "overweight" itself implies that there is a restricted range of legitimate weights with a definite limit that nobody should be allowed to cross. Being fat, that is being outside those limits, is regrettable. The same idea should be extended to all the euphemisms often used to replace the term "fat." Indeed, using euphemisms merely confirms and reinforces the prejudice (Peters 2018a: 20–1). The point in resisting fat-related stigma is not to minimize the health implications of being obese, but to recognize the asymmetry between fat and thin in the value judgments expressed within contemporary Western culture: while thinness is stigmatized only when it is excessive, fat is always undesirable. I have decided to use the unadorned term "fat" because I am interested in investigating the forms and causes of this asymmetry, which has significant implications for the fashion system, in a neutral manner with respect to the desirability of a specific body size.

The asymmetry between fat and thin in common value judgments is also manifested by the variety of adjectives used to indicate thinness: thin, slim, slender, skinny, lean, and willowy, to mention the most common ones. Of these, only skinny has a negative connotation; the rest have mostly a positive connotation. Slim is perceived as a compliment, lean is used for someone that is fit and healthy, slender is used in appreciation of a "ladylike" figure. Therefore, I will mainly use the term thin, which has a neutral connotation, reserving skinny for extreme, anorexic thinness.

Pillars of the Thin Ideal: Fashion and the Media

It is a commonly held intuition that the fashion system is strongly implicated as one of the main culprits in propagating the tyranny of slenderness. Indeed, ever since the first commentators began to observe the phenomenon around the beginning of the twentieth century, fashion has been held up as one of its main causes (Walden 1985). This is hardly surprising, since fashion's aspirational character means that it explicitly pursues the goal of promoting female beauty in production as well as communication and consumption. As the prevailing idea of female beauty demands that women be thin, it is natural for fashion to cultivate a thin ideal. Cultivating the ideal of thinness results in the attempt to get rid of fat bodies. Just as a woman, by dieting, seeks to get rid of her natural body and replace it with one which is closer to the ideal, so the fashion system tries to get rid of fat bodies because they go against the ideal. In Chapter 6, we will see that the fashion system produces a segregation effect in various ways by obscuring fat bodies from the clothing landscape. Furthermore, by functioning as a social norm, fashion exerts a coercive power over people and their behavior. Not only does the fashion system segregate fat bodies, but it also encourages consumers to do the same. The thin ideal is deeply embedded in fashion.

However, it would be naive to consider fashion the exclusive or even main cause of the tyranny of slenderness. Scholars have pointed to other culprits, most frequently the media—especially though not exclusively traditional ones.

The basic idea is that the intensive media representation of a particular ideal of female beauty (namely the thin ideal) has a long-term impact on women's idea of the "normal" female body, their own body image (normally significantly larger than their actual body size, as shown by Thompson 1986) and body (dis) satisfaction, the social acceptability of fatness, and the actions women take to better adapt their own look to the ideal. Bordo calls this a "perceptual pedagogy" and warns against its potentially distorting effect with respect to the reality of human bodies:

> Now, in 2003, virtually every celebrity image you see—in the magazines, in the videos, and sometimes even in the movies—has been digitally modified. Virtually every image. Let that sink in. Don't just let your mind passively receive it. Confront its implications. This is not just a matter of deception—boring old stuff, which ads have traded in from their beginnings. This is perceptual pedagogy, How To Interpret Your Body 101. These images are teaching us how to see. [. . .] Are we sophisticated enough to know the images are not "real?" (Bordo 2003: xviii)

The media, however, are just one part of a wider, more complex setting. As Bordo (1993: 23–6) further underlines, media messages are texts, and like all texts they become meaningful only in relation to the recipients' cultural context.[11] Since context is essential in decoding the meaning of the messages, they could not take the form that they take if there were no context in which they could be read and interpreted. They would be meaningless. To some extent, texts stem from the recipients' cultural context. Wykes and Gunter (2005: 39, 67, 73, 82, 95) conclude that the power of the media has been largely overstated. The media can spread an image of femininity characterized by the "slender-is-sexy" norm only because that image resonates with the expectations of the public, as it accords with the history of the recipients' experiences. Female magazines, for instance, mediate and circulate an already-current discourse on what is valuable and desirable in the feminine, a hegemonic discourse that identifies femininity with beauty and beauty with thinness:

> [S]uch a connection must make sense to readers on the basis of other experience; it has to have cultural consonance in that it fits prior knowledge that may have historical origins (as in the long history of representations of femininity) or occur elsewhere in the contemporary shared culture (newspapers, television, the Web) or social practices (family units, religion, employment). Magazines are part of broader discursive practices and power relations; they fit ideas within those and those ideas come from that context. (Wykes and Gunter 2005: 82)

To understand the link between the thin ideal and the fashion system it is vital not to overestimate the power of the media. It is tempting to create a short circuit between the media system and the fashion system and to assume that there is a sort of tacit conspiracy that brings together the interests of both. Yet the situation is not so simple and, as we shall see, has a paradoxical character. To attribute this phenomenon to the sole power of circulating representations would mean having a narrow view of the way representations work, as Entwistle and Slater have observed:

> The stereotypical young woman as potential victim of size zero imagery is not simply engaging with specific represented bodies in reiterated texts; she is engaging with body values through everyday dress practices; social networks and peer relationships and competition; regulatory structures (e.g. school or workplace dress codes, formal and informal); leisure spaces, practices and regulations; complementary commodities and aesthetic forms (e.g. the relationship between music cultures and fashion); domestic and familial dynamics; retail structures; aesthetic genres such as modelling competitions and reality TV formats; and on and on and on. (Entwistle and Slater 2012: 29–30)

The Paradox of Fashion

There can be no doubt: the fashion system is deeply implicated in the reproduction and circulation of the thin ideal. It contributes to the tyranny of slenderness by segregating "fat" bodies from our cultural landscape. This, in practice, means most actual bodies, since, due to the thin ideal, all non-thin bodies are somehow considered fat. This is what this book is about. More specifically, the crucial aspect to focus on is that the fashion system excludes real bodies not only from the media but also from the design and manufacture of fashionable clothing. The segregation of fat bodies is not just about featuring more or less drastically photoshopped images of skeletal bodies to be circulated in the media and the blogosphere. It concerns, first of all, the manufacture of clothing items with which to supply the retail system: *fashion brands provide clothes only in slim sizes.*

I highlight this point because this circumstance gives rise to a fundamental contradiction, which I call the paradox of fashion. On the one hand, the fashion system takes the thin ideal so seriously as to forgo the production and sale of garments for women whose body deviates significantly from the ideal.

On the other hand, the real-world bodies that the fashion system has to clothe increasingly diverge from that very ideal. Statistics based on the populations of Western countries show that the range of real bodies is much wider and has shifted toward larger average sizes than the clothing supplied by fashion brands, while the Global Database on Body Mass Index (BMI), available on the World Health Organization (WHO) website, shows that the average weight of the world population, and of Western populations in particular, has increased significantly in recent decades. Let us look closely at both these facts.

Christel and Dunn (2017) have convincingly shown that in the United States the average size worn by women is greater than sixteen (contrary to the widespread belief that it coincides with fourteen)[12]. In spite of this, regular clothing stores normally offer sizes between zero and twelve, while sizes from fourteen upward are considered plus-size and sold in designated sections within department stores or by "plus-size" specialty retailers (Bishop et al. 2018: 186). In Europe, similarly, according to a 2005 survey, 38 percent of Italian women wear sizes twelve (United States)[13] and over (Iannello 2006), and according to data published by the French e-commerce website ClicknDress (2016) collected without statistical sampling on the basis of self-declarations, 38 percent of the 55,000 customers registered on the site (women between seventeen and sixty-five years) wear a size between ten and twelve, and 40 percent wear a size fourteen or higher. The same study analyzed clothing on sale in French stores and found that the quantity of different available patterns was six times greater for size six than for size sixteen.[14] In Chapter 6, I will show that most high-fashion brands featured in Paris Fashion Week market sizes up to ten. These data show that the size of clothes worn by most of the female population in Western countries is significantly larger than the sizes in which the garments marketed by fashion companies are usually manufactured.

The WHO has been reporting for some time, with some concern, on the "fattening" of the world population, especially in Western countries. According to the most recent data, the proportion of overweight people is increasing, and is now close to two-thirds of the population in some English-speaking countries and around half in most other Western countries. These data are anthropometric in origin and are based on the BMI, which is obtained by dividing a person's weight by the square of their height in meters. For example, the BMI of a woman who is 160 centimeter tall and weighs 64 kilograms is twenty-five ($64/1.6^2$). Since the index has been developed by health professionals to monitor pathological deviations from body standards (anorexia and obesity), the statistics are informative only with respect to the thresholds separating underweight from normal weight (BMI 18.5), normal weight from overweight (BMI 25), and overweight from obesity (BMI 30). However, as the above example shows, a BMI of 25 or higher indicates a body that—setting aside the obvious, endless variations in shape—almost certainly wears a size greater than ten. It is enough, then, to consult the figure for the overweight category to get a rough idea of the percentage of the population that needs clothes in sizes twelve and over: almost 70 percent in the United States, about 60 percent in the United Kingdom and Canada, around 50 percent in Spain, France and Germany, 45 percent in Italy, 40 percent in Brazil, and 25 percent in Japan. Moreover, historical data show a continuous growth in the percentage of overweight people throughout the world population in the last fifty years, even though over the last few years the growth rate seems to have slowed. The data are not completely reliable,[15] but the trend is clear. These figures are a long way from the accommodation rate that handbooks term "typical" of the fashion business (Petrova 2007: 64).

Herein, then, lies the paradox of fashion: that *the fashion system is not optimized to serve the population of its potential customers.* This is a much more powerful contradiction than the apparent conflict between the cultural ideology about the ideal size of the body and the realities of people's bodies (Kaiser 1997: 135; de Perthuis 2008: 179). The latter is just one of many social phenomena that successfully cultivate a divide between the ideal and the real: others include for instance democracy, science, and art. Yet the paradox of fashion consists in the *economically absurd* fact that while potential fashion customers have shifted toward larger sizes, the industry has increasingly focused on smaller sizes not just by creating (through photographs, videos, and fashion shows) exclusive, aspirational imagery to capture the interest of consumers, but also in manufacturing the tangible goods it sells them. Not only does the fashion industry promote its products using particularly thin models, it also restricts those very products to small and medium sizes. One might expect that, as the population grows fatter, the fashion's addiction to the thin ideal would diminish. But it has not. Despite some noteworthy tendencies in the opposite direction—hitherto limited to the sphere of communication— fashion continues to confine fat bodies to niches in the fields of production (plus-size brands), distribution (plus-size retailers), and communication (fatshion blogs).[16] The fashion industry thus appears to be forgoing a slice of potential revenue, the size of which is hard to estimate but which, given how many are overweight in the West, cannot be insignificant.[17] What can explain this seemingly contradictory and ultimately disadvantageous behavior? This paradox of fashion is a telling indication of the power that the thin ideal wields over the fashion system.

What Makes the Thin Ideal so Resilient in Fashion?

Both "common sense" public opinion and scholarly articles have often blamed fashion, and in particular the fashion media, for the tyranny of slenderness. Yet, the paradox of fashion would seem to indicate that the fashion industry is the victim as opposed to the cause of the thin ideal. Should we conclude that fashion is blameless? That it must bow to the power of ideology and adapt to the demands made of it by the dominant culture through consumers' choices? We need to understand the actual role of fashion in this story. To do this, we will look within the fashion system and inquire into its internal dynamics and trends in order to understand what makes the thin ideal so powerful as to generate the paradox of fashion.

Several scholars have investigated what factors other than fashion may account for the tyranny of slenderness. Hillel Schwartz, for example, has inquired into the history of diets—which is closely linked to the history of the thin ideal— concluding that fashion plays only a secondary role:

> The desire to be slim is not simply a result of fashion. It must be understood in terms of a confluence of movements in the sciences and in dance, in home economics and political economy, in medical technology and food marketing, in evangelical religion and life insurance. Our sense of the body, of its heft and momentum, is shaped more by the theater of our lives than by our costume. (Schwartz 1986: 4)

For Schwartz, clothing is not the prime cause of the spread of dieting in the Western world over the last century or so. Quite the opposite: the modern obsession with weight and fat is an independent cultural element, stemming from a multiplicity of interlocking cultural changes that took place in the fields of science, religion, and everyday life at the turn of the twentieth century.

Naomi Wolf, as we have already seen, attributes the myth of beauty to the strategies of industrial patriarchal capitalism to thwart the emancipation of women. The growing emancipation of women during the twentieth century threatens the stability of a society based on male political and economic power and female restraint in the separate sphere of domesticity, care work, and personal services (Wolf 1991: 14). The myth of beauty forces women to focus assiduously on their physical appearance, which is both a physical and mental obstacle to self-fulfillment in their career and social life. According to Wolf, "the qualities that a given period calls beautiful in women are merely symbols of the female behavior that that period considers desirable: *The beauty myth is always actually prescribing behavior and not appearance*" (Wolf 1991: 13–14, emphasis in original). In particular, the thin ideal prescribes self-monitoring and self-control, which limits women's scope for action. According to Wolf, the modern economy is dependent upon the representation of women within the beauty myth, and the tyranny of slenderness derives not so much from the needs of fashion as from the need for the capitalist economic system to subject women to a condition of perpetual incompleteness, imperfection, and dissatisfaction with themselves, as this hinders their will to challenge men's political and economic hegemony.

In a similar vein, Susan Bordo sees thinness as a tool for normalizing the female body according to a contemporary ideology of femininity. She argues that the body should be read as a text through which women construct and symbolically represent their perception of what femininity means today. In contemporary Western societies, the idea of femininity moves between two contradictory standards. On the one hand, an ideal of domestic femininity persists which reserves the role of emotional and physical nurturers for women. On the other hand, women entering the professional arena are required to incorporate the "masculine" rules of that arena: self-control, determination, discipline (Bordo 1993: 171). The quest for thinness inscribes seemingly contradictory ideals in the body: the control of selfish desires and the discipline of other-oriented emotions. It does not consist, in other words, in an empty fashion ideal, but in a "citadel of contemporary and historical meaning" (Bordo 1993: 170), the interpretation of which requires multiple readings:

> Female slenderness [. . .] has a wide range of sometimes contradictory meanings in contemporary representations, the imagery of the slender body suggesting powerlessness and contraction of female social space in one context, autonomy and freedom in the next. It is impossible adequately to understand women's problems with food and body image unless these significations are unpacked, and this requires examining slenderness in multiple contexts. (Bordo 1993: 26)

For Bordo, then, it is important to investigate not so much the contingent causes that have fostered the spread of the thin ideal as the meaning it conveys and makes it so attractive to women: a complex meaning linked to the female condition in contemporary society, far more powerful and profound than the "whimsical and capricious enemy, capable of indoctrinating and tyrannizing passive and impressionable young girls by means of whatever imagery it arbitrarily decided to promote that season" (Bordo 1993: 46), that is to say, the fashion industry.

Such theories allow us to grasp the complex sociocultural factors that fuel the thin ideal, which extends far beyond the power of the fashion system. However, they have a flaw: they usually aim to identify one or more causes of the thin ideal *outside thinness itself*. They consider thinness the product of sociocultural dynamics, not a sociocultural dynamic itself. Thinness itself seems inert, neutral. An example from Naomi Wolf's book may help clarify what I mean.

Wolf's theory requires that each discrete manifestation of the ideal of female beauty be investigated in terms of how it can be useful to the dominant economic system. This also applies to women's magazines, characterized by a radical ambivalence between the transmission of positive messages for the emancipation of women and the constant use in advertising of an ideal of female beauty based on body slenderness. Wolf's theory is that this ideal serves the interests of advertisers, who are manufacturers and retailers of cosmetics, diets, slimming and body care devices. The advertisements that populate women's magazines artificially construct an ideal of beauty that is unattainable for real women by making it appear real and achievable, and then offering them the tools necessary to adapt to it. "The magazine message *about the* [beauty] *myth* is determined by its advertisers" (Wolf 1991: 73–4, emphasis in original). The myth itself seems to be devoid of agency, a mere tool in the hands of a patriarchal capitalist system that benefits from forcing women into a kind of consumeristic compulsion that produces wealth for the industry and, at the same time, restricts the scope for their aspiration to social emancipation. Yet, Wolf fails to take account of the fact that the beauty myth, and in particular the thin ideal, is not only cultivated in advertising but also permeates every part of women's magazines, including fashion editorials, articles, and columns.[18] Women's magazines conceal fat bodies even when they talk about current affairs, politics, work, feelings, and everyday life. The thin ideal spreads beyond the bounds of the advertising of products designed to make it achievable and contaminates the rest of a women's magazine—as well as clothing production. Ascribing the tyranny of slenderness to the interests of capitalism and patriarchal society certainly makes sense and is thought-provoking, but ends up embracing a deterministic approach if it induces us to overlook the capacity that the thin ideal has to dominate and resist in contemporary society even apart from those external causes.

By attributing the thin ideal to a cause other than thinness, many scholars fail to notice the intrinsic inertia of the ideal, its power of resilience. They ignore the fact that thinness exerts an agency that is independent, though not separate, from the actions and influences of external agents. I shall defend the thesis that *the thin ideal is characterized by an inherent inertia that determines its resistance over time despite the paradox of fashion to which it gives rise.* An analysis of the tyranny of slenderness in the fashion system, and the related segregation of fat bodies, will allow us to highlight such inertia and its power.

This Book

I will not address the topic outlined above with a reporter's eye and descriptive attitude, nor will I approach it from a historical perspective.[19] My approach is, rather, a sociological one. I wish to highlight the social mechanisms that have caused Western fashion to embrace the thin ideal and remain faithful to it all this time. We are often quick to understand the psychological and economic determinants of a phenomenon, perhaps a little slower to understand the biological ones, but often we find it difficult to grasp its social determinants. For example, we immediately see the relational and sexual implications of female beauty standards and also how they are connected with profit and wealth. If it is explained to us, we can also fairly easily understand the role played by appearance—differently for men and women—in the continuation and evolution of the species. Yet it requires application and study to grasp that the social structure, too, can benefit from the circulation of this idea, to the extent that the myth of beauty plays a hegemonic role in the conservation of existing hierarchies of power—in this case, in the preservation of the power structures of patriarchal consumer capitalism.

This also applies to the hegemony of the thin ideal in the fashion system. I will also deal with the psychological or economic mechanisms that sustain this hegemony, as this will serve to frame the phenomenon appropriately. However, my goal is to draw attention to the less visible underlying social dynamics, which I will discuss under the categories of discourse, practice, technology, and politics. *Hegemonic social discourses* produce representations of the human body, and in particular of the female body, capable of systematically forming the objects of which they speak, since in establishing the thin ideal they ipso facto establish rules of behavior and, consequently, practices that discipline the bodies of real people. *Dispersed fashion practices* that nurture the thin ideal have an inertia that resists external pressure for change exerted by economic power or cultural trends, and helps explain the emergence of the fashion paradox described above. These practices are also based on *techniques adopted by the fashion industry* that have incorporated the thin ideal and are endowed with their own agency; that is, they bring about the unplanned and unexpected effect of secluding clothing for larger sizes within a production and consumption niche—the plus size—that renounces the quality of fashionability. Finally, the thin ideal incorporated in discourses, practices, and technology generates "naturalized" *politics of slenderness* that have the effect of marginalizing "fat" bodies, namely the overweight bodies of ordinary people, inside and outside the fashion system.

The issue of fat fashion is a particular aspect of a more general trend toward thinness. My main objective in this chapter has been to deconstruct the naive idea that thinness is inherently an element of beauty, and that beauty is naturally a qualifying characteristic of the female body. Having clarified that the thin ideal is a social construction, we can now tackle without prejudice the study of the grounds for the emergence of the fashion paradox. The next chapters will address this along the following lines of reasoning.

Chapter 2 discusses some general theoretical issues that need to be clarified in order to correctly address fat fashion. I want to show that the tyranny of slenderness in fashion does not only have implications for the shared imaginary of clothing consumers and their consequent consumption choices, but also directly affects everyday life leaving its own imprint on the social interactions that pervade it. Fashion thinness extends its influence far beyond fashion itself. Although the thin ideal belongs essentially to the current fashion discourse, it also affects people's everyday inner lives, which are inherently social. To illustrate this point, I shall discuss how clothes come into our lives. Studies of fashion often insist on the power of trends, on the effects of social distinction, and on the role of social belonging and cultural identity, but overlook the experience of individuals when they wear clothes and—so dressed—move through the world. Hence, Chapter 2 focuses in particular on the latter aspect. The impact of the nonexistence of fat fashion, in fact, becomes evident when we do not only look at the policies of the fashion system, but relate them to the expectations and needs of consumers. The seclusion of clothing for overweight women within a separate market niche that largely forgoes the attention to aesthetic detail typical of fashion becomes particularly significant when it clashes with the need of consumers to use clothes to regulate their social interactions. And this is always the case, because *social interactions are dressed interactions*. Therefore, it is of fundamental importance to discuss in detail the inseparability of clothes from the body that they cover, and, vice versa, the body from the clothes. We need, if possible, to stop talking about clothes that cover the body, combine with it and expand its capabilities. We must learn to recognize the unique clothes-body complex which makes interaction with others and social life possible. Ample space will hence be devoted to discussing how the clothes-body complex works as an interaction tool, and what one should be understood when it is said that clothes are used to communicate. On this topic, in fact, studies are still rather uncertain and often based on a naive vision of communication, ignoring the role played by clothing in the process of "furnishing" the experience of others (as one furnishes a home) in order to influence their expectations of us. In this approach, it is the concrete and individual practice of dressing for social life that enables the adoption of costume and fashions in the situated circumstance. Dressing is a situated practice. Fashion discourse is able to exert its hegemonic power because clothing is not a communication tool added to social interactions as an enhancement of the body, but is *the* way in which the body enables and mediates social interaction.

According to Foucault ([1969] 2002), a "discourse" developed within a social field determines the rules and boundaries of what can be said, thought, and done within the field. Those who participate in the fashion system as practitioners or consumers share a series of catchwords, set phrases, refrains, and "obvious" ideas that predetermine the way in which topics are addressed in conversations, texts, and personal reflections. Today's fashion discourse implies that beauty should be thin, to the point that this condition has now been assimilated into the gaze, as well as the thoughts, of those who take part in the fashion world. I will deal more directly with this issue in Chapter 3. After a detailed discussion of the evidence for the tyranny of slenderness in Western societies and the power exerted by the thin ideal in the fashion system, which will corroborate the considerations advanced so far, I shall describe the aspects of fashion discourse that further the acceptance and circulation of the thin ideal. The aim of the chapter is to show that the thin ideal acts undetected in a multiplicity of events, situations, and practices concerning clothing and fashion, on both the industry and consumer side. It will become clear that photoshopped images and anorexic models are just the tip of the iceberg. The thin ideal dominates fashion in much more subtle ways.

In Chapter 4, I shall attempt an analysis of the conditions that have led to this situation. It is not so much the causes of the emergence of the thin ideal that merit consideration, as this issue has already been extensively discussed by scholars. What I am interested in here—in itself as well as in relation to the paradox of fashion—is the persistence of the thin ideal in the face of economic, social, and cultural trends that push toward its dismantlement. This persistence of an apparently 'irrational' ideal is hard to explain if we disregard the fact that it is embedded in a series of established practices within the fashion system (practices such as the fashion show, shopping, producing a fashion editorial, etc.). Practices are complex, structured forms of behavior based on the alignment of a multiplicity of elements (people, things, technologies, institutions, norms, etc.), and share the following fundamental characteristic: that the actions pertaining to them are not actions of the individuals concerned, but actions of the practice itself. Individuals are "carriers," and not agents, of the practice: they "interpret" and perform the plot delineated by the practice itself. As these practices are external to and override individual choices, and are rich in elements that are resistant to change such as bodies, routines, institutions and artifacts, they possess a peculiar inertial force, and as such are capable of "stabilizing" the actions of a multiplicity of individuals. If we view fashion as simply another dispersed practice, its resistance to external pressures for change becomes less obscure. The practitioners are forced to adapt to the thin ideal because this is how they are expected to behave by other actors within fashion practice.

As I have already pointed out, techniques are a relevant element of practices. All practices develop specific techniques for doing things, such as the Fosbury Flop in the high jump, caramelization in cooking, and fingerpicking in playing guitar. These establish themselves as standardized "doings" that practitioners acquire while familiarizing themselves with the practice. The emergence of the thin ideal in fashion has gone hand in hand with the development of a major technique for the mass production of clothing: sizing. Chapter 5 is devoted to an in-depth discussion of the sizing system to highlight the technological constraint that has favored and still supports the segregation of fat bodies. The technological constraint in question consists in the fact that the algorithmic size grading technique works effectively only for sizes less than or equal to twelve. For larger sizes, the accommodation rate falls dramatically. This fact, far from demonstrating the existence of "objective" boundaries between fashionable clothes and featureless garments, is the tangible outcome of a social turn, namely the transition from craft production to mass production of clothing. With the size grading technique, the fashion system has established a threshold that discriminates between what is admitted, inasmuch as it meets the thin ideal, and what is excluded, as it is too divergent from it. What is excluded constitutes a parallel domain in which the problem of covering bodies is solved by relinquishing the fashionable dimension of clothing.

The tyranny of slenderness in the fashion system does not only give rise to an autonomous plus-size market segment governed by principles different from the mainstream. It also results in active policies for the exclusion of fat bodies from the field of fashion. Of course, these are not "planned" policies, but spontaneous strategies dictated by the fat-related stigma that derives from the emergence of the thin ideal. Chapter 6 analyzes the marginalization of fat bodies in four key areas of the fashion system: manufacturing, design, retailing, and communication. In all of these areas, the separation between fashion for regular sizes and plus-size clothing has turned into a sort of segregation of the latter by the fashion system: high-fashion brands avoid marketing plus-size clothing, fashion designers and established art directors do not design plus-size collections or clothes suitable for enhancing overweight bodies, retailing of plus-size clothing is often located in urban areas that are distant from the centers of high fashion, and mainstream communication tends to conceal the very existence of fat bodies.

The final chapter takes a look—how could it be otherwise?—at future prospects. Such an enterprise is, in all likelihood, doomed to failure. In my defense, I must make it clear that I make no claim to see into the future and I have not written Chapter 7 to make forecasts. My aim is rather to draw some conclusions about current trends based on the considerations discussed in the book. In other words: given the situation described above, how should we interpret a number of emerging trends in the fashion system? These trends are there for all to see: curvy models begin to tread the runways in the major mainstream Fashion Weeks, fashion magazines increasingly publish images of "nonstandard" bodies, some high-street brands exploit the idea of "all bodies" to promote their collections, and so on. My conclusion is guarded, though not pessimistic. Given the power of the forces that govern this game (practices, techniques, discourses, spontaneous policies), I suspect that any decisive loosening of the grip that the tyranny of slenderness holds over fashion will have to come from antagonistic forces that are far more powerful than the arbitrary choices of a brand, magazine, or group of influencers. Hegemonic social discourses possess a resilience that allows them to adapt to outside pressures, often assimilating and reorganizing them so as to neutralize the threat that social actors pose to their existence. Fashion discourse has hitherto shown a remarkable ability to assimilate cultural trends that oppose or threaten it, fashion blogging being a case in point. Greater openness to fat bodies still does not constitute proof that fashion is breaking down the tyranny of slenderness. However, I will argue that social changes of a more general nature, brought about for instance by economic development, technological progress, demographic change, increased population fatness or migration flows, have the potential to transform fashion practice to such an extent that they undermine the resistance of the thin ideal.

What This Book is *Not* about

A number of major topics are not covered in this book. I will briefly discuss two which I have already mentioned. The first is clothing that is not womenswear; that is, mainly the vast fields of menswear and childrenswear. The second is clothing which lies outside the bounds of the fashion system; that is, non-Western fashion and, in particular, the vast area of national and local fashions and clothing cultures. Both of these topics deserve far more attention in contemporary fashion studies; however, both of them are inherently distinct from the issue of fat fashion in Western womenswear, as I will argue in this section.

Several reasons have induced me to exclude menswear and childrenswear from the discussion. To begin with, despite a recent tendency to break down barriers (think of such trends as genderless styles, soft masculinity, and non-binary fashion), as industries they remain disconnected from womenswear. They make use of different design departments, manufacturing companies, and retail channels, and therefore employ different people. In the communication field (photographers, stylists, editors), too, specialization in men's, women's, or children's wear is the norm, since the communication aims and rationales of magazines and brands are different. In short, practices, techniques, and products in the menswear and childrenswear sectors are so different from those in womenswear that it is impossible to treat them as a single field. This is especially true for the plus-size sector. My discussion of the sizing system and the segregation of fat bodies in Chapters 5 and 6, for instance, does not apply to menswear or childrenswear. At most, we might make some comparisons, for which data is in any case in short supply.

Another important reason to exclude menswear from the analysis is that the thin ideal is less coercive toward men than toward women, as mentioned above (Ålgars et al. 2009; Polivy et al. 1986: 95–8; Silverstein et al. 1986: 521–6). Historically, weight loss is not a female prerogative (Schwartz 1986: 16–17). However, it is women over whom thinness has exerted its tyranny during the last century or so (Mazur 1986; Wykes and Gunter 2005: 5–6), since thinness has become the main expression of the myth of beauty to which women, according to Naomi Wolf's theory, have been subjected since embarking on their quest for

emancipation and against exclusion from public life and the workplace. Susan
Bordo sums this up succinctly:

> Women in our culture are more tyrannized by the contemporary slenderness
> ideal than men are, as they typically have been by beauty ideals in general. It is
> far more important to men than to women that their partner be slim. Women
> are much more prone than men to perceive themselves as too fat. And, as is by
> now well known, girls and women are more likely to engage in crash dieting,
> laxative abuse, and compulsive exercising and are far more vulnerable to eating
> disorders than males. (Bordo 1993: 204)

Recent research has demonstrated that "appearance norms encountered by
women in daily life are more rigid, homogenous and pervasive than those for
men, and that more messages implying the attainability of the ideal appearance
are directed at women" (Boute et al. 2011: 322). In general, women are more
strongly encouraged than men to develop their bodies as objects of perception
for others (Gimlin 2002: 4; Shilling [1993] 2012: 71, 140; Tseëlon 1995: 78). All
of this makes the issue of fat fashion, and in particular, the segregation of fat
bodies from fashion, particularly apparent—urgent, even—for womenswear,
to which most research in this field is devoted. Menswear often remains in the
background, not to mention childrenswear, which raises extremely delicate
ethical and educational issues.

   The second topic that this book does not tackle is non-Western fashion.
The kind of fashion I am discussing is that which is produced by the fashion
system, an international network of production and consumption whose central
nervous system is still located in four "fashion capitals" in Europe and North
America. What distinguishes it above all is the fact that in Western nations—and
not elsewhere—it develops its own habits, routines, practices, ways of thinking,
idiosyncrasies, and styles. The thin ideal and the segregation of plus sizes arose
in the context of Western fashion during an era before globalization, when
the relationship between Western and non-Western cultures was essentially
colonial in nature. Non-Western cultures developed their own local traditions
and fashions, such as *qipao* in China (Liu 2017) and *hanbok* in Korea (Lee 2017),
which were originally associated with the modern look and changed rapidly
with time. However, they subsequently underwent the economic and cultural
aggressiveness of the (Western) fashion system, so that eventually they have
been reduced to mere cases of traditional garments, as opposed to the "modern"
Western ones. Globalization in fashion is based on this precondition: that a

Western fashion system spread all over the globe and colonized local clothing habits. The fashion system is global as regards consumption but is local, namely Western, as regards production (Gilbert 2000). Acknowledging this fact does not mean that we must accept the hegemonic discourse of fashion (Cheang and Kramer 2017; Kaiser 2012: 32–4) or believe that fashion must necessarily be "Western" in spirit. What it *does* mean is that we need to be aware of the fact that the transnational character of the contemporary fashion system does not exclude that there are asymmetries of power within it. Those asymmetries manifest their effects on how people actually dress in all corners of the world. Fashion is globalized, but globalization is not democratic (Bauman 1998), and fashion imagery (as well as fashion imagination) is still dictated by people based in the world's fashion capitals, as described by Iris Marion Young:

> Fashion imagery may be drawn indiscriminately from many places and times, and the clothes themselves come from all over the world, usually sewn by very poorly paid women. The fashion fantasies level and dehistoricize these times and places, often contributing to the commodification of an exotic Third World at the same time that they obscure the real imperialism and exploitation that both the fantasies and realities of clothes enact. (Young 2005: 74)

This impacts the body ideal as well as clothing styles. As we will see, the thin ideal originated in Western countries and is tightly linked with the industrialization of clothing manufacturing. It is an outcome of Western cultures of interaction, appearance, and the body, and only as such, and as an instrument of the fashion system to enhance Western clothing mass production, has it imposed itself over non-Western cultures and lifestyles. Clearly, today the thin ideal produces its effects all over the globe (Swami 2015). Yet to study its intricate connection with local cultures would require us to acquire specific expertise about each culture. Instead, by analyzing the way in which fashion's ideal of slenderness has stabilized within its original milieu, that is, the fashion system, we can discover its scope and mechanisms. By avoiding dealing with the near-infinite variety of national and local cultures and the complexity of intercultural situations, it becomes possible to frame and explain a phenomenon which, thanks to the power of the fashion system, unleashes its effects, more or less effectively, almost everywhere. A study of the thin ideal in non-Western clothing cultures and fashion environments, which requires acquaintance with those cultures individually, is a much needed but substantially different task.

Dress and the Body

Fashion and Communication

In Chapter 1, I argued that reducing fashion to merely material production, the development of styles, and the design of collections is limiting, as to do so is to overlook the inherently social character of fashion as a form of interaction and an instance of lived life. I have also argued that fashion is a type of practice, that is to say, one that essentially involves the activation of the body and the use of clothes and accessories. From this perspective, the body and clothes form an indivisible unit. Together, they define an individual's appearance, which stems from their interplay and is the ultimate purpose of fashion, what clothing choices are aimed at. This makes the paradoxical nonexistence of fat fashion not just relevant to fashion history, but a social problem related to issues such as social cohesion, unequal opportunities, and the rise of what neoliberals have termed a "consumers' democracy" (von Mises [1949] 2007: 813).

Such claims need to be suitably grounded in theory. Before discussing fat fashion, a thorough understanding is needed of the clothes-body complex, how it helps to create and perpetuate social relations, and what role clothing plays in all of this. This chapter examines these questions in detail and, drawing on established theories in the social sciences, sets out to provide a firm foundation for the subsequent discussion of the fashion paradox. To this end, I shall momentarily "step back" from my focus on fat fashion and return to it in the next chapter, having provided the reader with greater awareness of the issues at stake.

In this chapter, I shall first undertake a description of the clothes-body complex. The discussion will obviously touch upon the case of interpersonal communication, which necessarily leverages the body. In other words, I will argue that the clothes-body complex is essentially a communication tool. This places it at the center of social processes. But to emphasize this point requires us to address the very idea of communication. Fashion studies have long promulgated theories on the communicative function of clothing. However, a lack of insight into the matter has led to the proliferation of naive or weakly argued positions that settle for the simple idea that clothing is a kind of language. I, therefore, believe that there is a need to examine the mechanisms of interpersonal communication and the role it plays in the construction of social relations. My aim is to go beyond the vague idea of "clothing-as-communication" and flesh it out with a concrete examination of the way it works. This will eventually lead us to a better understanding of the function of fashion in the continuous work of bodily transformation that enables individuals to manage everyday social interaction and structured relationships in contemporary consumer-oriented societies. It is in the context of this "work of the body" that people usually encounter the issue of fat fashion in their lives.

The Clothes-Body Complex

The paradox of fashion springs from the fact that the fashion system seeks in various ways to exclude fat bodies, just as it does with many other nonstandard body types: old bodies, ethnic bodies, differently able bodies. And yet it is not so easy for fashion to truly be rid of unwanted bodies, because the human body as such implies clothing. We must therefore start from this observation: body and dress presuppose each other. The human body is a dressed body (Entwistle [2000] 2015: 6), and has therefore been called a clothes-body complex (Klepp 2011), clothes-body hybrid (Haller 2015), and body-clothes assemblage (Ruggerone 2017). This basic fact is the reason for which the fashion system attaches such importance to the shape, appearance, and size of the consumer's body, and why clothing occupies such a preeminent place in everyday life.

Clothing is created according to a certain body to be dressed. A skirt, shoes, jewelry, piercing: no matter how beautiful, elaborate or precious they may be as objects, they have that shape and features because they were designed to be used on a human body. While many human tools (such as a hammer) are designed to be used exclusively by a specific part of the body (such as the hand), clothing normally relates to the body as a whole, and as such incorporates this relationship into its own materiality and design. Not even a clutch bag is associated only with the hand in which it is held. It is also associated with the arm, armpit, shoulder, side, dress, shoes, jewels, and so forth, of the woman holding it. It is part of a look. This is even more true of the fabric garments we wear, which must fit on our body, that is, conform to our body in a desirable manner.[1]

Similarly, the body originally involves some form of clothing. By "originally," what I mean is that in daily life the body is first and foremost dressed. The body by its very nature is a vehicle for clothing (Hillestad 1980). While a dressed body represents normality, the naked body is a consequence of an undressing, an exceptional state reserved for special situations. Paradoxically, the naked body is no longer a "natural" phenomenon, but a product of civilization, as has been pointed out in various fields, including philosophy (Hegel 1970: 401–6), cultural anthropology (Lévi-Strauss [1971] 1981: 389), art history (Hollander 1993: xiii and 1999: 105–6), psychoanalysis (Lemoine-Luccioni 1983), sociology (Elias [1939] 2000) and fashion studies (Barnard 1996: 21–2; Calefato 1986; Entwistle 2001: 33–4; Polhemus 1975: 18–19). All of these fields of investigation insist on the fact that in societies for which historical records exist there is no "natural" form of nudity. The naked body is a cultural product,[2] and as such addresses others according to their culture. It is, in the strict sense of the word, a meaning. That is to say, it is not a bare fact, but a meaningful experience for someone, whether for the one who is naked or those who meet him or her. Therefore, being dressed is an essential condition of the body both when it is there and when it is absent.[3] Even the naked body speaks through dress—albeit in a privative way. The naked body that arouses modesty, shame, scandal, or excitement can do so precisely because it is uncovered. A particular state of dress—absence—makes the body meaningful. Indeed, we call it an "undressed" body (Klepp 2011: 453).

In short, the body becomes socially significant through dress, either by addition or by subtraction. *The indivisible pairing of body and dress elicits meaning in human interactions.* In the case of nudity, the clothes-body complex lies at one extreme of the spectrum of its possible states. However, in most cases, nudity works in a similar way to the silences in a melody. These silences speak through the same code as the sounds, the musical code. Only, they do it in a privative fashion. Although we call them pauses, these moments of silence are not interruptions in the melody but intrinsic parts of it. Likewise, body communication takes place thanks to a skillful dosage of full and empty (sounds and pauses), that is of the dressed and undressed body. The long or short skirt, the shirt with or without sleeves, the high or low waistline of trousers combined with short tops, fastened or unfastened buttons, necklines, slits, transparencies— these are just some of the tools through which nudity is combined with coverings to adequately articulate the clothes-body idiom.

I wish to emphasize the broad scope of this assertion. If the body is not "natural" before being dressed, and if dress does not fully exist without a body that brings it to life, it follows that the traditional distinction between dress and the body has to be shelved. It is a merely analytical distinction that separates two elements that in reality are inseparable—like a person's eyes and nose. According to Jennifer Craik, clothes "are activated by the wearing of them just as bodies are actualized by the clothes they wear" (Craik 1993: 16). And the bodies are actualized by the clothes because, as Cavallaro and Warwick (1998: 3) have noted, "it is dress that has time and again been assigned the responsibility of transforming the incomplete body into a complete cultural package." A garment deprived of its body is like a deactivated device, turned off. A body deprived of its clothing is unreal, abstract. It is in the unity of this relationship that the body is humanized and socialized, that is, becomes real and contributes substantially to people's everyday life—so that historically undressing has often been used as a tool of dehumanization (Soper 2001: 21).

Dress as a Technique and Practice of Acculturation

The mutual implication of body and clothing requires us to consider clothes and other body ornaments not as a later addition to an already given body, but as an essential aspect of body constitution: of its meaning, its abilities, and the experiences it conveys. Yet, the body does not only convey experiences. Social and psychological studies have acknowledged recently that several characteristics of social actors can become embodied: social relations, classifications, gender differences, emotions, and thoughts.[4] Elaborating on the idea of the embodied cognition, Adam and Galinsky (2012) concluded that even clothes serve as embodiment agents. In what they call "enclothed cognition," garments exert a powerful effect on the cognitive functions of their wearers. Wearing a garment makes the wearer embody its symbolic meaning. Empirical studies based on their theory showed that clothing is a fundamental part of the dynamic between body and environment and helps to define the position occupied by the individual in the surrounding world.[5]

Here, then, is a second key aspect to address in framing the study of the marginalization of fat bodies in fashion. Clothing by nature extends the body and defines it within the social space. Not only do bodies and clothes co-belong, but this mutual implication also occurs *in the presence of a community*. Interaction with others presupposes that the body is dressed in some way, while undressing is allowed only in circumscribed situations. It is therefore through clothing that the individual body becomes an element of social dynamics. In other words, clothes socialize bodies (Wilson 1992: 6).

Studies of fashion have recognized this fundamental characteristic of clothing from the beginning (Craik 1993: 1–16; Wilson 1985: 2–3), and the seminal work of Joanne Entwistle ([2000] 2015) has described it exhaustively. In this regard, Craik (1993: 9 and 2009: 136–9) has proposed that clothing be considered a body technique in the sense that Mauss (1936) attributes to the expression. Body techniques are forms of physical behavior learned through exercise. Such exercise can be informal or codified, but is usually learned from others, that is, socially acquired. For example, sports (swimming, running, jumping, cycling) always involve a body technique: they are cultural expressions. Yet, other everyday activities, such as walking, sleeping, and sex, are techniques learned from others, as shown by the fact that they change according to gender, profession, and society.[6] For Mauss, people's movements and postures never possess "purely natural" features, as they are always co-determined by techniques of cultural origin. Body techniques are the concrete means through which the acculturation of bodies takes place, that is their transformation from biological entities to cultural artifacts.

Clothing rightfully belongs to the category of body techniques. Mauss's example of walking in high heels is instructive. High heels play an important role in determining the social perception of the female body (because they "slenderize" it according to the thin ideal, reduce physical subordination to the male body, and symbolize values of elegance and style). However, walking in high heels with ease does not come "naturally": it must be learned. The body must undergo a lengthy period of training. Women capable of easily walking in high heels perform a body technique. The same concept can be extended, in a subtler way, to other clothing habits, such as wearing a skirt, using a tie, cultivating a particular look, or following a trend. Like other body techniques, clothing also plays a fundamental role in integrating the individual into the community.

The concept of "technique" might tempt us to overstate the rational, intentional aspect of body adornment, as if possible clothing choices were already there, preliminarily coded, and freely available. Clearly, this is not the case: we do not choose our clothing styles but develop them over the years through life experiences in our communities. Thus Entwistle ([2000] 2015: 11) opts to call clothing a situated bodily "practice," that is, an embodied activity embedded within social relations in everyday life. Practices, compared to techniques, involve more routine and are less conscious. It should be noted that Mauss already conceived of body techniques as a means of an embodiment of social practices. For him, by training their bodies individuals internalize social rules and routines, which eventually become habits. These habits are not individual but collective. They vary from one society to another but "amalgamate" the members of the same society, since for them they are established, taken for granted, embodied ways of doing things. Therefore Mauss (1936) and later Bourdieu ([1980] 1990) prefer to use the term *habitus*, as opposed to habit, for such embodied, routine practices. A *habitus* is the embodied imprint of the past, of the social trajectory that led the individual to occupy his or her specific, current position in society. It has been structured through social practices and consists in a wealth of competencies incorporated in a subject's body that make it "naturally" suitable to act in accordance with social expectations (Bourdieu [1980] 1990: 52–4). Dress as a social practice resorts extensively to *habitus*, which as principles that generate and organize practices predispose bodies to deal with clothes adequately with respect to others' expectations.

Both concepts, technique and practice, capture significant aspects of the clothes-body complex. Both allow us to recognize that the social dimension is an essential feature of clothing. Irrespective of other functions (such as protecting the body), clothing is essentially a means of mediation between the individual and the community. Therefore Turner ([1980] 1993) has called it "the social skin." In dressing, individuals prepare for the social world, they *equip themselves to face their community carrying their own interests and needs, with the goal of leading a fulfilling life*. Herein, clothing is just one of a range of tools—certainly a powerful one—that help to include the biological body in social life. Social theory has long shown that the biological body is a mere abstraction, a reference point, since the real body is "an object of labour" that is constantly "worked on by people just as are other aspects of the natural and social world" (Shilling [1993] 2012: 110). This "body work" consists of a number of aspects (Gimlin 2002 and 2007). Alongside the emotional labor involved, that is, the manipulation of feelings and emotional states (Hochschild 1983), much body work manipulates the body's physical appearance (Twigg 2013b): cleaning, cosmetics, hairstyles, tattoos, piercing, gymnastics, tanning, cosmetic surgery, and clothing. It is of fundamental importance not to separate clothing from the rest just because it is industrially manufactured separately from bodies and subsequently bought and worn. Exactly like other manipulations of appearance, clothes are body transformations that enable and arrange social relations. Wearing a gown is a form of manipulation of the body's appearance to fully enjoy the evening party, not unlike having a shower, brushing one's own hair, putting on makeup, and regularly going to the gym.

Shifting the Approach to Clothing: From Identity to Meaning

For a closer understanding of how this "socialization" or "acculturation" of the body takes place, or what is implied by the notion that individuals "equip themselves" to face the social world, fashion studies offer two kinds of analysis. One focuses on the development of an individual's social identity. The other concerns interaction with others and sees clothing as a tool to make the body meaningful in such interaction. The two approaches have much in common. They look at the same phenomenon from two complementary points of view, the former from a more ontological and the latter from a more genealogical perspective. However, I feel that the genealogical approach grounds the ontological one and allows for a less abstract explanation of people's behavior. Let us address the identity approach now, and postpone the discussion of the interaction approach to the next section.

The theme of identity has long been a concern in fashion studies, mainly in the context of symbolic interactionism (Davis 1992; Kaiser 1997), but also in other theoretical frameworks.[7] The concept of identity is usually not considered in terms of the constitution of a unitary ego through a multiplicity of life experiences, but rather the close relationship that exists between a person's consumption choices and his or her membership of particular groups or communities. Rather than identity, it is more accurate to talk about identities. Membership can be understood in two senses: belonging to a certain social category (e.g., a gender, a generation or an ethnic group), and belonging to a community (e.g., a subculture or a local community). In the first sense, membership is dictated by similar characteristics. In the second, it is dictated by social relations. In both cases, the idea is that having something in common (such as the same age or hometown) produces a sense of co-belonging that helps to place people within society and influences their choices and behaviors. People belonging to a certain class ("bourgeois") or a certain subculture ("punk") share the same social identity.

As far as the clothes-body complex is concerned, the underlying idea is that there is a connection between social identity and a person's clothing choices. If I identify with the bourgeois class, I dress in a certain way. If I identify with the punk subculture, I dress differently. Clothing is a major mediator between the individual and his or her social belonging, and this can manifest itself in two opposite directions, which we might term "real" and "aspirational." On the one hand, clothing can reveal an established identity that precedes it and is acknowledged by the community: a police officer's uniform makes his or her function clear, while a formal dress code signals the status of a top executive's son. On the other hand, clothing can help forge an identity "in the making," one which is desired by the subject but not yet recognized by the social milieu through which he or she (occasionally or permanently) moves. A formal dress code, for instance, helps a working-class law student to attain a new status. Toward the end of the last century this became the subject of an extensive debate between post-modern thinkers, who saw in clothing the potential to freely construct and effortlessly change between a multiplicity of identity "masks" (Featherstone 1991; see also Cavallaro and Warwick 1998), and their critics, who called attention to the fact that we do not choose our body, but we can at most work on the clothes-body complex to try to bring it closer to a fulfilling expression of our real or aspirational identity (Wilson 1992; see also Tseëlon 1995: 120–35).

By expressing identities (whether real or aspirational), the clothes-body complex elicits in others expectations of our behavior and predispositions to behave toward us in a way that is consistent with what we are or would like to be. It is therefore a significant means of facilitating interaction with others. The term "identity," however, has a number of flaws that should make us wary of using it indiscriminately. As Susan Kaiser (2012: 20–3) has pointed out, it tends to lead to typification of human behavior, classifying people according to predetermined general categories. A perusal of the main texts that interpret fashion through the concept of identity shows that they usually describe clothing as a means of expression or construction of class, subcultural, gender, sexual, and generational affiliations. It is thus apparent that the concept of identity tends to neglect the individual effort involved in individuals' conduct in everyday social life, instead classifying them rigidly by social type.[8] Both adherents and critics of the post-modern approach interpret a person's clothes as the consequence and manifestation of his or her being, for example (more or less permanently and unambiguously) woman, heterosexual, middle-class, middle-aged, as if she were basically determined by those characteristics. Furthermore, Kaiser has noted that the term identity implies a predominantly static view of the individual's social positions, that is, relatively persistent over time because they are determined more by belonging than by personal actions and experiences. To be clear, I am not claiming that we should ignore the dependence of clothing choices on social belonging. We must not disregard the fact, for example, that in less flexible societies clothing is often very static (Rouse 1989: 71–82). Nor should we assume, conversely, that the high degree of freedom of clothing choices in consumer societies is a sign of a high degree of social mobility. But if we shift our focus from the level of the social structure to the level of individual behavior of society's actors, it becomes clear that the static nature of the concept of identity obscures the daily work of construction of the self that individuals carry out through their ongoing interactions. The lived experience vanishes.

To mitigate these limitations of the concept of identity, Kaiser proposes replacing it with the idea of "subject formation," which emphasizes the continually evolving character of the individual's positions. Clothing, in her view, does not express stable memberships, but the transient social position of the individual in a given situation, determined in part by the "subjection" of the individual to cultural discourses which, as shown by Foucault ([1969] 2002), shape the understandings of subject positions, in part by the free agency of the subject, capable of constructing his or her position through everyday interactions, particularly by fashioning the body.

However, one aspect of the acculturation of the body through clothing is still overlooked here. In focusing on subject formation, not unlike focusing on identity, we disregard the fact that many aspects of the clothes-body complex are not related to identity at all. This is particularly true of aspects that concern this book most closely, such as body size and weight. Unlike "bourgeois," "punk," or "African American," "fat" does not express a social membership. No one manipulates his or her appearance to express belonging to the social milieu of fat people—nor, for that matter, to that of thin, tall or short people. However, this does not prevent possessing a fat or thin body, or a tall or short one, from influencing the types of social relations available to the subject. Hence people choose clothing in order to manipulate such variables, since being fat or thin does communicate something to the other. In other words, the clothes-body complex is inherently social not just because it is able to communicate or construct the individual's social belongings. It is social because it is capable of communicating in general, because it is a means of communication. That is, it helps manage interactions by shaping, negotiating, and sharing meanings. Clothing socializes the body by placing it in a relationship with others through the exchange of meanings, regardless of how strong the imprint exerted by social structure on this relationship. We must therefore shift our attention to the communicative function of clothing.

Understanding the Clothes-Body Complex
as a Means of Communication

A meaning-focused approach can overcome the problems raised by the concept of identity because it addresses the clothes-body complex as a means of communication, thus extending our insight. That the body—whether fat or thin, tall, or short—is a fundamental tool of human communication, goes without saying. However, it may be useful to highlight two aspects of bodily communication that are sometimes overlooked.

First: the body is a fundamental element and a necessary condition of *all kinds* of human communication. Consider, for example, mediated communication, which consists of the use of technological tools to bridge the gap between bodies which do not share the same spatiotemporal reference system, that is, that do not belong to each other's horizon of experience (Thompson 1995: 18–23). The use of a technological tool such as a camera or a telephone enables communication that otherwise would not take place by making it possible to transfer aspects of the body into the experiential horizon of absent others. Consider, too, verbal communication, which textbooks usually describe as the opposite of nonverbal bodily communication. As shown by Goffman (1959: 2), this distinction has only initial validity. In fact, verbal communication is a specific case of bodily communication. Speaking, like gesticulating, is a modification of body parts (in this case the vocal cords) with the aim of sending a message to the sense organs of others. Utterances are "vocal gestures," as Mead would say (1934: 61). Extremely complex, advanced gestures, but gestures nonetheless. The fact that the anatomical and neurological properties of the human body enable the use of complex codes when producing vocal gestures is an enhancement, however valuable, of characteristics that are proper to gestures in general.

The second aspect not to be overlooked is that nonverbal bodily communication is *by nature* clothing communication. The inherent relevance of dress for the body, discussed above, also extends to communication. In fact, communicating by means of the body consists of transforming it in the eyes of others, as much as communicating with words consists of transforming and articulating the voice. In a perceptual system that uses not only hearing, touch and smell, but primarily sight, the possible transformations of a body include modifications of the covering. *The covering, hence clothing, is an inherent part of body communication,* which is in fact clothed-bodily communication. This statement must be understood in a strict sense. Often in the literature dealing with nonverbal communication the function of dress is mentioned only with reference to the person's general appearance and not to individual gestures, as if these were distinct from the clothing context (see e.g., Argyle 1975). But on closer inspection, it is difficult in everyday life to imagine a movement, a posture, an act of body communication that is not mediated by some form of cultural adornment: a cloth, a metallic pendant, a painted or scarified decoration. Such adornment affects the way we communicate and the meaning of gestures. The way a handshake takes place changes depending on whether we wear a jacket or a hoodie, the way we sit changes depending on whether we are wearing a miniskirt or jeans. As a means of communication, the body never simply *is*, but it is always *in a certain way*: in a certain posture, making particular movements, and *dressed in some way*. Therefore, clothing is not just a form of spectacularization of the body, as with uniforms, formal dress, and subcultural styles. It is also a component of everyday practices of bodily interaction (Woodward 2007) and a tool for the body language from which they are mediated. Taking inspiration from Erving Goffman (1963: 33), who called bodily communication "an idiom of individual appearances and gestures," we will call it the "clothes-body idiom."

In this perspective, we should conceive of clothing as an extension inherent to the body (Kaiser 1997: 98), a prosthesis without which the body cannot control communication and hence govern interaction with the other. As a prosthesis, clothing has the characteristic of being relevant both inwardly (self-perception) and outwardly (interaction). Inwardly, it produces effects related to bodily comfort or to the stabilization of the self through the vicissitudes of life, that is, in other words, the construction of the sense of continuity that underpins the constitution of personal identity. Outwardly it produces manifold social effects: by making the body acceptable, appropriate to the situation, and possibly desirable, clothing keeps a channel of communication with the other open; by expressing the individual's social belongingness clothing facilitates interaction, since it enables processes of typification (Schütz [1932] 1967: 181–94) and role-taking (Mead 1934: 253–60) that simplify communication; by altering the perception of the body and characterizing its movements and adjustments during interaction clothing contributes to the production of meanings and, therefore, to the achievement of communicative objectives related, for example, to the momentary mood, sexual preferences, sense of group belonging, personality, and so forth. The latter aspect is what distinguishes a meaning-based approach from an identity-based one.

According to Hillestad (1980) the body communicates in three ways: through shape, surface, and movement. Now we can specify: the body's shape is normally clothed, its surface dressed, and its movement adorned (even facial expressions are mediated by grooming). Conversely, as a prosthesis of the body, clothing cannot be reduced to a mere mask, even in situations where the deceptive function of costume is predominant, such as in the theater. Nor can it be reduced to a mere object of consumption, even in situations that are expressions of consumer culture, as in the case of so-called fashion victims. In all situations clothing is also a fundamental ingredient of nonverbal communication, and as such cannot be separated from the materiality of the body which it seeks to dissimulate (theater) or standardize (fashion).

To summarize the argument of the opening sections of this chapter, three features of the relationship between body and dress should never be disregarded if we want to avoid a simplified view of the role of clothing in people's lives. First, we should avoid the mistake of considering clothing in any form (clothes, accessories, cosmetics, piercings, tattoos) separately from the body that it modifies. *Body and clothing co-belong*, and any non-abstract theory of clothing should consider it embodied. Second, the clothes-body complex is a social reality that takes shape *in the presence of an actual or imagined community*. It would be a mistake to think of the relationship between body and dress as a private affair. Third, the social character of clothing depends, even more than on its ability to represent and/or negotiate identities, on its ability to *enact body language* and thus activate interaction. To fully understand the clothes-body complex we must therefore analyze how the clothes-body idiom works in more detail.

Criticizing the Idea of a Language of Clothing

How, then, do clothes contribute to interpersonal communication?

In fashion studies, it is common to talk of the "language of clothes." This abused expression is often a refrain used to conceal the vagueness of a commonplace, while on other occasions it is deliberately used in a metaphorical sense, using "language" as a synonym of "communication" without claiming that communication through clothes actually operates as a proper language (see, e.g., Roach and Eicher [1979] 2007). However, there have been attempts in fashion studies, especially in the 1980s, to interpret variations in fashion and clothing literally as the manifestation of a linguistic code and thus apply the rules governing natural languages to the clothing system. The most well-known study of this kind was conducted by Alison Lurie in *The Language of Clothes* (1981), while similar attempts were carried out by Hillestad (1980), Polhemus (2011: 45–54), Rouse (1989: 20–7) and others. An authoritative precursor to these approaches was Roland Barthes in his influential essay "Le bleu est à la mode cette année" ([1960] 1993).[9] These theories, which obviously acknowledge the communicative function of clothes, presume to identify in clothing a system of signs governed by a code which, although very simple, functions in an analogous manner to a language code. Language codes are systems of rules that allow simple signs (e.g., words) to be assembled into meaningful sentences. The garments are the "words" of the language of clothes, and looks are the "sentences" that they make it possible to formulate. Each "speaker" masters a certain number of words and statements in proportion to his or her fashion competence. Like natural languages, Lurie (1981) observes, clothing is full of archaic (outmoded), foreign (exotic), and vulgar terms. Some elements of the language of clothes (namely ornaments and accessories) have the function of modifying the meaning of the sentence (the outfit), in a similar way to adjectives and adverbs in verbal language.

The hypothesis that clothing works as a language is based on questionable assumptions. On the clothing side, the semantic determinacy of garments and looks is overstated. It is assumed that they work through a relatively precise code, made up of a vocabulary and a grammar leading to the combination of terms into meaningful syntagmas. On the language side, communication is conceived of as a process of transmission (or sometimes sharing) of messages. It is assumed that the meaning of a message is established by the sender and decoded by the recipient. The combination of these two assumptions allows clothing communication to be thought of as a language. Yet, both assumptions are weak. The former has been widely discussed and criticized by scholars, so I shall limit myself to reporting the main aspects of the debate in the next section. I shall devote more space to a discussion of the second assumption, which is still common currency in fashion studies and appears almost incontrovertible at first sight. Moreover, it is by subverting the second assumption that the way clothes, or rather the dressed body, carry out their communicative function in society can be fully appreciated.

Why Clothing Cannot Be Equated with Language

The equation of clothing with language was strongly criticized in the 1990s by scholars such as McCracken (1990), Davis (1992: 1–18), and Campbell ([1997] 2007). At the heart of these criticisms lies the observation that clothing communication does not have a grammar, in contrast to Lurie's hypothesis. That is, it does not possess a syntax that allows different words to be linked together in a generative way. In a natural language such as English, the words "dog," "man," and "bite" have precise meanings, but do not identify a situation yet. When we combine them in the sentence "the dog bit the man" we do not obtain the mere sum of the three previous meanings, but a new meaning, the description of a specific action. The particular way in which we have connected (and conjugated) those three words has generated new meaning. In fact, we could link the same terms differently and obtain another meaning ("the man bit the dog") or no meaning ("dog the man the bite"). The laws that govern the assembly of terms in forming linguistic statements, that is to say, the rules of syntagmatic combination, characterize language as a form of communication but are substantially absent in the case of clothing communication. Available examples of syntagmatic rules applying to the combination of garments are extremely rudimentary: the meaning of the jacket changes according to whether its buttons fasten to the right or the left (Eco 1973: 59), whether it is worn with a tie or not, or whether the tie is dark or fancy. Even if such a clothing code did exist, it would reasonably consist in a collection of model messages rather than in a set of rules for the creation of new messages (Jakobson [1968] 1971).

From this basic observation, the authors mentioned above infer several characteristics of communication through clothes that prevent any comparison with language. Clothing is particularly ambiguous (Davis 1992: 7), since the meaning of its terms, and even more so of their combinations, varies considerably over time in relation to context and observers. Moreover, comprehension of the "texts" of clothing (namely outfits and looks) does not lend itself to a linear reading, which would imply that they are decoded according to the rules assembling the syntagmatic chain, but happens simultaneously and in an impressionistic way (McCracken 1990: 65). This entails that the meaning conveyed by such texts is always elementary and simple, and above all that they lack the generative capacity to produce new, complex, and unpredictable meanings in the way language does. The messages are not the result of combinatorial rules, but are "pre-fabricated," so to speak (McCracken 1990: 66). The interpreter does not read the text in search of a new meaning, but seeks to identify an old, already known one, albeit personalized. Finally, clothing does not enable the development of a conversation between two subjects or more (Campbell [1997] 2007: 164). For example, we rarely receive explicit feedback regarding our appearance, and when we do, it mainly addresses the appearance itself ("that jacket really suits you," "the colors don't match") as opposed to the meaning that we intended the look to convey. As Kaiser also notes (1997: 228), we can appear in front of others but we cannot engage with them through our appearance, nor can we substantially change our appearance quickly enough to adapt its meaning to the varying situations we are involved in.

The Lesson of Semiotics: Dress Versus Dressing

We must therefore give up the presumption of treating clothing communication as a language. How, then, can we describe the way clothing communicates?

Let us return to Roland Barthes. In his essay "Histoire et sociologie du vêtement" ([1957] 2013) he attempted to apply the semiotic categories of *langue* and *parole* developed by Ferdinand de Saussure to clothes. The Swiss linguist had argued that human language works by merging two different but complementary levels. On the one hand, we have the rules that govern the emission of sounds, allowing them to take on standard configurations and convey meanings that other people understand. On the other, we have the set of material sounds that we call syllables, words, sentences, that is, the concrete speech of individuals, which is not standardized at all.

In the terminology of Saussure ([1916] 2011: 7), the first level is that of *langue* ("language"): in order to work as a language, sounds must be articulated according to certain rules of composition, for example, pronunciation, spelling, grammar, and syntax. These are not artificial rules, like those governing formal languages (such as mathematics, in which the meaning of the sign π is arbitrarily assigned), but "natural" rules, which have arisen spontaneously from social life. In a literal sense, they are social institutions. A grammar rule, in fact, is the linguistic equivalent of a collective norm of conduct, which is independent of individuals and indeed coerces them to use it (if you do not correctly pronounce the sound "water" nobody will give you a drink, regardless of their good or bad intentions). As they are the historical product of a community that communicates, the rules of natural language evolve with the continuous transformation of the dominant culture.

The second level, the actual events through which language literally materializes in physical phenomena such as sound waves and organ vibrations, is what Saussure ([1916] 2011: 17) calls *parole* ("speaking"): language actualized in a specific speech act. The elements of *parole* do not belong to the linguistic rules, just as the shape of the king's crown and the design of the rook are not part of the rules of chess. They are optional features. Just as we can play chess with a bean in place of the king, so we can make ourselves understood whether we speak in a shrill or deep voice or with a southern or northern accent.

The fact that *parole* includes the individual and circumstantial elements of speaking does not imply that it is less important than *langue* in determining the human language. The two aspects are closely related and presuppose each other (Saussure [1916] 2011: 18). Without *langue*, sounds would be unintelligible or would be reduced to a set of merely denotative grunts. But without *parole*, language would not exist at all, it would neither be able to settle down nor change over time. The modifications of sounds that occur in every actual linguistic exchange lead to the development of grammatical rules. Language is simultaneously what "guides" the *parole* and an effect of it, as if it were an "instruction booklet" that is written as the device is used.

When Barthes ([1957] 2013) revived Saussure's distinction, he did so to obviate a shortcoming of fashion studies, which at that time was almost exclusively historical in focus, and systematically disregarded the normative dimension of dress, tracing clothing choices back to the random sequence of fashions or to cultural and social changes. At that time, fashion studies overlooked the fact that the nature of clothing behavior changes when passing from impromptu actions, often dependent on circumstantial objectives (such as throwing a blanket over the shoulders to protect oneself from cold and humidity), to systematic actions regulated by a set of collective norms (such as donning a cloak when leaving home). Buying and wearing a cloak of a particular shape and fabric, in fact, implies that there is a system of rules (about materials, shapes, colors, accessories, occasions, and ways of use) that have no other justification but the fact that the community considers them binding. The French semiologist terms *costume* ("dress") the set of such "normative links which justify, oblige, prohibit, tolerate, in a word control the arrangement of garments on a concrete wearer" (Barthes [1957] 2013: 7). Fashion is its most typical manifestation in the contemporary world. *Costume* corresponds to Saussure's *langue* in the field of clothing: a social institution that dominates and binds individual actions, a reservoir of norms that frames the contingent choices of individuals.

If Barthes's semiotic interest was focused on dress as an institutional, "sociological," and structural dimension of the clothing system, in order to fully understand the function of clothes in communicative practice we need to look at the side of *parole*, the act of dressing through which the individual handles ongoing social interaction by drawing on the reservoir of dress norms, thus actualizing it. Barthes ([1957] 2013: 8) calls this facet of clothing communication *habillement* ("dressing"), and stresses that it is essentially circumstantial, "psychological," the way in which the individual wears the *costume* proposed (and required) by the community. It manifests itself in multiple features including (1) individual forms and dimensions of the garment dictated by the body of the wearer and by the relationship that develops between body and garment through the movements and typical postures of the subject; (2) how worn out and dirty the garment is, which is an expression of its history and the situations in which it has been worn; (3) anomalies and exceptions to the rules established by *costume*, which are the effect of idiographic characteristics of the subject and his or her freedom from the norm; (4) individual or circumstantial variations in the mode of use, including the non-usage of some garments or accessories.[10]

Habillement intrigues Barthes especially as the initial stage in the institutionalization process that produces the rules of dress. This happens, for instance, when the casual wearing of a coat over the shoulders, sleeves dangling, gradually becomes expression of a lifestyle, a culture, a social group, and all this is incorporated into the coat in the form of a cut and accessories specifically designed for that use. However, wearing a coat over the shoulders communicates a meaning even when it has not yet been institutionalized in a *costume*, when no social norm has yet established the correct usage conditions. The interest in the structure of the language of clothes led Barthes to neglect the communicative function of the practice of dressing, which is nevertheless fundamental in shaping social interactions in everyday life.

The speech act is not a mechanical application of pre-established rules, but lives on the dialectic between the rule and its application. We must keep this fact in mind so as not to fall into a naive view of clothing communication. Let us consider verbal language again. The normative apparatus of *langue* is an inescapable precondition of verbal communication. Yet, since it is a normative apparatus, it is also a "hardening" of language, since it imposes constraints on speech acts. Following rules is the condition for communicating, but it can also be an obstacle to better communication, especially when the speaker has not perfectly mastered the "rules of the game." In that case the speaker may, on the contrary, be "played" by language, for example, when to extricate oneself from a difficult situation, one relies on proverbs, sayings, or set phrases. In such circumstances, language is no longer at the service of understanding, but puts the speaker, as it were, at the service of language (see also Bourdieu [1980] 1990: 57). Communication unfolds in the best possible way when *langue* is mastered so well that the speech act can become partly autonomous, sometimes drifting away from the rule and then conforming again. Some cornerstones of literature (James Joyce, Martin Heidegger, Carlo Emilio Gadda) owe their appeal to this skill. When it happens in everyday life, language fully fulfills the function of empowering understanding and does not subjugate the speech act to its own normative requirements. In clothed-bodily communication, too, the norm can subjugate the individual to the point of rigidifying, rather than empowering, communication. Here too the rule can gain the upper hand over its own concrete implementation. This is when fashion victims appear, those who take a fad too far, thus taking the look from the glamorous to the ridiculous. Such consumers are not able to personalize the rules of fashion according to their communicative and expressive needs, but instead subordinate these needs to the rules, thus becoming their victims. When this happens, fashion triumphs, and the social actor is reduced to a "mask." Conversely, when the individual masters the medium, fashion transcends into elegance, classy taste, a relaxed use of clothing that enables the body to communicate without being noticed. The person is then master of the medium and able to create his or her own "speech" freely by "contaminating" garments and escaping the standardized trends of industrial production (the old trap of the total look).

In conclusion, the practice of *habillement* is a fundamental aspect of clothing communication for at least two reasons. First, because dress cannot act if it is disembodied. It is a tool for aligning the actions and experiences of individuals, but it cannot be actualized except through their concrete, contingent, and individual behavior. Second, because the *costume-habillement* (*langue-parole*) pair does not only concern the composition of clothes (suit and tie), but also how they are worn and used (the tie knot tight or loose) embedded in individual life situations (early in the morning, late at night). All this has a high communicative value in social interactions. The institutional dimension is one crucial, but not the only, regulative framework.

The Lesson of Pragmatics: The Inferential Model of Communication

The dominant trend in fashion studies has long been to look at the institutional dimension of fashion, while neglecting that of individual practice. If Sophie Woodward's wonderful book *Why Women Wear What They Wear* (2007) marked a turning point toward a greater consideration of what individuals do when they dress, previously this kind of interest had remained mostly confined to social psychology, particularly the work of Susan Kaiser. The prevailing interest had been in fashion, historical trends, the relationship between clothing and social belonging: in short, everything that relates to the concept of identity described above. In this context, addressing the communicative function of clothing meant focusing on the linguistic rules that govern it rather than on concrete communicative interaction between people.

The scant attention paid to *parole* also derives from the fact that pragmatics[11] developed relatively late, in any case after Barthes had proposed his semiotic analysis of fashion. Pragmatics specifically considers language as the concrete action of a subject within a social world, thus restoring verbal language to its original status of social action or behavior. Speaking is as much a bodily action as screaming, laughing, or walking. A code regulating the emission of sounds (the language grammar) is added to this characteristic of the voice without changing its nature. In the command "Stop!" the articulation of sounds is coordinated with the tone of the voice, volume, facial expression, posture and body movements, to perform an overall act designed to interrupt the action of the other. What the verbal order performs is not substantially different from holding the other by the arm. For pragmatics, communication never takes place through purely verbal messages, but through complete behavior, or rather segments of behavior, each of which is "a fluid and multifaceted compound of many behavioral modes— verbal, tonal, postural, contextual, etc.—all of which qualify the meaning of all the others" (Watzlawick et al. 1967: 31). Verbal language, as I have argued above, is only one specific aspect and a limited, though fundamental, portion of communication in general, which is bodily by its very nature.

From this general observation, Watzlawick, Beavin and Jackson derive what they call the first axiom of the pragmatics of communication: "*one cannot* not *communicate*" (Watzlawick et al. 1967: 32). This is a fundamental principle for understanding the communicative function of clothing. It is impossible not to communicate because every act of communication is a form of interaction, a case of social behavior. And behavior has no opposite, that is, non-behavior. To be silent is to behave. To stay still is to behave. Not to dress (i.e., undressing) is to behave. In short, when we are in the presence of others, any action or inaction on our part is perceived by them as our behavior, and is therefore read by them as a sign of our explicit or implicit intentions, of our character, of our history (Goffman 1963: 35).

Everybody interprets the behavior of others, whether it is randomly observed or an intentionally communicative action. Understanding messages is equivalent to inferring from them information about the sender, his or her intentions and other manifest or hidden characteristics. This is true even for verbal language: in most circumstances the utterance "I am thirsty" is understood not as a description of the physical state of the speaker, but as a request ("give me a drink"). The meaning of the sentence is not the conventional one fixed by the code (English grammar, in this case), but that which the addressee infers from the utterance, how it is enunciated and the context in which it is enunciated, so that s/he will probably pour a glass of cool water instead of starting a conversation. This is all the more true, of course, for the clothes-body idiom, in which the code, as we have seen, is much weaker and undetermined. From the moving clothes-body complex we infer a great deal of information about the subject, who, indeed, cannot *not* communicate roles and typifying details (gender, age, social class, etc.) as well as personal and circumstantial data such as mood, current activity and immediate intentions. This is the reason why, if considered within the framework of social interactions, there is no room for dressing "randomly," without caring. Dressing randomly is also a way of communicating through clothes.

Pragmatics calls this fundamental structure of human communication the "inferential model" (Grice 1986), and contrasts it with the naive view implied by the code model, which Umberto Eco (1975: 51) also called the "hydraulic model," the first statement of which is usually attributed to Shannon and Weaver (1949). In its standard formulation, the hydraulic model envisages content that passes from the addresser to the addressee, without considering the problematic nature of its "passage." How does an idea, an item of information, an image, pass from one mind to another? What actual channel is opened between two communicating subjects? The naivety of the hydraulic model consists in its failure to address such questions, which instead concern a fundamental issue: ideas are closed inside brains and cannot be somehow "transferred" to another mind; nor can they be "shared" among two or more minds (see also Sperber and Wilson 1986: 1). Instead of thinking of ideas (or even, more concretely, messages) that inexplicably shift from one mind to another, the inferential model explains communication as the production and interpretation of clues. The sender creates useful clues for the recipient to produce certain meanings, and the recipient interprets the clues provided by the sender on the basis of his or her knowledge of the context in which the exchange takes place. An incisive formulation of this theory is offered by Sperber and Wilson:

> Communication is a process involving two information-processing devices. One device modifies the physical environment of the other. As a result, the second device constructs representations similar to representations already stored in the first device. Oral communication, for instance, is a modification by the speaker of the hearer's acoustic environment, as a result of which the hearer entertains thoughts similar to the speaker's own. (Sperber and Wilson 1986: 1)

Underlying communication, then, is the fact that human beings attribute to their peers mental states similar to their own, including the capacity to give meaning to situations. This faculty allows them to imagine the possible mental reactions of another to the perception of a state of affairs, hence to anticipate the meanings that this will elicit. Communicating means changing the experiential context of the addressees in a way that, presumably, will induce them to draw those inferences that we wish them to draw, that is to give the situation those meanings that we wish to instigate in their minds. The fundamental error of the hydraulic model is to imagine that the meaning of a message can be fixed into the medium by the sender by means of a code: that the meaning of a house is imprinted in the word "house" and the meaning of a look is imprinted in the style of its garments. It is, however, quite the opposite: the actual author of meanings is the recipient of messages.

The Lesson of Symbolic Interactionism: Communication as Performance

Given that the "transmission" of contents from one mind to another is not possible, and neither is their "sharing," behind these metaphors lies the fact that communication actually consists of a *performance* which the so-called sender puts on in the presence of the so-called recipient, so that the latter is able to produce the expected meanings. This is the main lesson of symbolic interactionism. This approach helps to place an understanding of communication based on the inferential model within a more general theoretical framework, in which the link between communication and social behavior is highlighted in both directions: a communicative act is actually a gesture, that is, a form of social interaction, while a social interaction is normally guided by the ability to influence the behavior of others by acting communicatively on the meanings that they produce.

George Herbert Mead (1934) summarized this fundamental structure of human interaction by observing that *gesture* is "the basic mechanism whereby the social process goes on" (Mead 1934: 13–14). In an interaction, Mead continued, gestures "are movements of the first organism which act as specific stimuli calling forth the (socially) appropriate responses of the second organism." They include not only hand gestures, but also facial expressions, postures and body movements. They can reveal the meaning of a person's conduct even when s/he is not aware of it, and thus enable extremely rich communication to be established between individuals, an "early stage" of communication that precedes—Mead concludes (1934: 15)—the symbol proper, and deliberate communication. The latter, that is to say natural languages, is only one particular aspect of social behavior, so that utterances are ultimately, as mentioned above, "vocal gestures" (Mead 1934: 61). In his focus on gestures, Mead considered the body alone, thus disregarding the indivisibility of the clothes-body complex. However, this aspect was later analyzed, in the tradition of symbolic interactionism, by Gregory Stone ([1962] 1995), who showed that the appearance of social actors— which in addition to body gestures and postures includes clothing, grooming, the use of objects, and the staging of the environment—constitutes the essence of that "early-stage" form of communication that precedes and makes verbal interaction possible. The clothes-body complex is the original, fundamental means of communicative interaction between humans. Any other language is but a byproduct and enhancement of it.

Moreover, Mead and symbolic interactionism show that social life is entirely based on this fundamental structure, in which interaction is mediated by the "reading" that each individual makes of others' behavior. This "early-stage" communication is therefore not something that human beings can exercise or not exercise, unlike running, singing or mathematical calculation. It is constitutive of social interaction and is always there wherever human life exists. Social interaction is originally based on the capacity of actors to give meaning to the actions of others, and this is the origin of the development of social relationships and structures. Therefore communication is the structuring power of society. As Mead says:

> [C]ommunication [is] in the significant sense the organizing process in the community. It is not simply a process of transferring abstract symbols; it is always a gesture in a social act which calls out in the individual himself the tendency to the same act that is called out in others. (Mead 1934: 327–8)

The final sentence of this quotation refers to the mutual dependence (or double contingency) of social actors when they interact with each other. The meaning of a communicative act is the result of a reciprocal adjustment between their gestures (Mead 1934: 75–82) based on the assumption of the role of the other and on the anticipation of his or her future actions:

> [T]he person who uses this gesture and so communicates assumes the attitude of the other individual as well as calling it out in the other. He himself is in the rôle of the other person whom he is so exciting and influencing. It is through taking this rôle of the other that he is able to come back on himself and so direct his own process of communication. (Mead 1934: 254)

In a communicative process, the alignment of the understanding of the meaning of the acts that are performed comes from a mutual adjustment of gestures.

The person who uses a gesture to communicate (e.g., by saying "I am thirsty") assumes that the other is able to connect that gesture to a specific course of action (pouring water), as does the addressee, reciprocally, in allowing the perception of the vocal gesture to be followed by a particular course of action (handing a glass of water to the speaker). Each behaves according to the expectations they have developed toward the behavior of the other.

It was Erving Goffman (1959) who applied the consequences of these ideas to describing social processes, since he developed a dramaturgical approach to sociology in which social interaction is basically explained as a kind of performance. Goffman argues that the individual is a social actor in the strict sense of the term, performing daily before an audience composed of others, who are interested in understanding who s/he is and what actions can be expected from him/her. Since it is the others who attribute specific characteristics to the actor, giving a meaning to his/her performance, the actor is called upon to perform according to certain strategies that induce others to attribute to him/her the characteristics that s/he wants them to attribute to him/her, so that they then behave toward him/her in the ways s/he wants them to behave. Daily life does not take place in a neutral space, but constantly in the presence of a public composed of the people we meet. Therefore social action is always, by nature, a kind of performance: "Half-aware that a certain aspect of his activity is available for all present to perceive," writes Goffman (1963: 33), "the individual tends to modify this activity, employing it with its public character in mind."

It is not a question of deceiving others. However, since the behavior of others toward us is influenced by the image they build of us, and since this image is a result of the fact that, according to the first axiom of pragmatics of communication, we cannot not communicate, it is only by managing our appearance that we can hope to transmit to them an "authentic" image of us, that is, an image that induces others to behave toward us in a manner congruous with our expectations and our abilities. Actors behave "so that [the] future consequences will be the kind that would lead a just individual to treat them now in a way they want to be treated; once this is done, they have only to rely on the perceptiveness and justness of the individual who observes them" (Goffman 1959: 242). All this precedes (although it then includes) verbal interaction:

> [W]hen individuals come into one another's immediate presence in circum stances where no spoken communication is called for, they none the less inevitably engage one another in communication of a sort, for in all situations, significance is ascribed to certain matters that are not necessarily connected

with particular verbal communications. These comprise bodily appearance and personal acts: dress, bearing, movement and position, sound level, physical gestures such as waving or saluting, facial decorations, and broad emotional expression. (Goffman 1963: 33)

Clothing and makeup, as elements of the clothes-body idiom, are part of the essential core of the human capacity to communicate as a whole. They are not embellishments but belong to the driving forces that hold society together. We can now return to consider more closely the fundamental features of communication through clothes.

Reading Meanings into Clothes

In fashion studies, we are accustomed to uncritically accepting a naive vision of communication based on the hydraulic model, which prevents us from acknowledging the crucial role played by the clothes-body complex in social processes. Of course, this is not universally the case.[12] Some scholars have been aware of the unsuitability of the hydraulic model to explain clothed-bodily communication. For instance Colin Campbell, one of Alison Lurie's leading critics, realized the need to abandon the simplistic view based on the hurried assumption that, as clothing is usually worn in public and mediates interaction between actors, those actors use it to make statements and transmit messages. Campbell's conclusions are clear and deserve to be quoted in full:

> The critically important point is that [. . .] since consumers cannot avoid wearing clothes they are unable to prevent others from "reading" meanings into the clothes they wear. Now they may be well aware of this: that is to say, they may anticipate that the wearing of an old, worn suit is likely to lead others to assume that they are relatively poor. But it does not follow from this that because they wear it they therefore *intend* to send such a message. Other considerations may have dictated the choice of clothes on this occasion. (Campbell [1997] 2007: 166)

The point is that we cannot in fact prevent others from reading their own meanings into our clothes, therefore we cannot intentionally send definite messages. The most significant contribution in this direction has come from Malcolm Barnard, who, having dedicated himself to the study of fashion as communication, understood the need to reject stereotypical conceptions of communication processes. In particular, in criticizing Lurie's overly close analogy between fashion and language, Barnard observed that it ultimately stems from a "mechanistic view of language and meaning" (Barnard 1996: 30), referring by this expression to something very similar to what we have called the hydraulic model. Subsequently, Barnard thoroughly criticized the idea that meaning can be *transmitted* from a sender to a recipient by sending a message. On the contrary, argued Barnard (2007: 171), meaning is a cultural construction that springs from the interaction between social actors. It is not fixed in the garment, nor does it coincide with the intention of the designer or the wearer. Instead, "meaning is constructed in the interaction between an individual's values and beliefs (which they hold as a member of a culture) and the item of visual culture" (Barnard 2007: 175). Clothes have no meaning until they enter the experiential horizon of a social actor with previous experiences as well as values and beliefs inherited from his or her community. Imagine meeting a young man wearing a hoodie in a lonely lane late at night. The meaning commonly attributed to the hooded sweatshirt in the United Kingdom in recent decades, that of an antisocial personality and hooliganism,[13] is not an inherent characteristic of the garment itself, nor does it derive from the designers' will or from the wearer's intentions. The wearer may or may not be a hooligan, but the meaning of the garment is produced by those who see him, as they are already embedded in a cultural context. The meaning of the hoodie in the situation described, and the fear it may engender in others, originate from the intersection between seeing the sweatshirt and the previous experiences of the viewer within the hegemonic system of values and beliefs which s/he shares (e.g., mediated by TV shows or post sharing on social networks).

Of course, the creators and wearers of the hoodie can "play" with the cultural context and take advantage of the meanings that are likely to be assigned to it. As human interaction is based on the relationship between mutual expectations, if we know that in a particular environment the hoodie is "read" as a sign of delinquency, we can decide to wear the hoodie to intimidate people. Like other objects of material culture, garments have affordances with which they interact with humans and somehow direct the meanings they produce. Garments are not neutral, inert, available to any reading that the viewer wishes to make of them, but instead encourage certain interpretations over others. They have an agency that they exercise over users and, in general, over all those whose experience they enter.[14] However, their non-neutrality must be understood in a strong sense: they are not inert even in the hands of their creators and wearers. The meaning they convey in a certain situation is not fixed into them by the designer or the wearer, but is the product of the situation in question, it is read into the situation by those who perceive them. Even the meaning imagined by the designer or the wearer is relative to their particular point of view, as they themselves are spectators of the event embedded in a specific cultural context.

The main preconceptions deriving from the hydraulic model prevent us from grasping the lively negotiation that takes place between social actors when they interact through their dressed bodies, and reduce clothing to a residual aspect of social communication, poor and of little use in people's lives. Those preconceptions can very often be found at work in descriptions of fashions and customs. Let us analyze, by way of example, the following description:

> The homosexuals of the mid seventies wanted to make the statement that fags were not weeds, that manliness has no necessary connection with sexual orientation. Out of this came the "clone" look. In a way, the clone was a caricature of masculinity. The clone wore jeans, lumber shirts and jackets, distressed leather and heavy boots, and although clean-shaven sported a moustache. This almost uniform style had a number of advantages. The clone was instantly recognizable to other gay men, yet did not invite violence from queer-bashers. The look would not offend at work for most colleagues would miss its significance; yet it gave the wearer the satisfaction of being able to feel that he was, in one sense, being openly gay even if most straights didn't realize it. The clone uniform emphasized the masculinity of gayness. (Wilson [1985] 2003: 202)

In this short excerpt, four preconceptions derived from the hydraulic model can be identified. The first assumes that *the meaning of a garment, an outfit or a look is encoded in it*, fixed for cultural reasons and recognized by all those who are familiar with the original cultural context. In this perspective, the clone look has a precise meaning because it emphasizes the masculinity of gays, so much so that it is "instantly recognizable" to other men who share the same culture. The very name with which it is identified implies the idea that its masculine meaning (as opposed to openly gay looks) is encoded in it. What gets lost in this description, however, is the everyday life of people who have worn that look in situated social contexts, having to interact with other gays who might not have recognized them as gays and with heterosexuals who might have equally discriminated against them, having sometimes to conceal their own sexual identity, sometimes to reveal it more openly, therefore interpreting the look day by day, that is, personalizing it according to experiences and expectations. From a general, abstract perspective it can be argued that in the case described above a particular meaning has been codified into a look. But in real life, choices, even when inspired by stereotyped looks, actually respond to circumstances that are never the same. The second preconception deriving from the hydraulic model assumes that *the meaning of clothes is shared and stable*—precisely because it is coded in a standardized look—and is therefore independent of the circumstances in which they are worn. Being an "almost uniform style," the clone look seems to have had a steady meaning for all those who wore it in all situations in which they wore it. This however discounts the possibility that while some were interested in the issue of masculinity, others instead were driven by the need to conform to the trendy style or by other specific communication needs. The third preconception, connected to the previous ones, implies that in the interaction between two or more social actors *the meaning of clothes is established by the wearer*, who chooses how to dress according to the meanings codified in garments. Choosing to wear the clone look would enable gays to "fix" the meaning they wanted to convey ("fags were not weeds"), that is, to determine the reading of gays and heterosexuals. This ignores the gap between the communicative need of the wearer and the multiple, contradictory readings that others make of his or her look. Work colleagues are not brutes who "miss its significance," they are subjects capable of signification who attribute a different meaning to that look than the one given to it by gays. Finally, the fourth preconception—perhaps the fundamental idea of the hydraulic model—is that the look allows gays to "make the statement": that is, *it enables the wearer to actually transmit to the public the codified meaning*. The hydraulic model by nature supports the idea that there can be a transmission of meanings from the sender to the recipient through the use of clothes, conceived of as messages or "vehicles" of meaning.

Since the hydraulic model is dominant in the common understanding of communication processes, it should come as no surprise that it also underlies a large part of fashion studies. I have purposely quoted an excerpt from an authoritative text, a classic of fashion studies, to dispel the suspicion that adhesion to the hydraulic model could be ascribed to an author's negligence. Instead, when considering fashion as a set of trends, styles or costumes to be analyzed as meaningful "texts," it is easy to overlook the work involved in the daily practice of dressing (Shilling [1993] 2012: 123–5). The inferential model, in contrast, makes it possible to appreciate the situated character of a look, which, like all practices, is embodied. Entwistle criticized Hebdige (1979) precisely for having textualized dress practices: "If practices are reduced to texts, the complexity of fashion and dress and the way in which it is embodied is largely neglected" (Entwistle [2000] 2015: 71). It is to Bourdieu's great credit that he highlighted the centrality of embodiment in human life, and the fact that meanings are mediated by situated bodies (Bourdieu [1980] 1990: 66–79). Responding to the opposite errors of mechanism, which reduces human action to the effect of natural causes, and finalism, which overestimates the power of consciousness and free choice, Bourdieu ([1997] 2000: 135–42) observed that the cognitive activities, including thoughts and choices, are inherent in the dispositions of the body. Before any conscious decision or rational calculation, social agents are endowed with schemes of perception, appreciation and action which are ways of being that result from the durable modification of the body. They have been shaped through that protracted exposure to the world that we call experience. Experience is practical experience, just as the comprehension we have of the world is practical, prepared by embodied dispositions. We understand a situation and we know how to act in it thanks to our practical sense, that is, because our body—having incorporated the right dispositions (the *habitus*) over time—is already inclined and able to act "rightly," adequately, by spontaneously adjusting its practices to the situation. The fact that Bourdieu insists on the alignment of tastes and dispositions generated by class membership helps to explain the uniformity of consumer choices without diminishing the situated character of choices and interactions.

This also applies to the field of clothing, and implies that the practical use of clothing can never be entirely traced back to the meanings designed into them by the fashion industry or by the fashion media. In other words, the actual daily use of clothing (Barthes's *habillement*) far exceeds the norm dictated by fashion (*costume*) through the industry's material creations and the cross-referencing of the images and statements featured by fashion media. The choice of garments, their organization into an outfit, the way they are actually worn and the way in which they are perceived by others—all these acts entail the embodied dispositions of consumers, which are the outcome of their individual life experience or unique biographical situation (Schütz [1955] 1973: 308). Companies' advertisements and magazines' editorials do contribute to meaning formation (Barthes [1967] 1983: 3–18), as they are part of our experience, but only insofar as they are mediated by the lived experience of individuals within social situations. Clothes and looks are texts in the sense that they carry meanings, but they are texts incorporated in situated and embodied practices, so that the meanings they carry can never be detached from the practices that generate them.

What Appearance Communicates: From Social Belonging to Personal Attitudes

When we choose day by day which clothes to buy and to wear, we aim to maximize pleasure in the social situations that we expect to encounter during the day. Expectations do not have to be conscious, nor does the relationship between appearance and expected situations need to be planned, or even effective. Furthermore, although the human capacity to signify exposes everybody to the need to communicate, the degree of awareness of such "exposure" on the part of actors is highly dependent on sociographic (age, gender)[15] and personal factors. We cannot *not* communicate through our appearance, but we are not always able to actively manage such forced communication, and certainly not all in the same way.

However, actors are normally aware that the reactions and behavior of others toward them depend on their appearance. Indeed, the clothes-body complex is already there when an interaction starts.[16] *Appearance* constitutes a primary element of social interaction, serving to identify the participants and establish the framework within which verbal communication becomes possible.[17]

What do we communicate through appearance? Many things. I will briefly focus on those that are most frequently referred to. For the sake of simplicity, I will disregard the very deep ties that exist between the clothes-body idiom and verbal language. Furthermore, I will also exclude those situations in which appearance is governed by a highly formalized code (such as uniforms and sumptuary laws),[18] as these are specific cases of little relevance to the issue of fat fashion. Let us focus, instead, on daily life situations.

In everyday life, the clothes-body idiom leverages a multiplicity of symbolic clues that contribute substantially to the development of interactions and the management of social life. Of course, appearance expresses such aspects as gender, social class, and political, subcultural, ethnic, or religious affiliations, as well as adherence to shared moral values (such as ecological awareness)[19] or aesthetic values (such as fashionability). According to several scholars, this ability is concretely used by actors to define their position in interactions.[20] Yet, as Sophie Woodward (2007) has demonstrated empirically, interactions are conditioned by a multiplicity of other elements that the spectator is able to read in a person's appearance, and that therefore materialize in his or her choice of clothes. Institutional and normative elements, such as fashion trends and the ideals of beauty and elegance, are always reinterpreted in relation to situated, circumstantial, and individual variables.

First of all, identity can be *qualified through clothing*. This is the phenomenon that Goffman (1961) calls "role distance." Briefly, while actors, in curating their appearance, can hardly divest themselves of clues that reveal aspects of their identity (such as their social origin), they can take a stance on them by declaring their non-compliance:[21] for example, young people sometimes wear sneakers with a formal suit to distance themselves from a stereotypical adult clothing style with which they are forced to conform for professional, class, or circumstantial reasons. The rarity of garments is often used in this same way (Roach and Eicher [1979] 2007: 111). Rarity is not necessarily synonymous with luxury. Clothes can be inexpensive but out of the ordinary because they are out of context, because they are out of fashion or anticipate incipient trends, or because they are difficult to find. Because of these characteristics, rare garments combined with a fashionable look are often used to express a personal character, to mark a detachment from the standardizing power of fashion without embracing anti-fashion.

A similar field of inferences from a person's appearance regards what Enninger (1985: 100) has called "clothing registers." These are expected clothing styles in specific situations in the context of a particular community. For example, ritual encounters (such as a Catholic mass), ceremonial situations (a wedding), and occupational contexts (a law firm) usually require a certain dress code and stereotyped forms of behavior. Yet, clothing registers also allow the wearers both to interpret and to detach themselves from their roles and thus negotiate their specific positions in the situation. These forms of disengagement from the dictates of the dress code can express particular power relationships (I am the son of the boss, hence I am exempted from compliance), disinterest for the event or community (I don't want to advance my career here, hence I am not interested in complying), or types of interpersonal relationships (I am a close friend of the groom, hence I refuse to comply), and so forth.

Inferences from a person's appearance can also relate to his or her *character and personality traits*, such as shyness, determination, sociability, authoritativeness, adaptability, even intelligence. The literature on these aspects, particularly in the psychological field, is extensive. Damhorst (1990) provides a thorough, albeit outdated, overview. In general terms, the possibility of inferring character and personality traits from the appearance of an actor affects his or her clothing choices. The tailored skirt suit became the style preferred by career women in the 1970s, that is, when they began to carve out a space for themselves in previously male-dominated professions, at a time when gender discrimination at work was stronger than now in Western countries. The skirted suit, reproducing and feminizing some fundamental elements of male dress, communicated personality traits (seriousness, power, commitment) considered important in the world of professions dominated by men (Entwistle [2000] 2015: 187–91).

A more changeable and serendipitous aspect than personality traits, *mood* is often mentioned by people to explain their clothing choice. It is equally considered by the public, so much so that appearance can be staged both to express and to conceal the wearer's emotional state (Roach and Eicher [1979] 2007: 110). Typically, colorful, unstructured clothes correspond more frequently to a positive emotional state (whether real or staged), while dark, linear, inconspicuous clothes convey a sad or introverted emotional state. Similarly, Efrat Tseëlon (1995: 61–4) has shown that taking care of one's appearance is often a powerful tool to boost one's sense of self-worth, as it checks negative opinions of others about oneself. Dressing up for the situation is therefore not just a way of conforming to a more or less explicit dress code. It also provides a kind of armor against an uncomfortable situation, a way of not becoming the subject of attention, of comparison with others, of explicit criticism. It is a way to claim the respect due by default to those who do not disturb the interaction order.

Finally, *attitudes*, that is to say, predispositions to behave in a certain way, can be discerned in the clothes-body complex (Stone [1962] 1995: 21; Kaiser 1997: 308–11). We should not forget that in social interactions participants' attitudes are not an objective fact but part of the subject's performance by means of the clothes-body idiom and which others anticipate according to that appearance. Thus, in the field of sexual preferences, clothing is often read by others to anticipate expectations about the homosexual or heterosexual choice that the person will make, in the field of political attitudes it is useful for prefiguring electoral choices, political values, and topics of conversation, in the field of social attitudes it elicits expectations about the degree of conformity or deviance, religiousness, fashionability.

How Appearance Communicates: The Frames of Reference

Mood, personality, attitudes, and even social belonging are not fixed data that interaction can convey through a codified language, as they are constructed and negotiated again and again through the mutual dependence of each actor on the expectations of others (Kaiser 1997: 186–90; Stone [1962] 1995: 27–8; Wilson 1992: 9). They are aspects which others infer from our appearance and which we can adjust by manipulating our appearance, which should not, therefore, be considered a tool of expression of predetermined conditions, but rather of definition and negotiation of the actor's position within the interaction:

> From the perspective of the decoder [. . .] her/his knowledge of what is rated as unmarked and marked vestimentary behavior for the event enables her/him to make inferences with regard to the social identity which a person vestimantarily

projects on his appearance on the stage of the event. That means that self's and other's clothing serves initial and tentative reduction of mutual uncertainty. Although the design feature of prevarication makes the feigning of false identities feasible, the identity a decoder takes from clothing will initially determine the kind of relationship s/he opens with the other. (Enninger 1985: 105)

Sophie Woodward has applied this concept to women's daily clothing choices, highlighting their essential function in the construction of interaction:

In dressing, the daily creation of [outfits] becomes a means through which women attempt to convince others that they are a particular kind of person. They wear the black leather skirt in an attempt to persuade their friends that they are sexy and chic. When they are successful, the item of clothing becomes an extension of the person, as the body, clothing, and person are fused. [. . .] When a woman chooses to wear a funky top, she not only has to believe that she is a funky fashionable person, but moreover when she actually wears the top, she has to both look and act in an appropriate manner. This acquires a particular poignancy as clothing is displayed on the body, because women have to measure whether their bodies live up to the clothing. A woman who desires to be fashionable not only has to wear the right pair of skinny grey drainpipe jeans, she also has to have the skinny thighs that go in them. (Woodward 2007: 12)

The situated character of the inferences that allow the clothes-body idiom to work becomes clear if attention is paid to the context that frames clothed-bodily communication. Several frames of reference enable us in any given situation to make sense of aspects of the look that would otherwise be meaningless (Goffman 1974). They are characteristics of the situation that influence the way in which the clothes-body complex becomes meaningful in the interaction.

First and foremost, the *public* of the performance is relevant. In communication, as we have seen, the characteristics of the recipient are just as important in determining the meaning as the characteristics of the message. Certain easily observable characteristics of the public perceiving a look, such as gender, age, occupation, social class, ethnicity, religious affiliation, or aesthetic tastes, are frequently considered by research. However, beyond these classifications the public that makes sense of a look is incredibly diverse, as it is made up of unique individuals. This makes the meaning attributed to the look unpredictable. Since meanings are not intrinsic to the appearance but attributed by others, they change as their publics change:

At times, appearance perception is on a more conscious plane than other times, but the important thing to remember is that perceivers are not merely passive receivers of information. Perceivers bring unique characteristics to social interactions, and these characteristics influence their frames of reference, world views (how they see the world), and levels of awareness. (Kaiser 1997: 271)

Second, the negotiation of the meaning of the clothes-body complex is dependent upon the *situation* in which the interaction occurs, that is, the physical frame that hosts the interaction. Again, general conditions may influence the meaning of clothes, such as the distinction described by Goffman (1959) between the front stage and backstage (and offstage) of social interaction: the loosened tie knot has a very different meaning if exhibited on the stage, for example during the wedding ceremony, or in the background, for example during a bathroom or smoking break. Yet the meaning of the look is also influenced by circumstantial conditions, such as the weather, other people's clothing or room decor. Consider the case of Rosie reported by Woodward (2007: 68–71): invited to dinner for the first time in a particularly fashionable restaurant, Rosie adapts her appearance to an anticipation of the situation based on photographs and descriptions. In other instances, to negotiate the expectations of others, we even change the environment besides our body (e.g., by adjusting the lights).

A third frame of reference that contributes to making the negotiation of meaning situated is *the dressed subject itself*, the characteristics of which are not stable over time. Our emotional state changes constantly, so that our motivation in our search for understanding in interaction is variable too. Our cognitive state changes constantly too, for instance, the degree to which we are aware of the effect produced by our appearance and the accuracy with which we anticipate the expectations and reactions of others. Even the state of the actor's body is rarely unchanging. Putting on or losing weight, or even the transformation of the body with aging, alters the perception of a look that others and the actor him- or herself have.

Finally, *the circumstantial use* of clothing is obviously occasional. If you have to run to catch a crowded bus to avoid being late for work, your outfit will not look the same compared to when traveling comfortably seated in the back seat of a taxi. Thus, it will have a different meaning for the viewers (and for yourself as well). The circumstances of life affect the meanings that are being constructed in interactions, and especially how looks are perceived by people.

The Function of the Clothes-Body
Idiom in Situated Interactions

A prerequisite for meeting the expectations of others is to anticipate them, hence to get an idea of the kind of social context in which one will act and the reactions that they may have to a particular look. If one has to show up at a formal dinner attended by people who view formal wear positively (e.g., as a sign of reliability, conformity, order, style, good taste, etc.), one is usually aware that the choice of casual dress is a strong, provocative decision that will draw attention to oneself, and maybe a hostile reaction. Often we wish to avoid both things: not only the ill disposition of others but also the mere fact of being in the spotlight of a group of people, exposed to their judgments and comments. Anticipating the expectations of others, therefore, helps us to make our appearance acceptable to them from the outset. To do so, we domesticate the clothes-body complex, civilizing it and molding it to expectations. Thus, in a culture in which fat bodies are perceived as nonstandard, "abnormal," anomalous bodies, so that the common expectation is that the appearance of a "normal" person is essentially thin, caring about one's look usually entails the construction of a lean silhouette. We do not care about our appearance in a generic, abstract manner, but always in relation to a specific social context, generally to a multiplicity of social contexts that we have to face throughout the day and in our lifetime, and into which we wish to integrate as smoothly as possible.

Yet, inclusion is not the only goal of interaction with others. Indeed, interaction is usually a prerequisite for attaining specific goals (we attend a dinner to have fun, to be seen, to make new acquaintances). For this reason, it must unfold in a favorable way that is beneficial to us. Detailed studies of the subjective motivations that underlie daily clothing choices, those of women in particular (Kaiser 1997; Tseëlon 1995 and 2012; Woodward 2007), have shown that in caring about our appearance, we do not only aim to make ourselves acceptable to others, but also to make a good impression on them. The focus shifts here from meeting the expectations of others to influencing them. Dressing to make a good impression means trying to govern those expectations, which no longer regard the generalized other—such as the expectation of formal wear at the dinner, which applies to anyone participating in the event—but ourselves in particular. Yet it is important to understand what is meant by "good impression" in this context. The case of the job interview, a frequently cited case in the literature, clarifies this point well thanks to its simplicity. Trying to make a good impression at a job interview through one's behavior—verbal as well as corporeal—means trying to influence the other's expectations regarding our personality, our abilities, our motivation. But in daily life, the negotiation of expectations is much more complex, since the objective is not as simple and temporally circumscribed as being hired, but multiple and extended over time: living in a fulfilling manner within a social context. Thus, to influence the judgment of others we may even dress to give them a bad impression. Favorably influencing the expectations of others does not exclusively mean making others expect something good from us. We "manipulate" our appearance in order to influence other people's judgment successfully. However, by "successfully" I do not mean "positively" but "usefully," that is, to achieve certain specific objectives. Adolescents in search of conflict with the adult world as their personality develops often use the clothes-body idiom to make oppositional statements and successfully elicit conflict. More in general, influencing other people's expectations means having others expect us to behave in ways in which we wish to behave, and at an acceptable cost. If you wear a funky top, you have to know how to behave like a funky, fashionable person; if you wear skinny grey drainpipe jeans, you have to have the skinny thighs to go with them. Using one's look to influence interaction is not the same as staying inside one's comfort zone, but part of an intense effort to achieve expected goals.

The Place of Fashion, the Place of Thinness

I have insisted on the communicative function of the clothes-body complex, stressing that the individual and situated practice of clothing, what Barthes calls *habillement*, is crucial in determining social interactions—more than Barthes was prepared to admit. The fundamental consequence of this is that dressing in situated interactions contributes substantially to determining the relationship of clothing with the body. *If a garment fits the body, it is because it fits the social life of that body, which is a situated life*, unfolding through the circumstances that follow one another throughout the day.

This obviously does not alter the fact that even general rules of clothing, whether long term (for example the male renunciation of the use of the skirt) or short term (as with fashion trends), are part of everybody's social life, and exert a normative force every day on the way we dress (Entwistle [2000] 2015: 37, 48–9). If on the one hand dressing means manipulating interaction with others, on the other hand interacting with others demands compliance with what those others consider a norm, otherwise the interaction fails. The rules of fashion are the aesthetic and stylistic manifestation of those social norms.

To begin with, fashion ratifies shared rules of clothing by developing and confirming aesthetic ideas around the garments. These are the rules that enable a style or outfit to be perceived as fashionable or unfashionable, contextually appropriate or inappropriate, ordinary or eccentric. They concern, for instance: colors, shape and fabric of clothes, so that a sweater that was trendy some years ago now lies abandoned in the closet; the appropriate way to wear them, so that an Italian man is unlikely to wear open sandals with socks even when his feet are cold; circumstances, so that one does not wear a cocktail dress to a funeral; rules of composition, that is, aspects of compatibility and incompatibility between garments (a tie goes with a shirt, not a T-shirt). In these and in many other cases, our behavior is governed by collective rules, whether we follow them or not.

Furthermore, fashion exerts its normative force on the supply side by establishing the style of clothes available in stores. In this case, it acts through the fashion industry, particularly design. Obviously, consumers are not compelled to adapt to what the industry supplies them with, and can in principle remain faithful to the garments they already possess and to the clothing rules they have learned in the past. Alternatively, they can invent new rules. But we know that this is not normally the case. In fact, the fashion industry is complicit in the relentless flow of fashion both by adapting to style changes and by governing them and making efforts to direct them in accordance with production strategies. As a result, fashion exerts its power over human behavior not only through the subtle system of informal social sanctions (such as disapproving glances or verbal abuse), but also through the much cruder system of industrial production: if a garment is not retailed, by definition it has little chance of establishing itself on the clothing landscape. What the fashion industry produces is the main determinant of the limits of the clothing possibilities that populate our cultural landscape and become conceivable ways for us to dress. Daily clothing choices constitute a sort of co-design experience which, through the garment's interaction with the body, elaborate propositions starting from the "rhetorical prompts" represented by designer garments (Lewis 2007: 309–10).

A third aspect of the normative force of fashion is more closely related to the issue of fat fashion: the ability to establish a regulating ideal for the body and for appearance. In human societies, not all bodies are equal, but they are subject to value judgments that are based on ideal models of corporeality and which leverage categories such as beauty and appropriateness. This power is fundamental with respect to our discussion, as in recent times thinness has become an essential ingredient of the dominant body ideal in Western countries. Moreover, this ideal is so ingrained in fashion that clothing that does not fit is, for obese people, one of the most frequently cited indicators—along with such things as small chairs—that their bodies do not fit normality (Degher and Hughes 1999: 18). As Bye and McKinney (2007: 489) point out, also for regular-size people "discovering that a favorite pair of pants or top no longer fits can be frustrating when the garment is too tight or satisfying if the garment is too big." The fact that a dress does not fit the body properly expresses a statement not only about the dress, but also about the body and its position in the social context. When it relates to size, any defect associated with an unsatisfactory fit does not only concern the inadequacy of the garment for the body, but also the inadequacy of the body with respect to a socially shared body ideal.

By virtue of this fact, thinness constitutes a regulative frame for the daily practice of dressing, a practice which aims to facilitate the negotiation of satisfactory interactions, but cannot disregard the regulative constraints imposed by fashion, since those constraints may play a part in determining whether these interactions are satisfactory or not. To the extent that they establish a thin body ideal, the constraints imposed by fashion substantially limit the communicative capacity of fat bodies: if you do not *look* thin, you enter a semantic frame burdened by stereotypes and prejudices that limit your ability to build an interaction consistent with your desires and expectations. The negative comparison with the regulative ideal of the body dominant in fashion deprives fat bodies of certain opportunities to negotiate and manage satisfactory interactions. Therefore, the clothing options that fashion places at the disposal of regular and fat bodies mostly conceal fat and construct the appearance of a lean body. This means, however, that they essentially deny the individuality of consumers' bodies and "standardize" them according to the thin ideal, as Alison Adam observes:

> A fat body is a body unwilling to conform. As [Mary] Douglas argues, there are sanctions applied to those who go beyond accepted boundaries, and margins are dangerous. [. . .] It is as if their bodies are refusing to conform, yet the clothes they are generally offered are very conformist and conventional, containing those bodies that threaten to break out. A more individual look is harder to achieve. Their choice of wardrobe is limited, although nothing like as limited as it used to be. Finally, they may well have to pay more for their clothes. (Adam 2001: 50–1)

Thus, specifically as a fundamental tool of interpersonal communication, the clothes-body complex has to deal with the institutional dimension of clothing, that is, social norms that bind people in general (Barthes's *costume*), and this affects fat bodies even more than thin bodies. As mentioned above, however, Barthesian semiotics somewhat restricts the normative dimension of languages to a closed, static system of rules (codes), while according a subordinate and less significant function to the social mechanisms through which those rules actually take shape. And yet, the rules of fashion do not arise from a kind of impersonal flow of collective life but rather from situated social interactions in which asymmetries of power, economic capital, and social capital between individuals or groups are at work. In considering the normative dimension of the clothes-body idiom, we should therefore focus not only on the abstract semiotic rules of construction and combination of garments—which, as we have said, are extremely rudimentary—but also on the concrete ways in which individuals and social groups construct their appearance in accordance with specific constraints and ideals as opposed to others. Especially the thin ideal. Our investigation will have to focus on the forces at work in actual cases rather than on the conceptual laws of *langue*.

To restate this from a theoretical point of view, I am arguing here that also in the study of fashion, at least as regards the issue of fat fashion, the structuralist approach of Roland Barthes can be enriched by a post-structuralist perspective inspired by Michel Foucault, which shifts the focus from the syntactic rules governing statements and discourses to the practices dictated by their actual social use. Signs and sentences are certainly enabled by the syntagmatic and paradigmatic structure of the language, yet not because of this they are used and understood by social actors. Countless possible sentences may have little or even no use in people's everyday lives. Thus Foucault ([1969] 2002: 41–2) suggests that, with regard to the institutional dimension of language, we should focus on actual cases of communication, the "discourses" that occur in everyday life. Indeed, of the infinite expressions that language makes possible in principle, only a few are really practiced. What makes certain ways of expressing a concept prevail over all other possible ways of expressing the same concept? What makes certain ways of using the clothes-body complex to manage a situation prevail over all other possible ways of managing the same situation?

While not specifically dealing with the subject of fashion, Foucault attempts to answer these kinds of questions and concludes that there is a strong, observable link between discourse and social structure, in particular the mechanisms of power. Any topic—for example, female beauty—can be approached in a meaningful way only by conforming to a socially pre-established frame of meaning, which makes consistent inferences possible and probably adequate.

This frame of meaning does not have the impersonal character of linguistic rules, but already contains a way of interpreting and making sense of the subject of the discourse. Linguistic rules allow us to affirm that "the fat body is more beautiful than the slim body," but this statement is not contemplated as a real possibility in current fashion discourse. The dominant frame of meaning makes it meaningless. According to Foucault, discourses are "systems of truth" ([1975] 1995: 23) that lay down the conditions of possibility for thinking and speaking. They do this, for example, by establishing a series of meanings taken for granted, which do not need to be expressed because they are the condition for talking about that topic. *That the woman must be tall and slender to be beautiful is, in contemporary fashion discourse, something that does not need to be expressed, because all speakers take it for granted.* It is the frame of meaning that enables meaningful arguments in fashion discourse. Moreover, fashion discourse gives form not only to real conversations about the body and fashion, but also to body techniques and fashion practices. For example, it implies that women's use of high heels is today, in the fashion system, a prescription of elegance that cannot be ignored, barring exceptional cases.

Stuart Hall (2013), whose interpretation of Foucault has had a significant impact on fashion studies, emphasizes in particular two aspects of the way in which for the French philosopher discourses operate in social life. First, the fact that highlighting the role played by discourses in the formation of the meanings we give to things and situations implies a substantial historicization of those meanings. Every epoch produces discourses of knowledge and truth that differ—sometimes extensively—from those of other times. For example, madness and the mad, as categories to classify and treat a certain state and type of person, have not always existed, but arose in a specific historical period and (perhaps) have recently been declining. This also applies to the thin ideal, as we will see in Chapter 3. Second, the fact that such discourses also exert their power to regulate human conduct. In fact, discourse disciplines bodies, and in disciplining bodies regulates social behavior. Power has always sought to discipline people's bodies through violence to normalize their behavior and thus maintain the social order. For Foucault ([1975] 1980), in modern Western societies this disciplining effort of power has gradually shifted from physical imposition through torture and corporal punishment to self-discipline on the part of individuals, who to comply with social discourses are expected to take responsibility for their health, physical efficiency, fitness for work, and so forth.

Fashion, too, develops discourses with the power to direct people's verbal and corporeal behavior. Even fashion, in other words, is an expression of the power asymmetries that run through society, as several scholars have noted.[22] It disciplines bodies through the words it uses, the images it circulates, and the clothes-body idiom it legitimizes. A blatant case is the construction of gender distinctions:

> The association of women with long evening dresses or, in the case of professional workplace, skirts, and men with dinner jackets and trousers is an arbitrary one but nonetheless comes to be regarded as "natural" so that femininity is connoted in the gown, masculinity in the black tie and dinner jacket. (Entwistle [2000] 2015: 21)

In establishing what is fashionable and appropriate for a certain situation, and in determining how bodies should look, fashion develops a discourse that circumscribes the field of what it is possible to think and say about the clothes-body complex. Current fashion discourse, which includes the thin ideal and the segregation of fat bodies, is part of daily interactions and thus plays a major role in determining our concrete options in using the clothes-body idiom. For example, it severely restricts overweight people's options in terms of fully exploiting their appearance in order to build interactions that are successful in meeting the expectations of others and making a positive impression.

Fitting Life

To conclude, I will return, with greater awareness, to my initial claim, which is that not only do body and clothes co-belong, but this mutual implication also occurs in the presence of a community. This is the point: clothes, whether they are casual garments or fashionable outfits, characterize a body that is already exposed to the "reading" of others, which determines the quality of the social relationships that social actors are able to establish. Dress "fits" when it is appropriate to a person's social needs, when "there is a fit between who the woman wanted to become and the final outfit on her body, as she both looks and feels right in what she is wearing" (Woodward 2007: 15). *How a dress fits is not exclusively about its relationship with the body; it concerns that relationship in relation to the social world in which it is staged.* If it fits, it is because it fits life, which is a social life, situated in a stream of interactions. To dress the body inherently means addressing some audience (Stone [1962] 1995: 28) whose responses essentially influence the actor's social life.

Clothing consumption—from the purchase of garments to the daily ritual of selecting them from a wardrobe and the "activation" of an outfit through body gestures and movements—takes place in this context. Dress must fit the body and the soul, the physical form of the body and its presence in the social world. The unseemly fold does not annoy us because it is aesthetically ugly, but because it may be noticed by others, thereby hindering the intensive work of constructing the most desirable appearance. No outfit does not fit in itself, but an outfit may not fit in relation to the self-image that it is intended to promote in social interaction. This is the most intriguing meaning of the concept of comfort, as Ruth Holliday ([1999] 2007; 2001) has shown. A garment is comfortable when it is "enjoyable" to wear. But we may enjoy wearing a dress for two reasons: because it feels pleasant on the body, and because it makes our interaction with others pleasant. Discourses that neglect the latter aspect and simply equate an outfit's comfort with physical pleasure tend to naturalize something that is intrinsically social. The situated character of the negotiation of the meaning of appearance makes the same outfit appear comfortable in one situation but uncomfortable in another. Even more than the physical comfort which a garment offers the body, it is the clothes-body complex that makes the subject comfortable or uncomfortable depending on whether it addresses its audience appropriately or requires considerable extra effort in terms of verbal mediation to be understood.

This is not to deny the importance of physical comfort in people's lives. I have deliberately emphasized the social function of clothing as doing so is essential if we are to adequately frame our discussion of the fashion paradox. Nevertheless, a thorough investigation of the clothes-body complex should clearly include an in-depth study of the effect of the sensory perception of clothes on the wearer's social behavior. Physical comfort is a fundamental goal of clothing choices, and sometimes constitutes an external constraint that limits their communicative possibilities (Eco [1998] 2007). As elements of the clothes-body complex, clothes possess the dual characteristic of being constantly in relation to the body without ever really being part of it. As a result, the need to feel good about oneself sometimes prevails over the specific aspects of the situation and interferes with the communicative function of clothing. Furthermore, the need to conform to expectations can be internalized within the individual's self-conception (Tseëlon 1995: 54). People, and especially women, often seem to have incorporated the sense of being exposed on the public scene regardless of the situation in which they currently find themselves. Negotiation of the meaning of one's appearance seems to be at work even in the absence of existing or expected social interactions, therefore in a way that is not dependent on concrete situations. Also, the type of clothing can limit the social negotiation of meanings. Ashdown (2014: 19) has noted that functional clothing, such as sportswear or protective clothing, provides special challenges to clothing fit requirements, and that their functional goals can take precedence over that of fitting our physical and social needs for comfort. In short, since the use of clothes produces effects on the body, it cannot be reduced to an exclusively symbolic use (Sweetman 2001). The act of dressing is extremely complex, and fashion studies as a discipline is still a long way from exhausting all of its facets.

The complexity of fitting and making an outfit comfortable becomes clear when dealing with bodies that strongly diverge from the ideal of beauty, which always faithfully serves social inclusion. This is the case, for example, of overweight and aged bodies. Twigg (2013a, 2013b) investigated in particular the latter group—which, incidentally, are often included in the former—and noted that the work of designers in dealing with clothing for older women consists partly in adapting the cut of the garments to the typical shapes of their bodies, which differ from the typical shapes of young, slim bodies on which the original pattern was based:

> In designing for the older market manufacturers need to adjust the cut of their clothes to respond to changes in the body that occur with age. Clothes lie on the interface between the physiological body and its cultural presentation. They directly reflect the materiality of the body, although always within a cultural context. Adjusting the cut, therefore, is a complex process that encompasses both the literal fit of the garment and its capacity to reflect norms about the older body and its presentation. (Twigg 2013a: 131)

An analysis of the issue of body representation that adapts to the social and cultural norms associated with the elderly body (as well as with the fat body) reveals a number of contradictory aspects. Adaptation serves to improve the physical comfort of the dress. Yet, the very same expedients that it uses, such as reducing the amount of skin exposed to the gaze of others, may in turn become signals that the older body underneath is unacceptable (Twigg 2013a: 134). Clothing fit is a delicate balancing act, since it concerns not only the relationship between the garments and the body or the relationship of the clothes-body complex with the needs of social interaction, but also the relationship of the body with a common ideal of beauty that relies on the value of youthfulness, which is deemed highly desirable and to some extent also achievable. Devices designed to give the older body a slender, youthful appearance, such as padded shoulders, nevertheless expose the wearer to the ever-present risk of making her appearance elicit expectations that do not correspond to the ways in which she is willing to act, for instance by creating in others expectations of physical performance that she is no longer able to fulfill.

What applies to youthfulness applies, with all the more reason, to thinness. Peters (2019a: 187) notes that, in the case of fashion, "garments that flatter the body both fit the body as the designer intended—that is, absent the real, fleshy body—and help the wearer to embody or inch closer to the prevailing corporeal norm." A prevailing corporeal norm is, in fashion, the thin ideal. We must now investigate how the thin ideal works within the fashion system.

Fashion Discourse

The Tyranny of Slenderness

Naturalization of the Thin Ideal

Fashion is thin. Simply flick through a fashion magazine, watch a fashion show online, or look at fashion advertisements on billboards to see this. Not only is fashion thin, it also theorizes the thinness of the body, in particular that of women's bodies. Fashion claims that the female body must be thin to be beautiful, and that clothes only fit well on thin bodies. It does this through articles, editorials, advertising, and statements by famous designers, as well as through the limitations of sizes available in fashion stores.

It could be argued that, even though fashion is thin, fat is becoming a current trend in fashion. Increasingly, there is news coverage of the inclusion of fat or average bodies in fashion events and photoshoots. For example, the diversity report of *The Fashion Spot* website announced in September 2019: "New York's Spring 2020 runways made historic progress on the body diversity front. Casting of plus-size models hit an all-time high" (Tai 2019). News like this seems to confirm the idea that fashion is changing its attitude toward fat bodies, finally embracing the opportunities they represent. Yet, in reality, it reveals the opposite: fashion is thin, and fat bodies are mere exceptions. The *Fashion Spot's* report goes on to comment: "A tiny milestone, but a milestone nonetheless." In fact, the sixty-eight curvy models that have broken all previous records account for less than 3 percent of all models featured in New York in September 2019, and—what is more—are an exception with no equivalent on the catwalks of Milan, Paris, and London. To use Winckelmann's metaphor, they are to the fashion system what the waves of a terrible storm are to the ocean's volume. If curvy models can make the headlines, it is because fashion continues to be essentially thin.

In general, the thin ideal is dominant in contemporary societies. It is particularly so in Western countries, but it tends to extend its influence wherever the media, fashion, and cosmetics industries penetrate. As we saw in Chapter 1, slenderness is not an "objective" feature of female beauty, but a social construct that has established itself over the last 100 years or so and is to fade away in due course, despite its enduring nature. Thinness is a contingent ideal, the product of a specific historical-cultural circumstance. The apparent naturalness of the idea of female beauty is, therefore, actually the product of the naturalization of expectations and behaviors that are cultural in origin and learned through the process of socialization (Butler 1990 and 2004: 40–56; Wittig [1980] 1993). Yet naturalization works, and to almost all of us a slim body seems obviously more beautiful than a fat one. Thinking the opposite requires reflexivity.

But how thin is fashion? Why is it thin? And how does the thin ideal manifest itself in the fashion system? This chapter addresses these questions. I shall discuss how the thin ideal features in fashion, and in particular what it means to say that fashion "theorizes" the thinness of the body. It will be seen that fashion can "theorize" thinness precisely because, as I showed in Chapter 2, it is permeated by a fashion discourse that stands above the participants and governs their thoughts and words. The idea that women have to be slim to be beautiful is such an obvious truth that it normally does not even need to be asserted.

Evidence of the Tyranny of Slenderness

Are we sure that the thin ideal prevails in Western culture? Yes, we are, and the point probably does not even need arguing. It is evidenced by consumer behavior (diets, cosmetics, gymnastics, fashion, beauty contests) and media imagery (photographs, films, models, actresses). Yet to corroborate this claim we must turn to academic research. The phenomenon has been studied and described in various fields, especially those that touch on the issue of body size. I am referring to studies of the media, body image, eating disorders, gender, and fashion. I shall now address the first four of these, postponing my discussion of fashion studies to the following section.

One of the elements that make the thin ideal pervasive in current culture is undoubtedly its pervasiveness within the *cultural industry*. Its dominant role in traditional mass media is well documented and has been widely discussed by scholars.[1] The hegemony of the thin ideal is especially evident in visual media, which devote a great deal of space to the construction of narratives (cinema, television, magazines), since they generally relegate non-slim bodies to niche products or marginal and exceptional roles (Giovanelli and Ostertag 2009; Schooler et al. 2004; Seifert 2005). However, the ideal pervades all forms of media. The gendered approach that expects women to devote particular attention to their appearance and beauty, that are identified with (among other things) thinness, is shared across the media as a whole, including newspapers (Wykes and Gunter 2005) and digital media (Rocamora 2019). The overall effect is that the prevailing image in our cultural landscape is of very thin bodies, even when they do not explicitly aim to represent ideal bodies (e.g., in images illustrating articles about politics, science, or sports in news magazines). Hence, the visual identification of the "normal" human body with a slim body pervades the cultural landscape far beyond the sphere of those industries that are essentially bound up with the idea of beauty, such as fashion and cosmetics. Arguably, this is why the statistics about the spread of obesity in contemporary society surprise many people, as the numbers are much higher than they expect.

This unrealistic predominance of slim bodies in the cultural landscape has long been a cause for concern among those who study the *psychology of physical appearance* (Cash and Pruzinsky 1990). In dealing with subjective representations of one's body and appearance, that is, what is called the body image, scholars have often noted the divide between actual bodies and the image of the "normal" body promoted throughout the cultural landscape. In fact, this divide has many adverse effects on people's lives. It often results in a distorted image of one's own body size and a tendency to overestimate it (Kaiser 1997: 100–6). Confronted daily with an unnaturally thin selection of bodies, we are led to perceive our bodies as fatter than they should be, as well as fatter than they really are. Moreover, and above all, this divide in many cases leads to dissatisfaction with body image and compulsive actions to attempt to realign the body appearance with the shared idea of normality. Research has repeatedly shown that in Western countries a significant number of individuals are unhappy with how they look. Since size is a key contributor to such dissatisfaction, the most obvious consequence is the spread of behavior aimed at weight loss, especially dieting. According to research, in Western countries at any given time about 40 percent of women are taking some kind of action to lose weight.[2]

Compulsive actions to recreate harmony between body image and the idea of a "normal" or "attractive" (i.e., slim) body can lead to eating disorders that endanger people's health and even lives. The literature on *eating disorders* has extensively discussed the tyranny of slenderness, ever since Hilde Bruch stressed its importance:

> The study of obese and anorexic patients brought strikingly into the open the extent to which social attitudes toward the body, the concept of beauty in our society, and our preoccupation with appearance enter into the picture. The obsession of the Western world with slimness, the condemnation of any degree of overweight as undesirable and ugly, may well be considered a distortion of the social body concept, but it dominates present day living. (Bruch 1974: 88)

It should be noted that anorexia is not the only eating disorder connected with the thin ideal. All eating disorders can be interpreted as the result of people's efforts to place themselves within the ideal, that is, as a consequence of dissatisfaction with their body image. If anorexia expresses extreme adherence to the ideal, obesity may express rebellion against the normalization imposed by the ideal as well as an abandonment of the pursuit of the ideal that nevertheless acknowledges its validity.[3]

Finally, *feminist studies* combine the perspectives outlined above and consider the tyranny of slenderness a distinctive feature of patriarchal consumer capitalism, and therefore of today's society (Chernin 1981; Orbach [1978] 2016). Feminist scholars observe that taking care of appearance and attributing value to beauty—which are now internalized by women as goals worthy of being pursued on a daily basis—are actually functional to the maintenance of gender inequalities and the subjection of women to the current social and economic system (Wolf 1991). In fact, they require women to exercise self-control and self-discipline which, for Foucault, take the place of external control and discipline, achieving the same effect (Bartky 1988). The thin ideal is widespread not because of the independent choices of groups of social actors, such as the media system and the fashion system, but because an entire social structure based on the asymmetry of power and opportunities between men and women strives to resist the changes brought about by women's emancipation. In other words, women constantly look for beauty and thinness because, in looking at themselves in the mirror, they are always looking through the male gaze:

> I cannot deny it: In clothes I seek to find the approval of the transcending male gaze; in clothing I seek to transform myself into a bewitching object that will capture his desire and identity. When I leaf through magazines and catalogs I take my pleasure from imagining myself perfected and beautiful and sexual for the absent or mirrored male gaze. I take pleasure in these images of female bodies in their clothes because my own gaze occupies the position of the male gaze insofar as I am a subject at all. (Young 2005: 67)

From this perspective, the thin ideal prevails in Western culture because it derives from the hegemonic position of the male gaze, which reflects the patriarchal structure of this society. This makes it pervasive and particularly resistant to change.

The Tyranny of Slenderness in the Fashion System

The thin ideal also prevails in fashion, as fashion studies have highlighted from the beginning. The entire fashion system is organized to serve slim bodies:

> Fashion colludes in society's obsession with thinness; the whole process of making and marketing a collection is based upon the production of clothing in the smallest sizes. This then requires models to be very slim to fit into the samples which are used for catwalk shows and photo-shoots, which then create media images that reinforce the received wisdom that clothing looks best on thin women. The phantasy created in fashion photographs emphasises that you need continually to maintain your body in line with the ideal model silhouette, as the only means to wear the latest, most desirable fashions. (Arnold 2001: 89–90)

It is worth noting that this collusion of fashion with the tyranny of slenderness is normally taken as much for granted by fashion studies as it is by participants in the fashion sector. It is discussed as a given, and as such is neglected—with exceptions. For instance, the link between the spread of the thin ideal in fashion communication and anorexia among young women became the subject of intense public debate around the turn of the century, especially in relation to the size and age of models featured in fashion shows, advertising, and editorials (Boselli 2012). Public statements by authorities such as the British Medical Association have sparked heated media discussions (BBC 2000) and even elicited policy measures to protect models' health.[4] Academic research, too, has demonstrated that the thin ideal dominant in fashion magazines has some influence on the eating disorders of vulnerable individuals (Thomsen et al. 2001). This discussion continues today, although the focus has now shifted toward the issue of diversity and problems generated by the cultural homologation and fat discrimination caused by a media system that tends to represent almost exclusively thin bodies.[5]

Denunciations of the tyranny of slenderness in fashion usually mention two phenomena: the representation of female bodies in advertisements, and the size of models.

Fashion advertising and photography have been intensively studied for the stereotypical nature of the situations and bodies they represent (Ruggerone

2006; Shinkle 2008). In creating an imaginary world for promoting fashion products and brands, they also inadvertently convey an image of women (and men) that is unrealistic and conflicts with people's actual bodies and lives. Body shape is not the only aspect concerned, since several other features—including age, ethnicity, social class, and the type of activity in which people are engaged—manifest and reproduce a standardized vision of being a woman (and a man). However, there is no doubt that thinness stands out against these features. Fashion advertising, in fact, particularly in the field of womens wear, makes continuous and unscrupulous use of photo manipulation in order to create representations of artificial, abstract, impossible bodies. Fashion images have typically favored the construction of an abstract and "synthetic" beauty ideal over a mere representation of the concrete beauty of the woman (or model) wearing the clothes (de Perthuis 2008, 2016). Their aim has often been to produce innovative imagery rather than the mere visual reproduction of a range of existing clothing possibilities. According to Elizabeth Wissinger, this trend is related to the digitization of images and communication in general, and has produced a tension between the fashion images in circulation and the actual people they supposedly represent:

> When fashionable equals thin, then looking thin from every angle becomes the Holy Grail for those caught up in producing the tsunami of images brought on by the cable and Internet revolutions. Achieving the fashionable look demanded producing a look that stood out and caught the attention of an increasingly fickle public, as well as maintaining the kind of body that looked like it had already been Photoshopped. (Wissinger 2013: 136)

Models perhaps bear the brunt of the blame for fostering the thin ideal, as through their work and their mere existence they not only sell people clothes but also sell people on an ideal of feminine beauty that implies extreme thinness (Entwistle and Wissinger 2012b: 4–5). Models' bodies are the bodies of fashion and, as such, they exemplify the ideal body that it promotes. Indeed, most models are extremely thin, even without postproduction manipulation of fashion photographs. As Ashley Mears (2011: 91–2) points out, fashion's ideal body can be inferred from models' "official" measurements, that is, those published by agencies for commercial purposes, which often do not coincide with their actual measurements but are instead manipulated to reduce any deviation between the model's actual body and what the fashion industry deems to be the ideal body. They thus reveal the industry's expectations of ideal body measurements. The average measurements on the Metro Models agency website in 2004 were 84.6

centimeters (bust), 61.2 centimeters (waist), and 87.6 centimeters (hips), and a height of 175 centimeters, according to Mears (2011: 92). In other words, a size two. Given that the most common sizes in Western countries are twelve to sixteen, as we saw in Chapter 1, models clearly play a role in establishing an ideal of extreme thinness in fashion.[6] Of course, there are also larger models. However, they are considered nonstandard, as the label plus-size suggests. In agency catalogs they typically have their own separate category, often going by the name of "curvy," and are rarely used by the mainstream fashion industry.[7] It is here, then, that we encounter an initial example of segregation of non-slim bodies as a result of the idealization of thinness in fashion. We will return to this in Chapter 6. Confining curvy models to a separate category that has little or no access to the most popular fashion shows (3 percent in New York in 2019) and mainstream magazines is equivalent to declaring their bodies unwanted, or at least eccentric, nonstandard. It should be borne in mind that "nonstandard" in this case—that is, curvy models—means a range of sizes from ten to fourteen (Czerniawski 2015: 9 and 174), in other words, a size range thinner than the majority of the female population in Western countries (Figure 3).

One aspect should be emphasized here: just as fashion photographs are manipulated, both rhetorically through the work of stylists and technically through digital postproduction, models' bodies are also manipulated through collective and individual labor (Mears 2011: 91–5). The human body changes over time, depending on age and lifestyle. Yet fashion models, who have been selected by some brands for fitting clothes, must maintain constant measurements over time, so as not to introduce an uncontrolled variable into the design and pattern-making processes: they should remain always identical to themselves, like a mannequin. At the same time, they must also subject themselves to the variability of seasonal trends, changing tastes, and evolving aesthetics (Wissinger 2015: 156–7). Clearly, the body cannot spontaneously adapt to either of these two needs, let alone both at the same time. We must therefore abandon the widespread, yet misleading, idea that models are particularly beautiful women who have received their body as a gift from Mother Nature, and that their job consists of simply making it available to fashion professionals. As Ashley Mears observes, the models she interviewed "were not mere lucky winners in some genetic lottery; they were fighters in an ongoing struggle against their bodies" (Mears 2011: 91). Elizabeth Wissinger (2015) has focused on the work that all this entails for the models themselves, whose success cannot be separated from the huge effort which lies behind this struggle and which images and fashion shows, with their ephemeral and visual character, end up hiding. This labor,

Figure 3 Curvy model Candice Huffine, dress size fourteen, catwalking for Elena Mirò, spring/summer collection 2012. Courtesy of Miroglio Fashion.

both material and immaterial (Lazzarato 1996), takes place behind the scenes, hidden from—and by—the outward appearance of the models. Thus, modeling is not limited to models' capacity to qualify industrial goods through visual culture, but actually involves self-commodification and transformation into a brand (Entwistle and Slater 2012). In working on herself, the model shapes and circulates a certain image of women, thereby playing a major role in stabilizing the hegemonic feminine ideal in our society.

Thus, the ideal of beauty embodied by models is constructed and at the same time naturalized, in Judith Butler's sense of the word (2004: 40–56). It is rendered apparently natural through a continuous artificial work of construction, revision, and adjustment of appearance. This appearance is what is normally called a person's "look" (Entwistle 2009: 6; Mears 2011: 5), and is the result—for models just as it is for all of us—of continuous work to manipulate the clothes-body complex, not just in terms of physical structure, makeup, and clothing but also postures, behavior, body language, consumption, and life choices (Wissinger 2007a and 2007b). This work is concealed, made invisible by the apparently natural character of the models' beauty. Naturalization does not only work in the eyes of the general public, as if it were a deliberately planned deception. It also involves experts, such as the models' agents. When asked the question "Why is the fashion aesthetic so slender?," Doreen Small, former vice president of the Ford Model Agency, answered: "I think beautiful girls are beautiful girls are beautiful girls and we're not size-ist" (quoted in Entwistle and Wissinger 2012a: 188). Analogously, George Speros, agent for New York Models, in describing what he perceived as a shift in modeling toward more "normal" body types, identified the latter with "Victoria's Secret-type girls" (quoted in Entwistle and Wissinger 2012a: 190). It should be noted that Victoria's Secret models normally wear a size two or four (Brar 2019; Pomarico 2018), and are therefore not exactly representative of "normal" bodies. A totally anomalous thinness—"abnormal" indeed—is perceived and passed off as normal.

In short, the causal relationship between models' bodies and fashion's ideal body must be reversed. Models must constantly meet the ideal parameters imposed by the fashion system: height, weight, breast, waist, and hip measurements. These parameters are extremely rigid in their regulatory function, but highly flexible in the models' daily practice, where it is common to lie about one's measurements (Mears 2011: 91–2). In fact, models are continually subjected to two conflicting demands: to conform to a common standard, and to have something unique that differentiates their look and makes them stand out from others. Like athletes and dancers, they use their corporeality as a form of capital (Wacquant 2004). Models must be able to express a "personality" that gives their look a hint of uniqueness and exceptionality. Modeling implies not only aesthetic work on the body but also emotional labor (Hochschield 1983) that enables models to express an intriguing personality merely by means of their appearance and look (Wissinger 2015: 154–6).

The work behind the construction of fashion photographs and models' bodies suggests that there is nothing "natural" about the tyranny of slenderness in fashion. Thinness is actively sought by professionals in the sector as well as by consumers with their diets and gym memberships. It is an ideal that lies at the outer bounds of attainability, or in the case of many manipulated photographs, far beyond them. And yet, as an ideal, it is capable of directing the behavior of those who participate, as professionals or consumers, in the great game of fashion.

This is confirmed by other, perhaps lesser-known, aspects of the fashion system, in which the power of the thin ideal becomes visible. Evidence of the type of work that models engage in to construct their own bodies can also be found, for example, among influencers. Yet in this case, too, such labor is concealed and disguised by the idea of a slim body "by nature." Agnès Rocamora (2019) has studied a number of Instagrammers who epitomize the idea-brand of the *Parisienne*, that is, the fashionable Parisian woman. The *Parisienne* is normally celebrated for her seemingly effortless style and beauty, which is a conventional and distinctly Caucasian beauty: white and lean. The Instagrammers analyzed by Rocamora embrace this ideal without questioning it, taking it for granted: "On their platforms, [they] do not disclose how they attain and maintain this bodily size. Their thin body, it is suggested, is an effortlessly thin one, a discourse that once again hides the labor that goes into both appearance and appearing on a blog/Instagram, that is, into blogging/Instagramming" (Rocamora 2019: 179).[8]

Finally, another aspect of the fashion system that reveals the power of the thin ideal is the development of clothing size standards. Consumers often use the size of clothes, along with their weight, as an indicator of the conformity or nonconformity of their body to the dominant ideal (Apeagyei 2008; Brumberg 1997; Russ 2008). The fact that high-end fashion houses very rarely produce clothes in sizes above twelve—which is at the root of the fashion paradox—constitutes an explicit, daily manifestation of the dominant body ideal: if clothes are small, the bodies for whom they were designed will necessarily have to be thin. Two other phenomena reinforce this effect. First, most "regular clothing" stores in Western countries offer items only up to size twelve, while for sizes from fourteen upward consumers need to go specialist plus-size clothing stores. This is another example of the segregation of fat bodies with which I shall deal in Chapter 6. The seclusion of plus-size clothing within dedicated physical spaces, separated from high fashion, immediately conveys the message that the ideal body is not to be found there. Second, the thin ideal reveals itself in so-called vanity sizing or size inflation, that is to say, the gradual increase over time in the physical size of clothes in the same nominal size (Alexander et al. 2005; Bishop et al. 2018: 187). Or, to view the same phenomenon from the opposite angle, the gradual reduction in the size number of clothes with the same measurements. If, from an economic point of view, this phenomenon can be considered a tool for the inclusion of increasingly fat bodies in "regular" fashion consumption, from a symbolic point of view it reinforces the idea that the body must be small in size to be considered normal.

Origins of the Tyranny of Slenderness in Fashion

Yet, this is by no means a recent trend. Fashion historians have shown that the fashion system has embraced the thin ideal since its emergence at the beginning of the twentieth century. Their reconstructions[9] show that the divide between fashion and fat bodies originated with the advent of ready-to-wear clothes, which became popular in the United States far earlier than in European countries, which implies that the thin ideal took hold in North America before it did in French fashion (Stearns 1997: 219–23). While French fashion celebrates Paul Poiret as the initiator, in 1908, of the revolution that led to the elimination of the corset and the radical simplification of the female silhouette through the neo-Empire style, the casting-off of corsets and voluminous skirts had already begun some decades before and the public was already prepared to accept the new style (Seid 1989: 82; see also Stewart and Janovicek 2001).

At the beginning of the twentieth century, American ready-to-wear clothing manufacturers began to introduce relatively effective sizing systems. While on the one hand these systems helped accelerate the spread of mass-produced clothing, on the other hand, being still approximate and based on a select-few wealthy white women, they promoted the standardization of clothes and the exclusion of larger or irregularly shaped bodies. To accommodate the needs of overweight customers, a specialized market niche soon developed, with its own design techniques and sizing systems. At the time it was not called "plus-size" but "stoutwear": clothing for stout women. From its very beginnings, Lane

Bryant was the largest and most famous retailer in this specialized sector, which included several players.

The segregation of fat bodies was not as marked as today, and Lane Bryant advertised in mainstream fashion magazines. However, the tyranny of slenderness was already detectable in several signals. The sketches in the company's advertisements, for example, represented basically thin women, and highlighted the slimming effect of clothes. Although "stout" bodies were not hidden by the fashion system, they were nevertheless presented as a "problem" which the stoutwear industry could help "solve." From the beginning, stoutwear was not conceived as the production of straight clothing in larger sizes, but of clothing capable of bringing overweight bodies back to within the standards of thinness that had recently become popular in fashion. This meant essentially masking, moving, dissimulating fat, which was considered a superfluous appendage to the "normal" body. The existence of a manufacturing sector specialized in stoutwear was therefore legitimated as empowerment of stout consumers, as it enabled them to cope with the growing demand for thinness. Only clothing specially created to *appear* slim could help stout women to comply with the dictates of fashion, whereas ordinary clothes made in larger sizes could not. Therefore, the main challenges associated with the design, manufacture, and promotion of stoutwear did not regard how to cope with the problems of fit that arise when mainstream fashion is worn by stout bodies, but rather how to strategically modify the body silhouette and create a flattering figure by slimming it down. Stoutwear design was mainly concerned with how to make the stout body look thin, using elaborate strategies of optical illusion, covering up, and camouflaging. "The clothing designed for the Stylish Stout was clothing designed to be inconspicuous, to fit in" (Schwartz 1986: 161).

The story of stoutwear reveals several things. To begin with, it shows that the identification of thinness with the body standard within the fashion system has a long history, coinciding with the initial spread of the thin ideal. This identification is contingent upon the close relationship between thinness and the myth of beauty. Unlike the movements against being fat or promoting dieting that spread throughout Europe and North America in past centuries, the contemporary ideal of thinness is closely linked to appearance as a tool for social interaction. Today, thinness is not cultivated primarily for physical well-being, to temper the spirit, or to please God, but to please others and adapt to their standards, so as to put the interaction on a favorable basis. Although many may say they want to lose weight to feel comfortable with themselves, we know that comfort and individual taste mirror the gaze of the generalized other, as shown in Chapter 2. The point is that when thinness is idealized for appearance and the beauty of the clothes-body complex, clothing and fashion belong straight away to the actualization of the ideal: they must enhance slenderness.

Furthermore, the story of stoutwear shows that the emergence of the thin ideal in fashion was accompanied from the outset by segregated clothing manufacture for nonstandard bodies, and in particular for fat bodies. The development of a market niche that was independent of mainstream fashion is not a phenomenon associated only with plus-size clothing in the second half of the twentieth century, but was already nascent in the early decades of the century. This separate market carried the stigma of the abnormal from the very beginning: the stout body had to be dressed with particular expedients to adapt it as much as possible to current beauty standards. This meant "slimming" the silhouette and concealing fat. The term "fat" itself was already stigmatized, as can be seen from the adoption of a different term ("stout"), which did not have the same negative connotation.

Finally, stoutwear can be seen as a major effect of the development of mass manufacturing techniques in the apparel industry. There is a clear connection between the industrialization of clothing manufacture and the spread of the thin ideal in fashion, which is contingent on the technology of mass production and its specific features when compared with tailor-made clothing production. Indeed, the mass manufacture of clothing incorporates and gives substance to the thin ideal. In Chapter 5 I will illustrate in detail this technological factor, which reveals that the thin ideal is no more "ideal" than it is "natural." What I mean is that it is not simply a dominant idea, nor a mindset or an ideology, but something much more stable and resistant to change, resilient to the forces that oppose it. Something that looks more like a practice than an idea: a "discourse," in the Foucauldian sense.

The Place of Thinness within Fashion Discourse

Since the thin ideal has dominated the fashion system for so long, we need to ask: exactly how does it exert such power? Clearly, it is a power that goes beyond the sphere of action of individual or collective subjects within the fashion system, however influential they may be.

I argued in Chapter 2 that fashion can be interpreted as an instrument to discipline the body. It develops a verbal, visual, and objectual discourse that enables certain looks and inhibits others, thus laying the foundations for what can be included in the sphere of clothing possibilities. Clothing possibilities are much more than just clothes, and the look is much more than pure visual appearance. It is not a mere covering of the body, but an extension of it. Therefore, fashion does not regulate clothes, as if they were a mask or an external shell, but the clothes-body complex, which is the elementary tool of social behavior and social interaction. This is masterfully summarized by Cavallaro and Warwick (1998: 15) when they argue that the subject is fashioned from the inside no less than from the outside.

Feminist theories and fashion studies, albeit operating within different frameworks and pursuing different goals, converge in arguing that the thin ideal plays an essential role in fashion's disciplining the female body. Joanne Entwistle has explained this clearly in a passage worth quoting in full:

> It is common to think about dress in the twentieth century as more "liberated" than previous centuries, particularly the nineteenth. The style of clothes worn in the nineteenth century now seem rigid and constraining of the body. The corset seems a perfect example of nineteenth-century discipline of the body: it was obligatory for women, and an uncorseted woman was considered to be morally deplorable. [. . .] However, this conventional story of increasing bodily "liberation" can be told differently if we apply a Foucauldian approach to fashion history: such a simple contrast between nineteenth- and twentieth-century styles is shown to be problematic. As Wilson argues (1992), in place of the whalebone corset of the nineteenth century we have the modern corset of muscle required by contemporary standards of beauty. Beauty now requires a new form of discipline rather than no discipline at all: in order to achieve the firm tummy required today, one must exercise and watch what one eats. While the stomach of the nineteenth-century corseted woman was disciplined from the outside, the twentieth-century exercising and dieting woman has a stomach disciplined by exercise and diet imposed by self-discipline. (Entwistle [2000] 2015: 20)

According to this view, the rise of the thin ideal in the fashion system, which took place at the same time as the process of "internalization of the corset" (Steele 2003: 143), exemplifies well how discursive practices can regulate people's conduct. As Foucault explains in relation to other fields (such as punishment and sexuality), in modern societies discourses often function as instruments of social control in place of violence and repression. According to this perspective, the idea that female beauty necessarily entails thinness is a fundamental aspect of the social effort to discipline female behavior. Power, says Foucault, "would be a fragile thing if its only function were to repress, if it worked only through the mode of censorship, exclusion, blockage and repression [...]. If, on the contrary, power is strong this is because, as we are beginning to realise, it produces effects at the level of desire" (Foucault [1975] 1980: 59). Fashion discourse, in particular, by imposing an ideal of beauty that is a far cry from real bodies and substantially unattainable, subjects women to constraints based not on the fear of punishment, but on the investment that they make in their body. The more they invest in the pursuit of beauty, the more valuable it seems. This is "a new mode of investment which presents itself no longer in the form of control by repression but that of control by stimulation. 'Get undressed—but be slim, good-looking, tanned!'" (Foucault [1975] 1980: 57). It subjects women to constant self-monitoring, as is illustrated by the increasing popularity of home scales at the beginning of the twentieth century (Schwartz 1986: 147–87). To be socially acceptable, attractive, or respected, women must exercise over themselves a form of surveillance that anticipates the expectations of others. They must weigh themselves and, based on the scale's response, exercise, diet, undergo surgery or medical treatments. Today, this is all taken for granted: we go from the scale's response to dieting perhaps grudgingly, but without doubting that we have to—that to be beautiful, attractive, healthy,[10] or even only in accordance with common expectations, one needs to be thin. Fashion discourse makes the equivalence of beauty and thinness appear self-evident or natural, concealing the work accomplished by an entire industry to establish and maintain such an ideal. Thus, through fashion discourse, the thin ideal becomes the undisputed frame within which we are caged, because only what is inside the frame is thinkable and speakable (Kaiser 2012: 21).

Not only does fashion discourse exert a disciplining power over the consumer's body but, in many cases, it also exerts this power hegemonically, that is to say, by disciplining not only those who benefit from discipline, but also those who only pay the price associated with it. The concept of cultural hegemony, developed by Gramsci ([1948–51] 2011), and a linchpin of cultural studies indicates a particular characteristic of power: that of working not only through the threat of violence but also through an ideological apparatus, capable of "recruiting" as followers of the holders of that power those who actually suffer the most under that same power. Hegemonic power is capable of imposing the cultural norms (i.e., beliefs, habits, explanations, and values) of the ruling class as legitimate and natural. As cultural norms, these are social constructs that benefit the ruling class; in other words, they help to maintain the status quo and existing asymmetries of power. But subordinate classes end up perceiving them as an immanent, rational, and inevitable order that is beneficial for everyone.

As Susan Kaiser has observed, the concept of cultural hegemony applies very well to fashion discourse, since it explains "how certain ways of knowing the world dominate and persevere, even when these ways are not in the best personal interests of those who seem to buy into them" (Kaiser 2012: 34). For example, the power of fashion discourse extends to non-Western populations and ethnic groups, who embrace and naturalize norms of beauty that favor white Western appearances, even if they are in contrast with the natural traits of their bodies. Likewise, the thin ideal not only affects young women with a slender physical constitution but also all other women who, in aspiring for it, strive for an unattainable condition and accept the asymmetry of opportunities[11] that it entails as if it were "natural."

Unpacking Fashion Discourse about Thinness

Concretely, how does fashion discourse work? How does it set the boundaries of what can be said or even thought about body weight, size, and shape? Let us look more closely at the aspects of the fashion system that imply the thin ideal.

As has already been clarified above, discourse is not the argument of a particular subject, but a complex practice that includes all individual expressions about a certain topic in a given sociohistorical context. According to Foucault, we must learn to treat discourses not

> as groups of signs (signifying elements referring to contents or representations) but as practices that systematically form the objects of which they speak. Of course, discourses are composed of signs; but what they do is more than use these signs to designate things. It is this more that renders them irreducible to the language (*langue*) and to speech. (Foucault [1969] 2002: 54)

In designating things, discourses establish how those things look and can be thought of. Therefore, they are practices that shape the world they focus on.

Fashion discourse manifests itself through different textual forms, through words as well as images, artifacts, or practices. Hence there are different manifestations of fashion discourse, some more evident, others more subtle and difficult to identify. We have already addressed the former kind in our discussion of the thin ideal in the collective imagination as represented by fashion photographs, which, whether used for advertising or in editorials, are often photoshopped to make the already unattainable thin body of the model even more similar to the dominant ideal. However, as Barthes's work ([1967] 1983) has taught us, fashion discourse also lives on words, which sometimes accompany images, and sometimes operate independently of them.[12] Examples of the latter can be found in certain public statements made by leading figures in the fashion industry who deem the equation of beauty or elegance and thinness irrefutable. Karl Lagerfeld, for example, has been quoted as saying that only "fat mummies with their bags of crisps in front of the television [say] that thin models are ugly" (Connolly 2009). Obviously, it matters little whether Lagerfeld really made such an assertion or not; what matters is the fact that such assertion is credited to him, thus playing a major part in determining the boundaries of what is conceivable, hence sayable. Similar is the perspective taken by Kirstie Clements, former editor of *Vogue Australia*, which condemned the use of anorexic models *because this undermines their health* (and not because it promotes an unnatural feminine body ideal), thus confirming the idea that "presenting a healthy, toned size 6" is an appropriate way of showing fashionable clothes (Clements 2014: 63).

The power of words is reinforced when they accompany images in the form the captions, when written clothing interacts with image-clothing (Barthes [1967] 1983: 3–4), as is the case with fashion blogs and magazines. By way of illustration, Figures 4 and 5 are taken from the August 10, 2019 edition of the Italian women's magazine *iO Donna*, which is published as a weekly supplement with the daily *Corriere della Sera*. They show, respectively, Zendaya Coleman and Kim Kardashian as featured in influential Italian fashion journalist Giusi Ferré's long-running column "Tocco di classe . . . e buccia di banana," a column on fashion "hits and misses." The captions for Zendaya Coleman on the "hit" side reads as follows: "Halfway between an evening shirt and a male tuxedo shirtfront, this sort of snow-white micro-bustier enhances the toned line of the figure, revealing the chestline," and: "The length, which stops above the malleolus, slenderizing the legs even more, is intriguing." In contrast, the caption next to the photograph of Kim Kardashian, on the "miss" side, reads as follows: "In keeping with the legend, in order to thin the waist and enhance the derrière, the socialite and 38-year-old entrepreneur has had two ribs removed. The curves, however, remain sumptuous and a little too visible." The overall message of the column, legitimized by the signature of one of the most influential experts in the field, is that a toned, slender body is elegant, while curves that are too "sumptuous" (i.e., a body that is much more abundant than the models' ideal bodies, although not more than the average body of ordinary women) are censurable and bringing them out is a mistake, and is not fashionable. A comparison of the two photographs would be enough to lead us to conclude that the body of Zendaya Coleman (who, incidentally, was twenty-two years old at the time of

Figure 4 Zendaya Coleman as featured in the column "Tocco di classe . . ." *iO Donna*, August 10, 2019, p. 14. Photo by Edward Berthelot, courtesy of Getty Images.

Figure 5 Kim Kardashian as featured in the column "... e buccia di banana," *iO Donna*, August 10, 2019, p. 16. Courtesy of Splash News.

the snapshot) is more fashionable than that of Kim Kardashian, because fashion discourse has long dominated the world we live in and influenced our perception of beauty. Yet, the mutual reinforcement of text and image makes both of them even more expressive and fashion discourse even more convincing (Wykes and Gunter 2005: 65–99).

Fashion discourse, then, makes use of texts that did not originate from within the fashion system but from the cross-contamination between fashion and other industries such as cosmetics and the media. For example, in the past, fashion magazines used to feature advertisements for body care products that leveraged the goal of thinness to enhance the properties of the product being advertised (see, e.g., Bordo 1993: 205, fig. 34). Naomi Wolf, in *The Beauty Myth* (1991), has highlighted the role played by the advertising of cosmetics and diets in developing and strengthening the thin ideal. More recently, a new form of collusion has arisen between the fashion and media industries, with television discovering how to leverage the thin ideal to create new forms of entertainment. TV shows such as *America's Next Top Model* and *What Not to Wear*, and their respective local versions around the globe, teach viewers how to create a clothes-body complex that is in line with the dominant ideals of beauty and elegance (Seegers 2019; Sender and Sullivan 2008). Such programs thus amplify fashion discourse. In the field of social media, too, fashion discourse circulates and proliferates relentlessly. Social media has embraced fashion in the form of apparently free advice on how to create an individual look. Both personal- and street-style fashion blogs were originally born with this spirit (Findlay 2017: 27–30). Indeed, the very term "influencer" implies the task of educating the general public in the standards of elegance and style shared by those "in the know"—that is, those who work in fashion. As thinness is part of those standards, it is not surprising that many Instagrammers do not even question it. Perhaps more surprising at first sight is the fact that many "fatshion" blogs—that is, sites and profiles of influencers expressly about fashion for fat bodies—are permeated by the very same discourse, and in particular the thin ideal, by providing a series of tips to lose weight, fight cellulite, or conceal the abundant body shapes with clothing.[13]

Other manifestations of fashion discourse are even more pervasive insofar as they are not linked to media or speeches, but dispersed in people's practice. Lauren Peters has highlighted this in relation to the body measurement habits that began to become widespread at the beginning of the last century:

> Early twentieth century practices, such as weighing the body, placing the body into height and weight tables or even classifying the body according to standard

sizing conventions may be theorized as political technologies of the body that ushered in new and more effective ways of quantifying and categorizing bodies [. . .]. Through these dispersed processes, which Foucault describes as "generative," notions of normalcy and deviancy—and specifically categories of normal and deviant bodies—are constructed. (Peters 2018a: 56)

Fashion discourse is rooted in the practice of measuring bodies, as this practice facilitates the definition of beauty standards and deviance from the standard. Measuring bodies allows them to be mutually compared according to a scale and a top (and a bottom) of the size range to be established. Each time we weigh ourselves, we nurture the conviction that there must be an ideal weight. Another practice which likewise helps fashion discourse to circulate is the ritual of gearing up for swimsuit season, which brings together women from many countries (*la saison des maillots de bain* in France, *la prova costume* in Italy) and is usually accompanied by a sense of panic due to the inadequacy of one's body when held up against the unrealistic expectations dictated by standards (Lomrantz 2009). Trying on a swimsuit hesitatingly and above all talking about it in conversations with friends are further examples of how fashion discourse exercises its power over consumers by means of their practices and behavior.

Yet Female Consumers are Not Dupes of Culture

Fashion discourse, therefore, permeates everyday life and makes it possible to conceive of beauty as an important goal for women, and thinness as an essential feature of the beauty myth. It occupies a special place among the discourses that play a role in determining social behavior, in that it speaks of the clothes-body complex, that is, of the basic building block of social interaction. Fashion discourse enables and frames social interactions both in contemporary Western and—increasingly—non-Western society, regardless of whether thin or fat women are involved, or whether they are satisfied or dissatisfied with their own body image.

The main reason for stressing the relationship between the thin ideal and fashion discourse is to circumvent the simplistic arguments that consider only the subjects' conscious intentions and rationalizations. As Moeran has shown, fashion journalists asked about their role in establishing the beauty myth and determining its salient features are likely to deny playing such a role. They will claim that fashion journalists, mostly women, have no desire to manipulate the tastes and values of female readers, nor would they be able to do so. All they do is make style proposals. "The women who are the objects of such proposals, they said, have minds of their own. It is up to them whether they accept or reject editors' various propositions" (Moeran 2015: 16). Having unpacked how fashion discourse works, its pervasiveness, and the complex stratification of its expressions, such justifications now appear to some extent naive and, above all, irrelevant. The question is not whether the tyranny of slenderness in fashion is the fault of journalists or other actors in the field. The question is why thinness continues to remain an ideal capable of directing people's behavior despite the fact that journalists, as well as all other actors in the field, are unable—they say—to manipulate consumer behavior. Discourse can work as a practice precisely because it is not conscious speech, but establishes the conditions for speaking, starting conversations, and developing theories.

At the same time, this should not lead us to conclude that fashion discourse and the thin ideal uniformly affect consumer behavior, as this would mean seeing female consumers as "dupes of culture" (Gimlin 2002: 8) devoid of autonomy and individuality. Above all, it would mean ignoring the fact that the clothes-body complex is an essentially *situated* means of communication. How the meaning of a certain look is negotiated, I have argued in Chapter 2, depends on multiple circumstantial factors, such as the situation in which interaction takes place, who is in attendance, the actors' individuality, and the circumstantial use of clothing. Similarly, the way each individual relates to the thin ideal, too, depends on the situation and can change over time and space. Sophie Woodward's ethnography has evidenced that women's relationship to their ideal body is complex:

> Women I have interviewed do not constantly see themselves as inadequate in relation to this media-presented ideal; in fact, women are considering themselves in relation to their own aspirational version of themselves, which may or may not be influenced by images in the media. This ideal is in turn mediated by women's experiences, upbringing and multiple other factors. (Woodward 2007: 89)

Her research and that of Lauren Peters (2014) show that women react differently to the dominant bodily ideal depending on the heritage of previous experiences, the current situation, and their own "projects" (de Beauvoir [1949] 1997; Moi 2005: 59–72, 74), which they develop for that occasion. Ruth Holliday (2001) comes to the same conclusion in her study of the clothing choices of queer communities. Even in this case of anti-hegemonic culture with its clothing outside the mainstream, the effect of a discourse of power can be detected. The protagonists' arguments and justifications, which highlight the authenticity of their individual choices against the inauthenticity and homogenization of fashion consumption, allow Holliday (2001: 223) to identify the effects of a subcultural discourse that is in its own way culturally "hegemonic," so to speak. According to this alternative form of regulatory "regime," there is a "right" way to dress queer, namely one that aligns individuals' behavior with the expectations of the community to which they belong, thus producing a comfortable frame of interaction. From this point of view, a subcultural community does not behave differently from mainstream society and, analogously to the latter, it seems dominated by its own discourse. However, a closer analysis of Holliday's field data makes it clear that in this case, too, the comfort produced by clothing is not just the effect of conscious conforming to an established model, but stems from the fact that the chosen look fosters a certain agreement between the self-concept cultivated by the individual and the way s/he presents him/herself in public, and between the latter and the reading witnessed by others. The standard established by queer discourse is not an undisputed imperative, but represents just one pole in the relationship between the individual and the community.

Thus, the beauty ideal circulated by mainstream fashion magazines, as well as the one circulated by subcultural media, does not coerce individual behavior, but is one of the elements that a woman normally takes into account—besides looking "individual," fitting in, and specific situations and roles (Woodward 2007: 28)—when arranging her look in view of upcoming interactions. This, on closer inspection, does not facilitate the job of getting dressed. As uniforms and sumptuary laws show, coercive fashion facilitates the task of dressing as it reduces the space for inference in the interactive working of the clothes-body idiom: what one can communicate is established in an *a priori*, top-down manner (Craik 2005). It is not negotiable. If the thin ideal were equally nonnegotiable, the current tyranny of slenderness would not only be perceived as "natural," but probably would not be perceived at all. As an element of fashion discourse, the thin ideal urges us to react.

To sum up, fashion discourse prevails over "speakers" and creates the space for arguments, concepts, and practices available to those who deal with fashion, but it does not predetermine the individual's stand. It is possible both to fully conform to the hegemonic ideal of thinness and to distance oneself through an oppositional and anti-hegemonic reading: fatshion bloggers, for instance, can both advise on how to lose weight and claim the beauty or legitimacy of fatter body shapes; similarly, overweight consumers can both look for clothes that conceal what they perceive as a flaw and clothes that help to enhance curves. Each and every one of us has to deal with the thin ideal, but *how* we deal with it is changing in relation to the individual and the situation.

Fashion Practice

The Persistence of the Thin Ideal

Inertia

To address the enigma posed by the paradox of fashion we need to ask why thinness has become so dominant in the fashion system. Since the thin ideal is not a natural disposition but a historically situated attitude, as we saw in Chapter 1, it must be rooted in sociohistorical circumstances. This chapter addresses the causes of the tyranny of slenderness. However, I must forewarn the reader that I am not so interested in the reasons for the emergence of the thin ideal in Western countries at the beginning of the twentieth century as I am in the forces that prevent it from declining quickly today. The emergence of a new phenomenon in society is not as interesting as the persistence of a state of affairs that apparently has no raison d'être. Therefore, this chapter will especially address the reasons why the thin ideal has persisted so long in fashion despite it being a limitation in terms of business, that is to say, the reasons for the persistence of what I have called the paradox of fashion.

Practice is the keyword here. Undoubtedly, the thin ideal is particularly resilient, as it has shown the capacity to resist contrasting forces. The very existence of a paradox of fashion testifies to both the forces that counteract thinness and the persistence of the thin ideal. I will argue that one way to highlight and explain this persistence is to interpret fashion as a practice. Practice is much more than mere action. Practices, such as playing football or driving, consist of bundles of actions, routines, habits, discourses, and standards which override individual decisions and which individuals have to learn if they wish to be able to perform the practice in question. As practices override individual choices, they have a specific inertia that is independent of individuals' aims, opinions, and values, as well as of economic or rational appraisals. They cannot be directed, but must be trained and accommodated. They cannot be changed by design. We need, then, to focus on fashion as a practice if we wish to shed light on the intrinsic inertia of the thin ideal, its agency, and its capacity to resist and endure despite the paradox of fashion to which it gives rise.

A Concurrence of Multiple Causes

Where does the tyranny of slenderness come from? What are the factors that have led to the success of this ideal in the fashion system over the last 100 years? Scholars have put forward countless hypotheses about this (albeit not always based on in-depth historical research).

The most commonly cited causes are wide-ranging transformations in the structure of society or general habits rather than clothing. Industrial capitalism is considered by many to be one of the main culprits in spreading the thin ideal (Seid 1989: 82–4). This has less to do with the specific interests of specific actors such as cosmetic surgeons, dieticians, manufacturers of cosmetics and food supplements, and so on, than with the economic system per se, which ends up producing a culture of the body that serves its own production and consumption needs. The profit-driven market requires ever-increasing levels of production, which are based in turn on ever-greater consumption levels that sustain increasingly "lavish" lifestyles, that is to say, lifestyles in line with ever-evolving notions of wealth. The ideal of the slim body took hold in this context. It served both mass production (which requires physical efficiency, speed, keeping pace), and consumption, as it established an imperative yet at the same time unattainable goal that drove consumption among working women. Hence, the cosmetics industry has been one of the main promoters of the thin ideal, by creating an objective that is completely unnatural and then promising to make it accessible through its products (Wolf 1991: 61–80). Furthermore, increased prosperity has allowed most of the population to be lifted out of food scarcity into a situation where food abundance is the norm. Accordingly, the value of fat as an indicator of wealth has been reversed. While previously the abundance of fat was an indicator of food abundance and therefore of wealth and status, when food became available to everyone, being fat came to indicate the opposite, that is to say, being disadvantaged, and being thin came to indicate the capacity to control one's appetite, as opposed to being controlled by it. Practices and attitudes such as choosing a healthy diet, giving priority to quality over quantity, dedicating time and resources to the cultivation of an athletic and therefore lean body, which involve the deployment of economic and cultural capital (money, education), became indicators of wealth and status (Polivy et al. 1986: 92). This explanation resonates with Bourdieu's observation that attention to body shape, rather than strength or floridity, is a characteristic of upper-class taste (Bourdieu [1979] 1984: 190).

A special case is represented by those latent conditions which already existed in Western societies prior to the emergence of the thin ideal and which, although they cannot be considered direct causes, have facilitated its propagation. One particularly important factor is traditional religious hostility toward being fat (Stearns 1997: 49; Tait 1993: 198–9). In the Christian tradition, which pervades the culture of Western countries, fasting has always been considered an instrument of purification and asceticism. Forsaking food, in contrast to the vice of gluttony, has been associated, in images and stories, with holiness and higher religious ideals. Naturally, thinness was merely a consequence of such practices. However, it was an inevitable one, and especially evident to all (overweight people cannot be particularly fastidious in their fasting practices, it was argued). Recent feminist theories, such as those discussed in Chapter 3, take a similar theoretical stance, as they consider the thin ideal a manifestation of the preexisting patriarchal social order sparked by women's emancipation at the turn of the twentieth century. In this case, the basic idea is that women's demand for more rights, greater sexual freedom, and work emancipation, that is, for a reduction in the control exercised over them by patriarchal society, pushed them into new forms of subjugation and control that were more effective precisely because they exploited that very same emancipation. According to this viewpoint, the idealization of physical characteristics that are difficult to attain and conserve, such as thinness, is therefore a tool for maintaining control over women's lives and their potential for social accomplishment (Walden 1985: 365; Wolf 1993: 9–19). In women's eyes, this idealization makes sense because, as Bordo has observed, thinness is overdetermined, meaning that it bears multiple meanings that respond simultaneously to the contradictory demands placed on women by contemporary society: on the one hand, it takes on the male attitude toward labor based on control and willpower, thus offering a promise of emancipation from family and household roles traditionally reserved for women; on the other hand, it simultaneously reaffirms the traditional idea of femininity characterized by denial, sacrifice, and control of desire (Bordo 1993: 168–74, 185–212).

Other factors deemed significant in causing or facilitating the rise of the thin ideal have to do with the cultural sphere more directly: beliefs, values, lifestyles, technologies. Stearns (1997: 52), for example, analyzing the North American context, points to the spread of white-collar jobs and cars and with them the spread of a sedentary lifestyle. For Stearns, a sedentary lifestyle entails weight gain for many, against which the stigmatization of fat serves as a deterrent. Walden (1985: 355–6) has emphasized the rise of youthfulness as a bourgeois ideal at the turn of the twentieth century. Youth established itself as an autonomous social group in more recent times. According to Walden's reconstruction, however, already at the beginning of the last century the wealthy classes, who could rely on ample resources to "manage" their appearance and combat the effects of aging, began to invest in youthfulness as a status symbol. Staying young, in fact, requires a good diet, a less-than-exhausting job, and both time and money to dedicate to activities and products designed to take care of the body. In an increasingly urbanized society, in which appearance became more and more important as a means of managing status relations in more impersonal circumstances, the opportunity to rely on something more stable and less imitable than clothing styles became a key factor in the strategies of social distinction. The ruling classes therefore idealized a kind of appearance—youthful, slender, sprightly—which distinguished them from the lower classes, who lacked the time, money, or mindset to develop such personal attributes.

If we turn our attention to causes more closely related to the fashion system, Hollander ([1975] 1993), interestingly, refers to the spread of photography. Since photography (followed by cinema and then television) accentuates the width of the body, as photographs became customary in the fashion press the height and size of models assumed particular significance. In addition, according to Banner (1983: 287–8), it was fashion photographers who introduced the idea that a dress is enhanced if the underlying body does not interfere with its shapes. Fashion photographers increasingly favored models with visually "nonintrusive" bodies, as they were interested in representing clothes as free-standing objects disconnected from the circumstances of their use, aimed, as they were, at the "artification" (Heinich and Shapiro 2012) of their profession and creations.[1] Finally, Wilson (1985: 116) has also suggested "that the slender figure fits with the modernist artistic love of form suggestive of movement and speed, and also with its rejection of the 'natural.'" The cult of thinness was, thus, how the dominant aesthetics of the early twentieth century—well represented by such artistic movements as Cubism, Expressionism, and Futurism—influenced fashion photographers and designers.

As far as the fashion system is concerned, however, the factor that has most significantly influenced the spread of the thin ideal is the industrialization of clothing production. As I have already pointed out, mass production of apparel initially took hold in the United States at the beginning of the twentieth century, and expanded to the rest of the fashion system after the Second World War. Previously, consumers would turn to tailors or make their own clothes.[2] In the transition from sartorial to industrial fashion, the making of clothes has undergone a fundamental transformation: the creative process is now separated from the body to which the garment is destined (Bertola 2014). In sartorial fashion, prototyping is normally carried out directly by the tailor on the client's body, while in mass manufacture it is performed by the pattern maker on an "abstract" body (Corrigan 1997: 64), that is, the model's body, which is theoretically representative of all possible customer bodies. As might be expected, the use of this kind of "impersonal" body has led to a gradual "splitting" of the dress from actual bodies, since now clothes "encounter" the body only after they have been manufactured. This encounter may be successful or unsuccessful: in the latter case, the customer simply does not purchase the garment. In short, clothes have become abstract and standardized with respect to the endless variety of actual bodies. Thus, the transition to mass manufacture has split the clothes-body complex and consequently facilitated the propagation of body standards in fashion, in the form of clothing sizing systems. In the world of haute couture very little use was made of the sizing system. A tailored suit does not need to conform to a size, as the measurements are taken directly on the body, and the garment, be it draped or tailored, is adjusted to the body that will wear it. In fact, in the world of haute-couture thinness has never been a dominant value (see Mears 2011: 182–3). Ready-to-wear fashion, on the other hand, can only work by standardizing processes and products and then demanding that actual bodies adapt to standardized products (Seid 1989: 94). "Ready-made clothing demands ready-made bodies," notes Corrigan (1997: 64). This standardization constitutes a condition for the establishment of body ideals based on dimensions and, in particular, for the establishment of a slender body ideal. Thinness became imperative with the emergence of the sizing system in conjunction with the transition to mass production.[3] This relationship is key to understanding the effects of the thin ideal in fashion and merits a thorough discussion, which I shall undertake in Chapter 5.

The Conundrum of the Persistence of the Thin Ideal in Fashion

A more interesting question than why the thin ideal first arose in fashion, and yet one that has received far less attention, is why it has proven to be so persistent over the last 100 years. Indeed, the paradox of fashion raises the question: Why does the thin ideal continue to dominate fashion even when the fattening of the world population and the democratization of consumption have given rise to a huge potential market of overweight customers? The paradox of fashion is not that the thin ideal came into being 100 years ago, but that it endures today, apparently running counter to business interests. There must therefore be some kind of force that accounts for its persistence.

One factor that may help explain the persistence of the tyranny of slenderness in fashion is the fact that the thin ideal pervades not only the fashion system itself but also social and individual life. Its influence is not limited to the manufacture of clothing and fashion communication, but involves people's conception of the body, the person, and social relations. The fashion industry has to respond to the broader social context in which its customers are immersed and which continues to consider thinness an essential characteristic of female beauty. And yet, the fashion industry takes the thin ideal seriously and, far from opposing active or passive resistance, has championed its diffusion.

The reasons for the tyranny of slenderness in fashion normally given by industry professionals are unconvincing. They can be encapsulated in the notion of "hanger models." As seen in the previous section, fashion professionals (not just photographers, but also designers, editors, and modeling agents) are inclined to embrace the idea that models are thin because they have to interfere as little as possible with the clothes they wear. The clothes fit well if the underlying body disappears, just like a hanger. This is commonplace in the fashion system, as a cursory perusal of the fashion media will confirm.[4] Some examples of this are reported by Ashley Mears in her stimulating research into the thinness of fashion models (2010), subsequently included in the book *Pricing Beauty* (2011: 182–8). She cites, for example, the answer given by Nev, a New York-based magazine editor, when asked why models are so skinny. Like "dozens of producers" she interviewed, Nev believed that thin models are an obvious choice, as they serve to make clothes look good. Or as Nev put it, quite explicitly: "Designers want them to look a certain way. Like the clothes that hang, like a hanger, as they say. You know, originally models were just hangers" (Mears 2011: 182). I find this line of reasoning, which naturalizes the thinness of models, unconvincing for three main reasons. The first is that it is underpinned by a judgment of beauty, therefore by a cultural motive that is the fruit of an implicit social agreement, a contingent alignment of taste cultivated by agents in the field. It is not beauty that constrains, but the community of those that share a certain idea of beauty. The second is that it takes for granted a misleading idea, namely that the natural state of the garment is when it is separated from the body. Claiming that the body must not interfere with the dress in order not to ruin its shape implies the splitting of the clothes-body complex to which I referred above, rendering the garment essentially useless, an object to be photographed and looked at, and not to be worn, in stark contrast with the ultimate goal of the fashion business, which is selling clothes to be worn. The third reason is also the most striking: fashion professionals do not even believe what they say themselves. As Mears points out in her book, most of them do not directly address how the garment actually fits thin bodies rather than fat ones, but refer to what they consider a general, inevitable law of fashion, to which they must defer as it is required by some other actor of the fashion system. In the words of one interviewee: "If you can't beat 'em, join 'em, honey! That's the way it is. We're not gonna change the majority here" (Mears 2011: 187).

Let us follow this suggestion then, and seek to understand how this "internal law" of the fashion system works. Instead of only looking for external causes of the persistence of the thin ideal in fashion, or denying its paradoxical character, let us investigate whether the thin ideal is supported by an inner drive, whether the reasons for its persistence can be found in its very existence. Once it has established itself, I posit, it also reproduces against adverse forces, including economic interests.

Resilience is a key characteristic of discourses. Foucault ([1977] 1980: 194–6) recognized this and attempted to explain it through the concept of apparatus. Discourses, he argued, are resilient because they are the discursive manifestation of underlying ensembles consisting of institutions, architectural forms, laws, scientific statements, administrative measures, etc. For Foucault, these apparatuses, such as imprisonment, have the characteristic of originally arising with a strategic function, that is, in response to an urgent need, but then of perpetuating themselves, once instituted, beyond the will and strategies of historical actors. Thus, the birth of the institution of prison had the effect of producing a professionalized, well-integrated delinquent milieu which legitimized the need for the prison itself, and which did not exist before.

Apparatuses are not only responsible for the resilience of discourses. They also account for the fact that discourses, far from just describing the world, are involved in shaping and structuring it. In Foucault's view, as we have seen above, discourses are not limited to designating things, but "systematically form the objects of which they speak" ([1969] 2002: 54). That is to say, discursive formations are in themselves discursive practices, ways of making things happen. It is as practices that discourses are resilient against opinions, actions, and the interests of individuals and groups.[5]

In short, to tackle the persistence of discourses, their nature as practices should be addressed. This applies to fashion discourse, too, particularly to the thin ideal. In enunciating the thin ideal, fashion discourse also establishes it as a reference model for the behavior of fashion professionals and consumers, and determines that fat bodies are nonstandard, inadequate, "abnormal," eliciting countless actions and strategies aimed at reducing or concealing the fat present in real bodies. The discourse of thinness is in itself a practice of thinness. To understand how a practice works, particularly its resistance to the forces of change and its intrinsic inertia, I will refer to the rich pool of heterogeneous theories put forward in the past twenty years that can broadly be grouped under what is called the practice approach. My claim is that by abandoning the points of view focused on human actions—individual or collective—and social structure, and assuming a perspective based on practice as a unit of analysis, the persistence of the thin ideal should become more intelligible.

The Practice Approach

The practice approach seeks to explain how social subjects adapt to the world they live in, internalize the social order, and thus learn to govern situations. According to such an approach, it is at the level of practice that social order is reproduced and the behavior of different actors is aligned. Several scholars[6] have developed alternative ways of thinking about social phenomena as expressions of practices in action. Following Davide Nicolini's suggestion (2012: 8–10), I prefer to refer to a practice "approach," as opposed to a theory, not only to reiterate that a single theory of practices does not exist, as Schatzki (2001: 2) has already noted, but also to clarify that this perspective may serve our purposes not as a single theoretical framework, but as a conceptual toolkit capable of opening up new perspectives on known phenomena.

Practices are forms of collective behavior. In everyday life, collective behavior typically involves many people who do not know each other and have not previously planned their actions. Nonetheless, such behavior unfolds in an orderly and disciplined way, following, as it were, self-evident paths: everyone knows what to do, and all act in a coordinated way. Going to the theater, taking the subway, or going out for dinner are examples of such practices. Moreover, social practices are forms of behavior which recur in analogous circumstances, take place as routines because they appear habitual and obvious to those who participate, and can arise only thanks to certain "stabilizing" factors that make them possible, such as embodied routines, shared knowledge of the practice, or dedicated artifacts. The practice of theatergoing, for instance, involves embodied routines such as applauding (or booing), acquired knowledge such as the fact that at the theater, unlike at the cinema, you do not eat, and dedicated artifacts such as the seats that firmly invite you to stay in your place during the show.

A key feature of practices is the fact that they are complex formations. They involve multiple interdependent bodily actions, mental states, objects, material and social structures, rules, meanings, and many other things besides (Reckwitz 2002: 249). Sports practices are an area in which this is apparent. Indeed, scholars working in the field of practices often expressly refer to them.[7] For example, in the practice of Nordic walking, a type of sport walking assisted by sticks similar to ski poles, the shape of the poles is closely connected not just to the movement of the body, but also to the imagery traditionally associated with the act of walking with a cane, clothing conventions, the users' spending power, the technologies available for the manufacture of poles, predominant design, walking styles and rules, and so on. This is not to say that the shape of the poles is the result of all these factors, but rather that all of these factors evolve together, each being the result of the constraints imposed by the others.

The recognizable structure of social practices is apparent in many other areas of consumption, daily life, and work: performing music, cooking, attending a religious ceremony, and voting are all practices. A distinctive case of practice is, for instance, the fashion show. It involves various interdependent aspects, such as the general layout of the catwalk, the bodies of the models, the clothes displayed, the conventions of the fashion system with respect to sizes, current fashion trends, social hierarchies within the fashion industry, and communication technologies. For example: there is a mutual link between the T-shape of the catwalk, the number of guests attending the show, the time available for the show, the fact that guests have different degrees of influence in the fashion system and can therefore be organized into successive rows of seats, the presence of photographers upon whose photos the success of the collection partly depends, the limited performance skills of the models, who are not actresses, the way in which they have learned to walk when they parade in a fashion show, the fact that they normally use high heels, and so forth. A fashion show is a form of action that conforms with a set of constraints imposed not by a single entity, for example, an authority, but by a vast array of human and non-human stakeholders involved in the practice itself. Authorities (such as the Chambre Syndicale de la Haute Couture in Paris), despite their privileged position, are in turn part of practices and must respond to the constraints that those practices impose.

This is reflected in individual actions. Like institutional authorities, and like technical objects, humans are also part of practices rather than governing them. Mastering a practice does not mean being its master. In Andreas Reckwitz's (2002) terminology, individuals are "carriers" of a practice, which means that they carry patterns of bodily behavior with routinized ways of understanding, knowing how, and desiring. The important aspect is that these conventionalized bodily and mental activities "*are necessary elements and qualities of a practice in which the single individual participates, not qualities of the individual.* [. . .] A practice is thus a routinized way in which bodies are moved, objects are handled, subjects are treated, things are described and the world is understood" (Reckwitz 2002: 250, my emphasis). Of course, in practice too, compliance with those constraints implies that people can distance themselves from them and change their course of action. In their role as carriers, individuals must interpret the behavior that the given set of constraints make possible or desirable. They, therefore, do not replicate predetermined courses of action but create actions compatible with the bundle of constraints imposed by the practice (Bourdieu 1990: 55).

Adopting the practice approach therefore means, essentially, accepting the idea that certain courses of action in human life are routinized for a community of practitioners. In relation to these courses of action, the practitioners themselves are interpreters of the routine, "carriers" as opposed to agents of the practice. This further develops our understanding of social interaction. Classical sociology (Goffman 1959; Parsons 1951; Schütz [1955] 1973) has accustomed us to thinking in terms of mutual expectations of behavior: social interactions are determined by others' expectations of us and by our anticipation of the reactions that our action will elicit (the self-reflected expectation). In Chapter 2 I described the clothes-body idiom according to this pattern. Now, the practice approach makes it clear that in certain situations the expectations of the practice itself are also relevant—by this I mean that which the practice expects from us. In stating this, "practice" does not mean the mere sum of other subjects participating in the practice. It also includes the set of material configurations, embodied skills, norms, and shared meanings that guide individual performances and ensure that they can be read as interpretations of a consolidated practice. The agent is never completely the subject of his or her practices, because the practices act in him or her through incorporated dispositions, which are acquired schemes that inhabit our choices and our behavior (Bourdieu 1997: 166).

Like walking the catwalk, dressing is a human practice, but not in the same way. Walking, as well as dressing, is a social practice of a general kind; but walking the catwalk and Nordic walking are different and more special. All these actions that depend on the socio-material setting in which they take place are expressions of a practice and its internal organization. Yet in the case of the fashion show, as well as Nordic walking, the practice has some additional features. For example, it requires special, dedicated training; it cannot be learned simply by living daily life. It takes place at a particular time clearly demarcated from the rest of the day. Its performance requires suspension of all or almost all other practices of the same kind (one either walks the catwalk or does Nordic walking). It establishes a community of practitioners whose primary social bond consists in the practice itself, not in other interests or affective relationships. In a sense, such practices may be considered distinct "entities" (Shove, Pantzar and Watson 2012: 7): circumscribed fields of action and demarcated social spheres that are easily recognizable through certain signs (Warde 2014: 291). Using a well-known terminological distinction drawn by Theodore R. Schatzki, I shall call entities of this kind "integrative practices" (Schatzki 1996: 98), contrasting them with "dispersed practices" (Schatzki 1996: 91), which are distributed across many domains of human life. While walking is a dispersed practice, walking the catwalk is an integrative one. In the case of integrative practices, according to Schatzki (1996: 99) particularly important roles are performed by "explicit rules," such as precepts and instructions, and "teleoaffective structures," such as ends, beliefs, and emotions. In fact, it is evident that whereas everyday walking does not normally have specific rules or purposes but simply body techniques and routines, and does not arouse particular emotions, walking the catwalk involves joining an entity in which these things are important.

Fashion is something much more complex than just participating in or attending a fashion show, if nothing else because wearing clothes is not limited to a set time of the day. Life is dressed. Therefore, wearing clothes is not reducible to an integrative practice. And, yet, opening the wardrobe and deciding what to wear, adapting one's bodily movements to the clothes that one is wearing, buying clothes and selling them, arranging a shop window, and so forth, are all actions typical of a socially constituted practice (Entwistle [2000] 2015: 11). It is impossible to be fashionable without practicing the social game of fashion. I therefore suggest that, in fact, fashion can be analyzed through the lens of practice theory. It can be considered a wide-ranging dispersed practice distributed across several domains of social life, although it may also include some examples of integrative practices. As a (dispersed) practice, fashion has a number of features that are typical of practices, and which help explain certain manifestations of fashion, including the persistence of the thin ideal.

The Inertia of Practices

Something that the practice approach can do very well is to explain the inertia of social behavior. This has often been considered a shortcoming of practice theories, which have been accused of focusing too much on inertia and failing to adequately explain social change (Turner 1994: 78–100).[8] However, I am not interested so much in whether the practice approach enables us to explain the change. It does explain inertia very well. Inertia does not imply immobility but continuity: it derives from the bond that each new action necessarily has with an array of actions, relationships, objects, and situations that pre-exist it. This bond is twofold. It takes the form of routines, habits, and conventions produced by reciprocal expectations of behavior within the community of practice—what Barry Barnes (2001: 25) calls "alignment" and Joseph Rouse (2007: 669) the "mutual accountability" of the agents. And it takes the form of embodied experience, a system of durable and transposable individual dispositions that generate new actions that conform to "correct" practices, therefore reflecting the weight of the past on the individual him/herself (Bourdieu 1980: 87–91). Both of these forces play a part in "hardening" people's patterns of behavior.

Shifting the unit of analysis from the subjects that act (individuals and organizations) and from social facts (institutions) to practices enables us to understand not only why individuals normally find it difficult to deviate from the norm, fashion, or habit, but also why they usually do not want to do it. Each practice is characterized at any time by a set of established understandings, procedures, and objectives (Warde 2005: 140). What needs to be done, how to do it, and why—these are all aspects dictated by the practice, concerns that the agent has acquired in the course of his or her trajectory, while learning to practice it. There is no need for set rules to be explicitly learned. Moreover, a practice incorporates in those who practice it ways of doing and thinking that, being incorporated, appear obvious, natural. This is particularly clear in the case of sports, as they channel the behavior of sportsmen and sportswomen toward routines and standards. No skier who is even remotely experienced has any doubts about what to do when s/he goes skiing (Nicolini and Monteiro 2016: 116). Where to go, how to dress, how to move, or what to talk about are all aspects that come naturally even though there is nothing "natural" about them. This is possible because the practice has "arranged" the agent in such a way as to act in a manner consistent with the practice itself, in various ways. To name just the most obvious ones, it has arranged the agent by incorporating in him or her a *habitus*, that is, orienting the body toward the "correct" practice and predisposing it to respond with the "right," direct action, appropriate to the demands that come from the environment (Bourdieu 1997: 170–5); it has also arranged the agent by immersing him or her in an environment of artifacts and infrastructure that exercise their agency over him or her, in the sense that they prescribe certain doings, channeling his/her behavior toward certain standards (Latour 1992); finally, it has arranged the agent by setting the goals, that is, determining the objectives to be achieved through practice, objectives that the agent can (and indeed usually does) perceive as his or her own, but which are set by the practice itself (Schatzki 2002: 80–5).

One of the main causes of inertia is the key role played by routines, habits, and tacit knowledge in the performance of practices. Another powerful source of inertia is the fact that many dispositions of the actors engaged in a practice are embodied: the affected gait of the models on the catwalk is the result of hours and hours of exercises and constrictions (Hesselbein 2019), but also an embodied *habitus* which is difficult to deconstruct when, as sometimes happens, the fashion show director decides to abandon the privileged setting of the central T-shaped runway (Mears 2011: 107–10; Wissinger 2015: 59–79). Finally, the things involved in a practice resist changes by the mere fact of existing, since they are produced by an industrial system that has invested capital in their manufacture, and are made in that particular way. Practices thus possess an inertia deriving from the fact that in their framework individual goals, models and constraints must constantly deal with goals, models, and constraints dictated by the practice itself (namely, by the fact of practicing that practice, *not* by the sum of other practitioners' goals, models, and constraints).

When individual goals, models, and constraints prevail that are too heterogeneous compared to those of the practice, the individual is simply doing something else. Since such a rift endangers the possibility of practicing the practice, it is not surprising that most times the goals, models, and constraints of the practice not only prevail, but shape the individual goals, models, and constraints. The agent engaged in a practice experiences acting in a world "taken for granted," which s/he inhabits like a garment or a familiar habitat. This presupposes agreement between the dispositions of the agent and the expectations that are immanent in the world (Bourdieu [1997] 2000). In general terms, it implies that the social order inscribes itself in the bodies in the form of dispositions attuned to the structures of the world, so that the individual knows exactly what needs to be done and when it needs to be done.

The practice approach allows us to focus on a social force that would otherwise escape the observer's eye, namely, the power of practice. This sheds new light on the tyranny of slenderness in fashion, as I shall show in the following sections. The persistence of the thin ideal in the fashion system seems paradoxical if analyzed on the basis of economic interests, individual beliefs, or social structures. But if studied with the conceptual tools of the practice approach, it appears as the striking manifestation of the inertia that bodies, materials, routines, skills, and meanings of fashion practice impose on its participants. These participants, in turn, do not perceive such inertia as a constraint because they are the carriers of the practice, actual interpreters of what the practice expects to be done. Fashion's forsaking the potential profit from fat bodies is neither a choice nor a true renunciation, since fat fashion is not a possibility that fashion practice currently contemplates.

The Thin Ideal Embodied

Let us examine fashion practice and thinness more closely. The power of practices is perhaps most evident in embodiment: that is, when the practice successfully disciplines people's bodies and is strengthened by the force of inertia that embodiment produces. In the case of fashion, a significant contribution to the structuring of the thin ideal has come from the modeling industry, as discussed in Chapter 3. The focus on slim sizes in mass manufacture has created a demand for slim bodies to use for fitting clothes, their display at fashion shows, and the communication of products and brands through the media. During the 1950s and 1960s, the in-house mannequins of high-fashion *maisons* were gradually replaced by freelance models, usually supplied by agencies (Koda and Yohannan 2009). Hence, modeling gradually became institutionalized as an independent profession with its own standards. The ultra-thin bodies of models increasingly became *the* bodies of fashion: the bodies which fashion could not do without.[9] For fitting or communication, these are now the only bodies available. It is thus all the more necessary for the design of collections to be based on those bodies. To be able to create a collection in a size other than four, designers would have to have bodies other than size four at their disposal. However, this is not the case.

Nevertheless, we cannot draw the conclusion that fashion's resistance to overthrowing the tyranny of slenderness is the effect of the characteristics acquired over time by the modeling industry—just as we cannot say that this persistence depends on the prevailing ideal of the female body in the media industry, or that it is the consumers who refuse to include larger sizes in fashion. None of these explanations works because none of them acknowledges the complexity of fashion as a practice.

Viewed from a practice perspective, the thinness of fashion models appears different. Models are not thin because this is an "objective" aspect of female beauty according to some aesthetic law or a mere constraint imposed by market needs or a cultural ideal shared by the fashion system. They are thin because the practice of fashion modeling has incorporated not only the ideal, but the very fact of slim bodies: the routines of designing on thin bodies, the materiality of dummies and samples, and so on. As mentioned above, Ashley Mears has observed that fashion professionals often blame other actors in the fashion system for models' thinness, claiming that they feel forced to enhance it. Especially agents, stylists, and editors, if pressed to explain, blame the thinness of models on fashion designers, who allegedly ask for very thin models because, according to the hanger model thesis, clothes fit better on tall and slim bodies. I have already explained why I find this argument unconvincing. However, there is one more point to add here. If designers are asked why they develop their designs in such small sizes, they answer, as Mears (2011: 184) points out, not so much with economic or aesthetic arguments as with an appeal to tradition: the sample size is the one they have learned to use at school, that of the dummy they use to develop their creations, that of the models supplied by the agencies. Moreover, in all settings (design, fitting, show, photoshoot) the size standard must be the same, because in the hectic moments preceding the fashion show there is no time to make adjustments to the clothes on the bodies of models of different sizes.

Based on Howard Becker's (1982) theory of art worlds, Mears ties all of this to the concept of convention:

> As in other art worlds, the accomplishment of fashion looks requires conventions, shared ways of doing things. Conventions are especially important [. . .] for cultural intermediaries to navigate uncertainty and ambiguity in the production process. Conventions can also make the accomplishment of fashion difficult, should producers ignore them. (Mears 2011: 175)

However, a careful examination of Mears' data shows that much more is at play here than just convention (although this is an important aspect of practices). In the field of fashion we encounter, to begin with, ideals and goals such as the thin ideal and the goal of achieving and preserving small body measurements, which are established by the practice itself, learned and incorporated by the individuals while learning and training in the practice, and shared and naturalized by the protagonists in the field, often against their own interests. Furthermore, we encounter moods that the practice instills in participants, such as the shame of having put on weight or, in the case of plus-size models, lost weight (Czerniawski 2015: 95; see also Czerniawski 2012). We encounter specific doings and body techniques that have to be trained in order to be accepted in the field, such as the walk on the catwalk, a highly affected gait that can only seem natural and elegant because it has been naturalized. We encounter instruction manuals that codify behavioral standards, such as the "how-to" books described by Wissinger (2015: 146–61), which lay down rules and "best practices" for those who wish to join the field of fashion modeling.[10] We encounter artifacts that have incorporated the rules and routines of the practice into their form, stabilizing them and making them resistant to change thanks to the solidity of materials, such as the "emaciated" dummies used to display clothes in department stores (Bentley 1999: 211). We encounter material settings and space arrangements, such as fashion store environments, that "encourage shoppers to compare themselves with the images of models," intimidating "women who feel excluded from the lifestyle that they convey" (Arnold 2001: 94; see also Gruys 2012). And we encounter bodies (the models' bodies, in fact) that through hard, painstaking labor have incorporated what the practice imposed on them and have turned it into a disposition to appear and act appropriately.

This all forms a "bundle" of activities and material settings that cannot be attributed to the participants' individual or collective choices, but in a sense constitute an external power that forces agents to act as they do:

> Ask designers why they book skinny models and they'll reply that that's what the agents are providing. Ask agents why they promote skinny models and they'll reply that that's what the designers want. And around we go. As a structural

organization system, the modeling market appears to be an external force to bookers and clients. (Mears 2011: 188)

However, this "external" force, which is external not only to bookers and clients, but also to models,[11] is not extraneous to them, but acts through the performances of the participants in the practice. It is external to their free and conscious will, not to their actions. The agents carry the practice and, by practicing it, enable it to establish itself. Fashion professionals and consumers, including models, enable the practice of thinness to become a standard in our cultural landscape, so that the tyranny of slenderness is not perceived as tyranny at all. The way in which they interpret and perform the thin ideal helps to perpetuate or modify it.

The persistence of the thin ideal is due to the inertia of the practice of fashion. Every agent in the system must adapt to this ideal if they want to continue to work, because every other agent expects them to behave consistently with the thin ideal. Modeling agencies do so to reduce the risk of being unable to meet the demands of brands (Sandre-Orafai 2016: 112). Fashion editors do so because they are forced by modeling agencies, the fashion industry, and colleagues from other magazines (Wykes and Gunter 2005: 53). This also applies to models,[12] with the not-insignificant detail that this ideal is incorporated in their bodies, allowing or not allowing them to enter the profession, and forcing them to exercise iron discipline over their corporeality (Wissinger 2015: Chapters 4 and 5). By embodying the thin ideal, models, not because they are ontologically beautiful or desirable but because they are necessary for the functioning of the fashion industry, contribute substantially to the persistence of the thin ideal notwithstanding changing economic interests in the sector.

Inertia of the Tyranny of Slenderness

The paradox of fashion is less puzzling if instead of conceiving of the thinness of the female body as an ideal to be achieved, that is as a cultural value, we conceive of it as a practice of which women, as well as professionals of the fashion industry, are carriers. What seemed to be a contradiction from an economic point of view and irrational behavior from a cultural one, emerges as a consistent expression of the inertia of a dispersed practice.

In fact, if we shift the unit of analysis from the subjects to the practice, we discover a viscous system of doings, artifacts, routines, and incorporations that channel the way individuals and organizations interpret and carry the practice. It becomes clear that the tyranny of slenderness in fashion is not due to single factors, but to the bundle of artifacts, actions, and situations in which the practice consists. We should not, then, blame, alternately, fashion designers' aesthetic choices, companies' marketing policies, the imagery conveyed by the media and the blogosphere, or consumers' aspirational expectations. None of these factors, taken in isolation, could conceivably produce fashion's "great renunciation" of the world of fat bodies. Of course, designers "choose" to keep on designing exclusively on underweight bodies, but it is actually the practice of fashion that chooses through them by means of the way it is taught in the fashion schools they attended, the fact that, as a rule, the bodies provided for fitting by the modeling industry are underweight, the technical limits of the automated size grading systems,[13] the aspiration of consumers to attain or preserve a thin and youthful body, a sales network that displaces stores specializing in plus sizes mainly to outlying districts and small towns, a fashion press that literally hides fat bodies. The same observation, of course, can be extended to the choices of those who plan the contents of fashion courses, those who develop the technologies of automated size grading, consumers, retailers, and editors. As well as modeling agencies.

The practice of fashion, like all practices, evolves slowly on the basis of a sticky dialectic between factors of change and of inertia; and the thin ideal is part of that dialectic. Of course, fashion thrives on change. The concept of fashion itself implies the idea that a style is bound to end very soon and be replaced by a new style in the cyclical sequence of trends. But this change, which makes fashion what it is, requires conventions and routines, shared ways of doing things, habits, artifacts, and alignments among the various actors involved. All of this makes fashion discourse surprisingly stable and resilient to attempts and reasons to change, and gives the thin ideal a persistence that the reasons offered by the subjects involved cannot explain.

Fashion Technology

The Sizing System

Mass Production and the Standardization of Clothes

In the previous chapters, I discussed the link between the rise of the thin ideal in fashion and the industrialization of clothing production. Both phenomena arose concurrently within the space of a few decades at the beginning of the twentieth century, so much so that the first appearance of a market niche dedicated to ready-made clothing for non-slim women, stoutwear, was already burdened with the mission of concealing the nonconformity of stout bodies to the ideal of female beauty. I have also argued that this concurrence is not fortuitous but characterized by a causal link. The transition from custom-made to ready-made clothing has entailed, as a necessary condition, the standardization of sizes, thus reversing the relationship between dress and the body: clothes no longer adapt to the body that must wear them, but the body adapts to the standard dimensions of the clothes manufactured and retailed by the industry. As mass production of clothing advanced, it became possible to think that body dimensions are important, that they are a key aspect of physical appearance and beauty, that they can be compared, and that it is necessary to be concerned with them. The standardization of clothes entails the standardization of bodies, and this is the condition for a standard based on size, such as thinness, to be raised to the state of a bodily ideal to be pursued.

Yet, the link between the inception of mass production and the rise of the thin ideal does not stop there. It has very deep roots in the technology of clothing manufacture and produces effects that play a significant part in the persistence of the thin ideal today. We, therefore, need to study it more closely. In this chapter, I will show that, for technical reasons, the standardization of clothes brings with it the establishment of a size threshold above which mass production becomes complex and unprofitable, so that companies prefer to avoid it and concentrate on slim sizes. Standardization was a major innovation for the fashion system, and was at the origin of the democratization of fashion, but it could only take place at the cost of a new form of segregation, this time based on size rather than wealth.[1] This form of segregation arises because standardization works adequately only for slim bodies. The emergence of this threshold and new segregation was at the origin of the plus-size apparel sector, a segment of the clothing industry that has traditionally been excluded from the fashion system.

The standardization of clothes was based on an innovative production technique for the time: the sizing system. It was this technique that made it possible to remove the dress from the body and consider it an independent object that can be proposed for a multitude of body types (Bertola 2014: 117–21). It was this technique that made it possible to separate the clothes-body complex into two mutually disconnected parts and systematically treat the garment as a self-sufficient artifact, separated from the concreteness of the personal body and relative only to the generality of a body idea. This observation supports this chapter's main thesis: *it was not so much the aesthetic choices of fashion designers or companies that determined the tyranny of slenderness in fashion as the advent of sizing in the manufacture and sale of garments for mass production.* The thin *ideal* was actually a consequence of the new *practice* that prevailed in fashion in the twentieth century in connection with the introduction of the sizing system.

In conjunction with these transformations, the reference to size has quickly become a significant aspect of the way bodies are considered by the fashion system. Size has become one of the distinctive features of dress, like shape and fabric. In fashion, body dimensions are not identified by weight or quantity of fat (although these characteristics, being addressed by the cosmetics and diet industry, feature prominently in fashion magazines), but by its measurements, especially the size of clothes, which is a synthetic, rather approximate measure, yet functional to the standardization required by the industry. I will therefore begin with a brief summary of the main features of the sizing system. This will allow us to lay the groundwork for a full understanding of how this technique has affected the thin ideal in fashion and still affects its persistence and the existence of a separate market for plus-size apparel.

A Technique to Bridge Clothes and the Body

The importance of the sizing system for today's fashion industry can hardly be overstated. Far from being just a technique, it is broadly responsible for how people dress in contemporary societies. Its agency affects the everyday life of individuals and the society in which they live.

To standardize is to classify. Each kind of standardization involves a process of classification, namely the reduction of the boundless variety of actual cases to a limited and manageable number of classes, types, or categories, which form the standard to which that field refers. For example, measurement systems establish standards to allow the infinite number of possible distances between two points in the real world to be compared and measured. Similarly, the standardization of clothing by means of the sizing system is based on the capacity to classify the infinite variety of possible shapes and sizes of clothes, thereby ordering them into a manageable number of types.

To be more exact: the sizing system is the technique that makes it possible to classify not just clothes, but clothes-body complexes. Classifying clothes would be neither problematic nor useful (except for fashion history purposes). The thorny issue here is the classification of clothes as body extensions: not objects of visual or tactile perception, but worn objects, clothes-in-action. Hence, the true purpose of the sizing system is the determination of standard dimensions not for clothes, but for the interface between dress and the body, an interface that in principle can never be fully standardized, because it is an intimate expression of the individual's singularity. This makes the development of an effective sizing system difficult, prolonged and demanding. Yet necessary. If clothing mass production splits the clothes-body complex, abstracting the first from the second, the sizing system is necessary to reconstitute the unit, that is to restore the prosthetic function of clothing within the clothes-body idiom and prevent clothing from being reduced to mere covering or masking of the body. Paradoxical though it may seem, it is thanks to the sizing system that the actual body can appropriate an impersonal garment created for standard bodies, and use it as an effective expression of the self in the circumstances of life.

This should also be understood in a second way, as the sizing system reconstitutes the broken unity of the clothes-body complex by other means. In fact, it bridges consumers and producers in a production system that has separated them. In today's fashion industry the issue of the relationship between a garment and the body is tackled in two separate phases: pattern making, which relates the design to a standard and hence abstract body; and purchase, which has been reduced to the consumer's choosing from an array of ready-to-wear clothes. The sizing technique makes it possible to combine these two phases. A sizing system is designed to guarantee the best fit for purchasers of ready-made clothes, "providing enough variation to accommodate all customers, but limiting the number of sizes for efficiency of production and distribution" (Ashdown

2014: 17). The smaller the number of sizes, the lower the accommodation rate of customers. The larger the number of sizes, the higher the manufacture and retail costs and the complexity of the purchasing process. The goal of a sizing system is to identify the best balance between these two opposing needs. By activating the connection between those who manufacture clothes and those who wear them, the sizing technique is a tool that enables the clothes-body idiom and reconstitutes the unit which mass production in principle would break.

The function of the sizing technique in the fashion industry is therefore complex. Correspondingly, it plays a multifaceted role in fashion practices as well. First of all, it is a means of facilitating the purchasing decision in the context of mass production. It allows consumers to navigate their way around what the industry offers:

> The theory is that clothing produced using a standardized sizing system based on scientifically derived anthropometric data will provide consumers with a product that they can rely on to fit in the same way, purchase to purchase. This consistency should reduce dissatisfaction with the fit of apparel, increase purchases, reduce returns and heighten profits for producers. (LaBat 2007: 89)

The purchasing processes that had established themselves over time in the consumption of consumer-made garments gradually became obsolete as the practice of buying ready-made clothes spread. The transition from the process of "constructing" clothing on the body to consumers choosing from several ready-to-wear clothes made the fit of the dress a crucial factor in their choice and size a key characteristic of the garment. In-store purchasing accelerated the decision-making process compared with that for traditionally tailored clothes. Moreover, in the United States, where the consumption of ready-made clothing spread considerably earlier than it did in Europe, the rapid growth of the population scattered across its vast rural areas favored the expansion of mail-order distribution (Ashdown 2014: 20). Naturally, mail-order customers could not try on a garment before purchase, meaning that their purchasing decisions were based on a catalog that allowed them to imagine the fit of garments on their body. To make this possible, a reliable sizing system was required.

Furthermore, the sizing system has an important function for retailers, who must bear the costs of matching an infinite variety of fitting requirements and a supply of clothing that is limited insofar as it is prearranged. They include not only storage costs but also costs of modification. This asymmetry between the variability of actual bodies and the standardization of clothing supply can be tackled by customizing garments by means of post-purchase alterations. A well-tuned sizing system that matches the predominant body shape of a store's clientele allows costs related to post-purchase alterations to be reduced. Indeed, as Ingrid Jeacle (2003) has shown, the improvement of the sizing system during the period in which ready-to-wear clothing came to prevail was key to reducing department store overheads, which were largely accounted for by the modifications needed to achieve a correct fit.

Finally, if we look at the industry, the link between mass production and the establishment of a sizing system is even stronger. Sizing facilitates standardization in several ways. First, it stabilizes measurements, and therefore machinery and storage, thereby reducing costs. Second, it rationalizes the use of fabric, thereby reducing waste. Next, it simplifies the variability of the product, hence making it easier to modify. Finally, it also simplifies the design process because it allows production patterns to be created by means of a simple algorithmic derivation from a single original pattern designed on a base size. The design and pattern-making process can be (ideally) reduced to just one for all possible bodies: for bodies that are larger than the fit model's body, it is enough to add fabric and move cuts and seams according to predetermined criteria. This gives rise to an economically viable system that produces a wide (albeit finite) range of products from among which the consumer can choose the one that best suits her body.

The Miracle of Size Grading

The last aspect mentioned in the previous section, that is, the role played by the sizing system in the simplification of the design process, is perhaps the one that has the greatest economic impact. Certainly, it is a primary cause of the exclusion of fat bodies from fashion. Its power originates from a specific technique called size grading (Moore et al. 2001). Size grading makes it possible not to repeat the body measurements for each size, since garment measurements in larger sizes are obtained by means of rules defining the incremental changes to be made with respect to the base size. These rules make up the size grading algorithm and normally have the characteristic of being proportional: they reproduce the shape of the base pattern by enlarging it proportionally in all its parts. When applied to production, this means that the prototype garment must be developed only for the base size, and that the production of all other sizes does not require further design effort. However, the enormous reduction in costs made possible by this technique brings with it a concomitant reduction in the variability of garment shapes:

> As the great majority of grading systems used are strictly proportional, the sizes in the range will only fit customers who are different from the fit model in overall body dimensions, but are identical in body proportion. Many of the fit problems encountered by apparel companies can be traced to this dependence on sizes that are proportionally developed based on one fit model. (Ashdown 2014: 23)

Basically, the use of algorithmic size grading implies that the body shape of the company's fit model becomes the ideal body shape for garments that the company manufactures in all sizes. Yet as we shall see, the divergence of real bodies from the ideal body cannot easily be counteracted for all sizes by the versatility of designs and elasticity of materials.

The size grading technique is the heart of the sizing system, the innovation that made the transition to mass production possible. In this respect, two related, but independent, historical processes should be distinguished (Aldrich 2007). First, full-size patterns and tools were developed to reproduce a garment in its absence, that is, without the need to have it physically in one's hands. Patterns were provided with marked rules at the relevant points and perforated with holes to allow the pencil to mark the point. Such tools have also been used in mass production, but they developed before the technologies of the clothing industry (such as the sewing machine) and served initially the tailors' craftsmanship. Sizes were developed for military purposes when armies began to dress their soldiers in uniforms in the eighteenth century, long before the advent of the apparel industry (Conti 2014; Godley 1997). In contrast, the introduction of size grading and other tools to automate the production of a garment in different sizes for different bodies was an innovation of a completely different scope. These tools are also useful for artisan tailors, but essentially they enabled the transition to an apparel industry based on mass production and consumers who, unlike the military, are free to choose. The sizing system developed long after the pattern technique, and also after the institutionalization of stable (metric or imperial) measurement systems and the invention of the sewing machine.

Another feature of the sizing system that has a bearing on our discussion of the issue of fat fashion is its fundamental inaccuracy. The system was first developed by apparel companies independently, based on their customers' body shapes and through trial and error. Manufacturer and retailer sizing initiatives were private and kept secret, but the results were very approximate and inconsistent between companies, so that the system had to rely heavily on the use of alterations to customize the fit. It became clear that an adequate sizing system would have to be based on systematic anthropometric studies that reliably represented the actual shape of the bodies of a certain population. For this reason, as the market expanded, governments funded statistical surveys of the population's body size.[2]

Although anthropometric studies have enabled companies to improve their ability to make clothes suitable for real bodies, some limits of the system have never been overcome. For example, since national populations differ from one another for ethnic reasons, national surveys produce different measurements that are difficult to compare. Variations between consumers from different geographical regions cannot easily be accommodated by theoretically homogeneous variations in body scale. Although the goal of anthropometric studies is to render an infinite variety of actual bodies manageable, the fact that they are carried out on a national basis introduces a further factor of complexity. Also, the transfer of anthropometric data to the clothing sizing system is substantially arbitrary even today (Christel and Dunn 2017). Various countries have published size standards, which however are national and therefore not comparable,[3] and their adoption by manufacturers and retailers is voluntary. Companies freely decide which size labels to attach to clothes, and labels do not normally show body measurements but the garment size, that is, a number or other symbol which is abstracted from the garment dimensions and only vaguely indicative of them. In other words, labels are not part of a garment's technical specifications, but a marketing tool to enhance customer loyalty and facilitate the purchasing process. It is for this reason that, as mentioned in Chapter 3, labels quickly became an instrument for the thin ideal to exert its influence in the fashion system. Vanity sizing is, arguably, to be interpreted not so much as a deliberate strategy to manipulate consumers, but as the natural tendency to lower size codes in a context where, on the one hand, there is no obvious connection between index and garment measurements, and, on the other hand, growing measurements of the clothes-body complex are increasingly source of the fat stigma.

How the Sizing System Encourages the Marginalization of Nonstandard Bodies

In short, a substantial characteristic of the sizing system is that it does not enable the production of ready-made clothes suited to accommodate all women's body shapes. Undoubtedly, reliable knowledge provided by anthropometric studies about prevailing body shapes in a particular population would in principle be useful for the development of a sizing system with a high accommodation rate. However, it would not eliminate the problem of extremes, namely deviant bodies, all those bodies that depart significantly from the most common measurements.

The truth is, a single sizing system seems unattainable.[4] Companies adopt very different size standards, and several clothing firms have changed their fitting measurements over time, so that consumers are faced with inconsistencies surrounding different sizing systems. This has produced a situation that Ashdown (2014: 27) summarizes thus:

> Most apparel companies create their sizing systems by defining their target market in a way that gives them a loyal following of customers, who appreciate the styles, fit characteristics, level of quality, and cost provided by the company. Different companies have fit models of different proportions; therefore each company provides [a] good fit for those customers whose body shape most resembles their fit model.

Ashdown's observation makes it clear that the sizing system, due to its imprecise character, reconstructs the unity of the clothes-body complex by adapting the body to clothes, and not vice versa. In principle, it should be a tool for making garments that fit bodies. In practice, it ends up "manufacturing" bodies that adapt to clothes. Each brand constructs its own audience by deselecting certain bodies. Thus, the partiality of the multiple sizing systems has the effect of marginalizing bodies that diverge excessively from what are considered the standards, even if these do not coincide with the most common body shapes. In 2007 Jennifer Bougourd described the situation as follows:

> At present, large segments of the population are regularly unable to find the right fit for the products that they like, because many fashion designers, retailers and manufacturers tend to build their products around stereotypical consumers. In doing so they neglect significant and expanding consumer segments with differing morphologies: ethnic groups with different morphologies, consumers aged over 60, and extra-large sizes which are increasingly common in affluent societies. (Bougourd 2007: 108)

Things have not changed radically in the last two decades. Many commentators have placed great faith in the expectation that digital technologies, in particular body scanners, will lead to more accurate, reliable anthropometric surveys and therefore a sizing system suitable to all bodies. However, results have been slow in coming, possibly because the very idea of size, due to its approximation, is at odds with the ultimate objective.[5]

In closed systems, the solution is simple: ban deviant bodies. Armies, for example, do not recruit outsize soldiers, and not for military reasons alone.[6] However, ready-to-wear clothing manufacturers cannot readily "dismiss" consumers. They can cultivate the homogeneity of their clients' bodies only by means of their products. The sizing system thus becomes a device for selecting and disciplining customers: if you wish to wear my products, you must match the body shape of my fit model, albeit in a larger size; if you do not, you must actively adapt. Inadvertently, it is not the consumer who chooses the brand, but the brand that chooses the consumer.[7] The technology for manufacturing clothes turns into a device for normalizing the body ideal and disciplining customers' actual bodies, that is, in a fundamental element of fashion discourse, which establishes norm and deviance. *Bodies that are accommodated by the sizing system are included in the fashion system, while those that are not accommodated are excluded.* Thus fashion becomes a disciplining discourse with respect to real bodies:

> By "natural" order of things I mean the tendency to go to a shop to try and find clothes that fit one's body. Here, clothing is made subordinate to the demands of the body. But if the store manages to create a stylized image, an abstract model of a standard female body, then the body must be made to fit the clothes that the store makes available. Here, the body is made subordinate to an abstract model that stands outside it and is shaped by marketing. (Corrigan 1997: 64)

The paradoxical character of all this needs to be recognized: the survey of actual bodies and the translation of the collected data into an arbitrary sizing system becomes the basis for the marketing of clothes that, in reality, are designed according to an ideal body that the fit model embodies. The ideal body is then incorporated into clothes as a sort of "model reader" of their meaning, in the sense that the garments have been designed for that body and incorporate it in their own characteristics, just as books incorporate a particular type of reader in the way they are written (Eco 1979: 7–11). Accordingly, the materiality of fashion becomes independent of actual bodies (Haller 2015: 190) and exhibits an autonomous agency (Latour 2005). The shape and size of clothes for sale produces an unintentional but real discrimination between consumers, as they generate the social and commercial marginalization of those bodies that are physically marginal compared to the ideal.

The Inherent Technical Limit of Size Grading

The sizing system serves to standardize clothing, yet why is this standardization geared toward slim as opposed to average sizes? The answer lies in the nature of size grading. At the very moment in which it made mass production possible, the size grading technique also introduced a constraint that proved to be decisive in establishing the thin ideal: *size grading can be extended to larger bodies only up to a certain size.*

To appreciate this point, it is necessary to reflect on the structure of the human body, in particular the female body, and how it changes with body mass. The fact that the skeleton cannot be easily altered, unlike fat and muscle mass, means that, regardless of basic differences dictated by the former—normally closely correlated with height—the great variety of bodies is mostly due to the latter. The variability of body shape resulting from different skeletons is relatively manageable, since such differences are limited and proportional. Variability which depends on the increase or decrease of fat or muscle mass is less predictable, and becomes predominant when body weight increases significantly with respect to height, as this is obviously indicative of greater presence of such mass (Boorady 2014).

If we now focus on the need to manufacture clothes that, as they are mass-produced, adapt to bodies of various types, it is clear that shape and size differences between bodies belonging to a range of slim sizes are more likely to conform to similar proportions, whereas for bodies above a certain weight that proportionality tends to be reduced, as fat and muscle mass prevail. Heavier bodies are more heterogeneous in their forms, as these words of a pattern maker underline:

> We know pretty well what a size 6 woman will look like if she edges up to a 10; her bust line might increase an inch. But if a woman goes from a size 16 to a 20, you just can't say with any certainty how her dimensions will change. [. . .] You'll have some people who gain weight entirely in their trunk, some people who will gain it in their hips. As someone getting into plus-size, you can either make clothing that is shapeless and avoid the question altogether or target a segment of the market that, let's say, favors a woman who gets larger in the hip. You really have to narrow down your customer. [. . .] If you have decided to go after the woman who is top-heavy, well, some gain weight in their upper arms and some do not. There are so many variables; you never win. (Kathleen Fasanella, quoted in Bellafante 2010)

The implications of this for the sizing technique are that, as compared to a slim size of one's choice, body-size variation generally follows a proportional trajectory only to a certain extent. Beyond size twelve most variation typically takes shape outside the proportions of the original model: more on the hips, bottom, bust or belly (Boorady 2014; Grana and Bellinello 2004). While in slim bodies the ratio between girth at chest and secondary measurements (such as waist and hip size) typically follows fairly uniform proportions, in overweight bodies it becomes difficult to standardize the drop. For the apparel industry this means that up to size twelve proportional size grading enables a large proportion of the population in question to be accommodated, while beyond size twelve the accommodation rate falls.

The apparel industry realized this limitation inherent in the size grading technique very early on. According to a reconstruction by Lauren Peters (2019a: 174–6) and Carmen Keist (2018: 32), as early as the 1910s, Albert Maslin, husband of Lena Bryant and her partner in the establishment and development of the plus-size brand Lane Bryant, had already noted that the ordinary size grading cannot be applied to the manufacture of clothing for stout women. Interviewed in 1916, he noted:

> The layers of flesh which bring stoutness are not added to the human body with anything like mathematical regularity. Sometimes this added flesh appears only in the woman's bust, her hips and abdomen remaining entirely normal. In other cases, it is only the hips or only the abdomen that becomes fleshy. Even when bust, abdomen and hips all take on flesh in about equal amounts, her arms, her lower limbs and other parts of her body may be of normal or possibly of less than normal size. (Quoted by Peters 2019a: 175)

These observations, accompanied by systematic research into the measurements of Lane Bryant's customers (Women's Wear 1915), show the origin of the idea that plus-size clothing should occupy a separate market niche in the apparel sector. The impossibility of extending the size grading of a base pattern indefinitely upward was indeed addressed by the industry through the multiplication and differentiation of patterns according to different exemplary shapes of stout bodies: apple, pear, inverted triangle, and so forth (Figure 6). Stoutwear, and later the plus size,[8] have since become a sector of the clothing industry specializing in conforming clothes to different body shapes.

Over time this limit inherent in the technique of size grading has stabilized around sizes twelve and fourteen, thus establishing a fairly clear threshold between two different fields. Below this threshold, size grading, especially after it has been automated and digitized, is quick, profitable and effective. The creative process is usually carried out on a very slim size, typically between zero and four

FASHION DESIGN FOR THE PLUS-SIZE

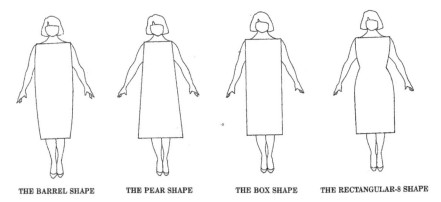

THE BARREL SHAPE   THE PEAR SHAPE   THE BOX SHAPE   THE RECTANGULAR-8 SHAPE

Figure 6 Body types for the plus-size woman, in F. L. Zangrillo, *Fashion Design for the Plus-Size*, New York: Fairchild Publications 1990, p. 4.

(Mears 2011: 183). Once the garment has been patterned and modeled, it can be reproduced automatically in other sizes using pre-set algorithms in CAD systems, save for possible subsequent custom fitting. Yet, this extension of the product to larger sizes usually reaches only size twelve (varying depending on brand). Larger sizes require the creation of a dedicated pattern for each specific size and body shape (Lottersberger and Pradel 2014: 164), so that mass production becomes much more complicated and hard to standardize. Accordingly, a significant proportion of apparel created by the fashion industry will never be manufactured for average and overweight bodies. Mass production of larger sizes is thus discouraged by issues related not only to profitability, but also to professional practice. Designers working in plus-size fashion, for example, must "reinvent" their creation several times. They must also pay special attention to the relationship between the garment and the body that wears it, relinquishing the use of clothes-hanger models for fitting and fashion show purposes.

This turns on its head—at least in part—received wisdom regarding the relationship between thin body imagery and thin fashion. With industrialization, the fashion industry restricted itself, through its own technological development, to a limited range of body sizes. The imagery of thin bodies seems to be more a consequence of this state of affairs than its cause. The culture of slenderness is difficult to fathom if we disregard that it is a hybrid of symbolic values and material constraints. It is not the thin ideal, appearing out of nowhere, that induced the fashion industry to limit itself to slim sizes. Rather, the thin ideal evolved alongside a fashion industry that was technologically discouraged from producing large sizes, and consequently developed practices that were technically within its possibilities. An industry that has a strong incentive to produce slim sizes logically develops communication strategies focused on slim sizes. At the same time, in a system based on the standardization of sizes, having a standard body becomes an increasingly important professional requirement for models, whose bodies became more and more homogeneous (Soley-Beltran 2004). The industrial fashion system thus began to promote its products and its brands through the uniform representation of slim bodies: the bodies on which the garments are modeled and for which they are produced. As a consequence of practices within the fashion industry, the cultural landscape began to be populated by images of women who were decidedly thinner than most women. Those images, and the collective imagination to which they belong, constitute a considerable part of the culture of slenderness prevalent in late-modern societies.

Size Grading is Consistent with the Thin Ideal

Some might argue that I am contradicting myself here. They might think that if there is a technological constraint at the origins of the segregation of fat bodies, segregation is necessitated by a reason that is somehow "objective." The focus of fashion on the thin ideal, from this perspective, is rooted in what is the currently most effective technology for clothing production, and not in the inertia of practice. The persistence of the thin ideal in fashion, far from being a paradox, is a consequence of technological innovation and a necessary condition for being able to market mass-produced ready-to-wear clothes for slim bodies. According to this view, not only is the thin ideal more than a mere cultural "perversion," as shown in the previous chapter. It is also something other than the manifestation of a practice that persists by force of inertia, as I have argued. Rather, it is the manifestation in the symbolic sphere of a manufacturing need dictated by technical constraints.

Although at first glance this view makes sense, it is based on a deterministic notion of the relationship between technological progress and society that has long been controverted by Science and Technology Studies (STS). Technological determinism is the idea that innovation arises in a linear fashion from scientific research and industrial applications (Flichy [1995] 2007). According to technological determinism, science and technology proceed in a substantially rational manner, which is constantly expanding human knowledge and finding the most useful, functional ways of applying new knowledge to people's lives. Innovations succeed because they work. If they fail, it may be because they do not work or because society is not ready to adopt them, but their adoption depends on the sole fact that they work and respond to a natural need for well-being. Of course, even technological determinists acknowledge that the processes by which innovations are adopted are influenced by psychological and social factors (Rogers 2003). However, their underlying assumption is that technological innovations per se must work and are the expression of the continuous progress of human knowledge and of our ability to exploit accumulated knowledge to our advantage.

In short, technological determinism is the view that technologies progress with a kind of intrinsic inevitability, dictated by the fact that they are effective and efficient, they work, and therefore determine social events (Sismondo 2010: 96). Yet STS has shown that technology does not work independently of social processes but is embedded in them. To say that a technology "works" is not equivalent to claim that it is objectively effective and efficient, but that it responds well to the specific needs, expectations, beliefs, and symbolic constructions (meanings) of a historical community. Each technological innovation develops in relation to a social context made up of "relevant social groups" that are affected by it and determine with their needs and expectations the direction in which it develops (Bijker et al. 1987). Different social groups can push technology in different directions, so that the perception of the efficiency or inevitability of a case of technological innovation is subject to interpretive flexibility. This means that technology ends up incorporating into its own structure and outcomes not only the needs of the social groups concerned, but also their beliefs, habits and idiosyncrasies. Those features that seem to be intrinsic qualities of technology are instead the ways in which it responds to the expectations of the social groups concerned.[9]

Like all technologies, size grading incorporates the needs, expectations, beliefs, habits, and idiosyncrasies of relevant social groups. The fact that there is an upper threshold of applicability of this technique, above which it becomes inefficient, is not a fortuitous consequence of how it was developed, but an inherent condition of the *fact* that it was. The threshold is a non-marginal aspect of the technique because it is part of its development, no less than, for example, the use of bust, waist, and hip circumferences as basic measurements. Therefore, it is both one of the reasons the technique was adopted and one of the reasons for its success. The fact that the emergence of such a threshold was unexpected only serves to highlight the difficulty of governing technological processes. Yet the crucial point is that the size grading technique was able to establish itself only because it adequately responded *as a whole, including the intrinsic technical "limits,"* to the needs of the relevant social groups. The exclusion of large sizes did not occur after the implementation of the technology, but was a condition for it to develop. That is, the size grading technique was able to establish itself and become an essential feature of the fashion system only because it is consistent with the thin ideal that fashion discourse was embracing at that time, and the practice of fashion has progressively developed since then. Technological innovation and cultural values often co-produce each other (Jasanoff 2004).

For this reason, I have argued above that the technique of size grading is a major aspect of fashion practice and a contributory factor to the stability and persistence of the thin ideal. In fact, it incorporates in the materiality of the manufacture of clothing (e.g., the physical machinery and its performance, forms of master patterns, algorithm-based rules, etc.) the standardization of garment shapes and sizes, the consequent standardization of clothes-body complexes, and, accordingly, the decision to sacrifice the capacity to accommodate fat bodies to the efficiency of the production process. Sizing is a powerful instrument for the normalization of bodies as it places bodies within a hierarchical system of classification that actually excludes from the game individuals on one end of the continuum, ipso facto stigmatizing their bodies as non-ideal. What makes the size grading technique particularly important in this process of body discipline is the stability and persistence that it brings to practice. With their normative power, techniques standardize and stabilize people's behavior. With their concrete materiality, the technologies that implement techniques strengthen the resistance of these practices to change. This is why the materiality of technologies, like that of objects and human bodies, must be considered a major contributory factor to the inertia of practices (Morley 2017). Regarding the specific field of fashion, the technique of size grading contributes, as much as modeling, to the persistence of fashion practice, a practice that has embraced the thin ideal.

The Unfashionable Plus-Size Market

The most evident consequence of the current practice of fashion, with its ideals, discourses, and techniques, has been the development of a market specializing in large sizes which is separated from the fashion system. The features of the sizing system discussed above have pushed in this direction. To summarize how this has come about: first, a hard technical constraint makes the production of smaller sizes easier and cheaper than larger sizes. This does not happen gradually, but with a marked discontinuity. For sizes over twelve, costs increase, profit margins diminish, patterns need to be simplified and the variety of clothing on offer must be reduced. A body ideal that exalts thinness creates the cultural space for this technology to establish itself. Accordingly, overweight bodies are gradually excluded from the fashion system because they are too costly to dress, unprofitable and—originally, at least—a small part of the whole. The distinction for technical and economic reasons between production for "regular" and "plus" sizes has ultimately given rise to a segregation of the latter. Although I shall put off describing this segregation until Chapter 6, I shall nonetheless clarify here in what sense the sector dedicated to large sizes constitutes a distinct market. Distinct from what?

Proof that it is a separate market lies in the name itself: plus-size. Unlike the term "regular," the term "plus" does not indicate a segment of a larger sector, but a market in itself that is outside the main market. Once, in the United Kingdom, it was more transparently called "outsize," that is, clothing outside of what society deems normal (Adam 2001: 46). In principle, plus-size clothing is simply clothing proportioned specifically for people whose bodies are larger than that of "regular"-sized people. Yet, for the reasons set out above, a threshold has established itself between size twelve and fourteen, which does not reflect the divide between average and extreme sizes (since the average sizes are twelve to sixteen) or between regular and fat bodies (as calling size fourteen bodies "fat" is irritating for size twenty-four wearers, as shown by Adam 2001: 45, LeBesco 2004: 105 and Sarbin 2005: 242). It is certainly not the size of garments alone that makes this segment a separate market.

That it is a separate market is also demonstrated by the fact that most firms that conduct market research produce specific analyses of the plus-size segment, treating it as separate from and contrasting it with the regular fashion market. Such market reports also show that the plus-size segment follows independent market trends. The most significant point to note is that, at least since the mid-1990s, it has expanded considerably faster than the "regular" fashion market, and has continued to grow even during downturns in the regular fashion market.[10] Nevertheless, it still represents a remarkably small share of the total women's apparel market. In the United States, for example, plus-size apparel sales were estimated at $20.4 billion in 2016, or 16.6 percent of the total market which was worth $120.3 billion.[11] For the same year, in the United Kingdom, the plus-size market was estimated to be worth £6.4 billion (including womenswear and menswear), or 12.5 percent of a total market worth £51.2 billion (PwC 2017). In countries like the United States and the United Kingdom, the plus-size market serves a majority of the population while contributing well under 20 percent of added value. There is evidently a strong imbalance in the value and volume of marketed products.

What does this imbalance depend on? To answer this question, we must analyze some characteristics of the plus-size market, and in particular of its players. There are two types of players (PwC 2017). "Generalists" are manufacturers and retailers who specifically design plus size ranges as part of a core clothing line, while "specialists" are manufacturers and retailers who exclusively serve the plus-size customer. The first type is mainly large clothing chains (H&M), variety chain stores (Marks & Spencer in the United Kingdom, Walmart in the United States), and fashion brands offering a plus-size clothing line (Asos Curve). The second type includes both retailers that target the general clothes-buying public through chains of stores (Lane Bryant in the United States, Evans in the United Kingdom), E-commerce (Igigi in the United States), or mail-order catalogs (N Brown in the United Kingdom), and specialized brands sold in independent plus-size shops or in their own single-brand chain stores (Carmakoma in Denmark, Yoek in the Netherlands, Marina Rinaldi and Elena Mirò in Italy). It should be highlighted that while the specialists are the most representative players in the segment, it is nevertheless the generalists that have by far the greatest sales volume, especially in Anglophone countries. Generally, when the size of garments exceeds the critical threshold, the landscape of brands, manufacturers, and retailers changes completely. While the brands and stores that sell size four almost always sell size ten, it is much rarer for brands and stores that sell size ten to sell size sixteen as well. Conversely, brands and stores that sell size sixteen usually offer size twenty-two too. Only generalists serving the mass market are an exception.

A long-established feature of the plus-size market is the limited willingness of women to buy in-store, meaning a greater tendency to use home shopping channels (Haswell 2010: 40). There are probably many reasons for this tendency, ranging from a poor assortment of plus sizes in high-street stores (Otieno 2005) to the sense of anxiety that bricks-and-mortar stores arouse in plus-size customers as they force them to compare regular and overweight bodies (Borland and Akram 2007). While, traditionally, this trend has generated purchases through mail-order catalogs, in recent years a significant proportion of purchases have been made on e-commerce platforms. In fact, overweight consumers seem to have been particularly willing to adopt new technologies, probably more out of a perceived necessity than out of choice (Greenleaf et al. 2020: 8). As industry expert, Nadia Boujarwah,[12] has pointed out: "The plus-size shopper [. . .] moved into e-commerce for apparel much more quickly than straight-size women did because most options are online. Even for most traditional retailers, the vast majority of assortments for plus [sizes] exist online only" (quoted in Bhuiyan 2017).

Other peculiar features of the plus-size segment concern communication. The sector features a number of specialized exhibitions to present its collections. The most popular was the Full Figured Fashion Week held in New York from 2009 to 2018 (and canceled in 2019). Conceived as an alternative to the New York Fashion Week, it focused exclusively on plus-size fashion and featured mostly size fourteen models. It was not a size extension of the North American mainstream fashion week, but a separate event dedicated to the plus-size market. In contrast, similar events in the European fashion capitals are of little importance. As for the media, it was only with the advent of the so-called Web 2.0 that the plus-size clothing industry could count on a wide range of channels to reach its public, in particular through "fatshion" blogs, plus-size influencers, and specialized e-commerce sites. Over the years, only two magazines specifically dedicated to plus-size fashion have had any significant influence, both of them based in the United States (Sarbin 2005): *Big Beautiful Woman* (*BBW*), edited by Carole Shaw between 1979 and 1996, and *MODE*, which became very popular during its short life (from 1997 to 2001). *MODE* resembled a typical mainstream fashion monthly, but only showed plus-size models in its editorials and on the cover.[13] Moreover, the niche of plus-size fashion communication obviously needs specialized models, who are represented by curvy modeling agencies (Bridge, Agence Plus, Ciao Magre, etc.), or grouped in the curvy division of full-service modeling agencies (Ford 12+, Wilhelmina ten20, etc.). As with regular fashion, the size of the models is significantly smaller than that of target consumers. While plus-size models can range from size eight to size twenty and beyond, those represented by the main agencies rarely exceed size sixteen, especially in the case of fit models.[14] And, as with regular fashion, plus-size models rely heavily on labor practices based on the aesthetics of the thin ideal (Czerniawski 2015: 23). If the bodies of ultra-thin models are the product of meticulous individual and collective adaptation to the current bodily ideal, this is even more true of the bodies of "curvy" models, which are average bodies.

We should not overlook the fact that there are significant variations between the plus-size markets in different countries. They are sometimes based on the structure of the local apparel sector, which may be more or less strong, dominated by major players, or highly fragmented into small and medium-sized companies, either based domestically or offshore. Other times, they depend on the structure of the retail sector, where large malls or small independent shops may dominate. Such differences can affect both the degree of openness of mainstream brands toward plus sizes (Boorady 2014: 164) and the quantity and quality of small specialist brands belonging to the field, as well as their willingness to invest in fashion and design. However, the distinction between two essentially separate markets, dominated by different players with different market strategies targeting different audiences, remains a constant, regardless of such national differences.

Above the critical threshold, companies basically pursue one of two alternative strategies (Pipia 2015). The first, favored by generalists, is to grade up patterns that have been designed and developed on small sizes. The second strategy is to adapt designs to the variety of plus-size body shapes, creating or recreating master patterns on a size around fourteen according to specific body shapes, and then studying the size grading according to the typical measurements of the relevant body shape. This is the strategy normally pursued by specialists, precisely because they specialize in plus size.

What is the outcome of these two strategies? I argue that both lead to the same result: the removal of the plus-size segment from fashion. The strategy of grading up patterns does not work technically, due to the limitations of proportional size grading mentioned above. As a result, companies that pursue this strategy tend to drastically reduce the number of designs offered for sizes over twelve. Officially, stores stock all sizes. However, in practice, the assortment for plus sizes is much smaller than for regular sizes (Boorady 2014: 163). Moreover, the selection preserves loose-fitting garments, as these create fewer fitting problems as size increases. The outcome is a reduced range of plus-size clothing on offer compared to the range for regular sizes: a common complaint among consumers. The other strategy, generally adopted by specialists, requires major investments in the manufacturing process (in particular, a great quantity of highly-skilled design- and pattern-making work) and the development of a larger number of articles, which is why it is based on highly specialized companies which are exclusively dedicated to their core market, the plus size, and which rely on that very specialization to successfully supply such a difficult, select market niche. The plus size, as opposed to fashion, is their core business. This gives them a competitive advantage over generalist players and brands in the regular fashion system.

In short, in both cases the same result is obtained: what this separate market is separate from is the fashion system. In the first case, this is due to the low quality of the products. In the second case, it is a consequence of specialization, which has isolated the plus-size segment within a space of its own and erected an impenetrable barrier between it and the fashion system. For fashion brands it is extremely difficult, both technically and financially, to extend collections above size twelve; for brands specializing in plus-size clothing, it is very difficult to carve out a space and position themselves within the fashion system and all that it entails (such as fashion weeks, mainstream magazines and fashion institutions). The fashion show held by the plus-size brand Elena Mirò at Milan Fashion Week from 2005 to 2012 is often mentioned as a unique case (Figure 7). Significantly, this ended at the behest of the Camera Nazionale della Moda, the institution responsible for organizing the Fashion Week. After 2012 the brand continued to present its collections through fashion shows organized during the Fashion Week, yet not as part of the official calendar. Nor have the other fashion weeks performed better. In 2013, the New York Fashion Week officially hosted a plus-size fashion show for the first time for the Cabiria line by designer Eden Miller. In 2017 the retailer Torrid put on a runway presentation, followed in 2019 by 11 Honoré, a size-inclusive e-commerce website founded in 2017 in Los Angeles. Any other cases of participation by curvy models in New York fashion shows have been exceptional appearances in standard collections.

Figure 7 Carrè Otis catwalking for Elena Mirò, fall/winter collection 2012. Courtesy of Miroglio Fashion.

Extravagances, we might say.[15] It is therefore inevitable for the plus-size sector to resort to its own devices in order to develop the symbolic content and aesthetic value of its clothes, for example by creating independent events such as the Full Figured Fashion Week.

Thus, while the simplest way to understand the separateness of the plus-size clothing market is by referring to the sizing system and the technical threshold of size fourteen, there is another, perhaps more important reason. While clothing for regular sizes constitutes the realm of fashion, *plus-size clothing is largely extraneous to fashion both because plus-size products are mostly poor in fashion content, and because the plus-size industry remains external to the fashion system*. Indeed, while in Western societies regular-size clothing has expanded its fashion content while extending it to mass production and making it increasingly available to the majority of consumers, plus-size clothing has remained at the margins. It has not been able to develop its own autonomous fashion content appreciably, thus missing out on the opportunity to participate in the spread of fashion. Admittedly, the plus-size segment also includes premium brands and designer fashion brands, some of which were founded by overweight women dissatisfied with the fashion on offer for plus sizes (Czerniawski 2015: 142–4). However, only a very small number of these brands have managed to get themselves accepted by the fashion system. As Brooklyn fashion blogger "Carine" noted, interviewed by Lauren Downing Peters, "there is a difference between plus-size 'fashion' as it is sold at stores like Lane Bryant and *Fashion* with a capital 'F,'" because "the point of capital 'F' Fashion is to have a point of view, not to try to conform to an ideal or merely being content in covering oneself" (quoted in Peters 2014: 57). In Carine's perception, what clearly separates the plus-size clothing market from the fashion system is that the former at best produces fashion, while only the latter produces capital "F" Fashion capable of having "a point of view." Of course, it is highly debatable to what extent Fashion, especially cutting-edge fashion, is truly capable of not conforming to a pre-established ideal. However, it is a common view among those involved in the plus-size segment that its products are lacking in aesthetic quality and fashion content compared to their counterparts in "regular" fashion. Those who take a different position or point to an improvement in the quality of plus-size fashion, such as Boorady's respondents (2014: 164), are often managers of plus-size companies, making it difficult to disentangle their opinion from the dictates of corporate marketing.

6

Fashion Politics
The Segregation of Non-Thin Bodies

A Matter of Discrimination

Just as plus-size clothing is confined to a separate market niche, plus-size bodies are excluded from the fashion system, in the sense that they are not visible within its landscape. Several observers have termed this exclusion "marginalization,"[1] emphasizing the stigma that the thin ideal projects onto "fat" bodies: fat is ugly, cumbersome, undesirable, to be amended. But the concept of marginalization seems inadequate in this case. The marginalization of fat bodies results in a reduction in opportunities; it is a major obstacle to the democratization of fashion. Nowadays body shape, as opposed to economic status, is the barrier preventing many women from gaining access to fashion. Hence I prefer to use the term "segregation."

The opportunities to which I am referring here are opportunities for building fulfilling interactions. As clothing is an extension of the body and an essential part of the clothes-body idiom, which is what mediates social interaction, access to a wide range of garments that offer a high level of aesthetic and semantic performance expands the range of social opportunities offered to the individual. And vice versa, exclusion reduces that spectrum. The segregation of plus-size bodies means not only that the fashion system does not include overweight consumers among its customers. It also means that overweight consumers are denied access to the wealth of products offered by the fashion system (Bougourd 2007: 108, 127). As I will show, women over size twelve perceive this reduction in opportunities through the limited assortment of clothing stores, the poor fashion content of clothes on sale, and the stigmatization of available clothes as nonstandard cases at variance with the ideal. They express this perception through a high degree of dissatisfaction with the offering. First I shall start by analyzing this dissatisfaction on the part of consumers, and then describe in detail how the segregation of plus-size bodies takes place in various areas of the fashion system, from production to design, from retail to communication.

The segregation of plus-size bodies is a subtle form of social discrimination. In accordance with what I argued in Chapter 2 when discussing Foucault's theory, I will claim here that the segregation of plus-size bodies—or, to be more precise, the segregation of non-thin bodies[2]—is a case of a discriminating rule which is unconscious because it is part of a hegemonic discourse. As such it is a tool for preserving social order by leveraging the self-control and self-discipline imposed by fashion discourse, rather than physical coercion. Moreover, it is a tool of the hierarchical organization of society, in which the link between body slenderness and social status or ethnicity is anything but accidental (Mason 2012). From this point of view, I will argue that the segregation of non-thin bodies in fashion is a political issue that is very closely connected with the distribution of power and social opportunities in society (Bishop et al. 2018: 185).

The Discomfort of Large-Sized Consumers

According to the results of a 1995 survey reported by Scaraboto and Fischer (2012: 1238), 84 percent of plus-size consumers felt that stores offered less choice in their sizes than in others, and 70 percent felt that the choice of brand names was too limited in their size. Several studies have evidenced that large-sized women are dissatisfied with the range of clothing available for them.[3] They show that, in the face of a plus-size market niche that provides mainly cheap, unfashionable clothing, and a popular misconception that overweight people are not interested in fashion and body enhancement, large-sized women do wish to have access to a similar choice to that available for smaller sizes, and are willing to pay a good price for quality clothing.

Plus-size consumers attribute their dissatisfaction resulting from a lack of appealing products to various factors: for example, the difficulty of finding stores offering plus sizes, both because such stores are few and inconspicuous, and because they are rarely located on main shopping streets, and must be sought out in out-of-the-way locations. This is also why plus-size customers prefer to shop online (Greenleaf et al. 2020). Another, even more frequent factor, is the limited range of designs available in store. Clothing display stands become smaller and sparser as size increases, and often, if a garment does not fit, there is no alternative garment available. The experience of leaving a store without having satisfied one's needs is relatively frequent among large-sized women. Further dissatisfaction stems from being unable to find products that match one's own taste (McReaddy 1988), in contrast with the "regular" market in which the range of fashions and styles on offer seems inexhaustible. According to the results of a survey conducted by Otieno and colleagues in the United Kingdom in the early 2000s (Otieno et al. 2005), only 24.4 percent of women in the UK size sixteen plus subsample reported being able to find fashionable clothing, half the percentage reported by the overall sample. Frustration arises in this case from feeling excluded from the fashion system, which is a field of possibilities to manage social interaction. This sense of exclusion can refer both to the absence of well-known brands and to the low quality of designs. Both these deficiencies combine to give clothes a sense of being ordinary and impersonal, given that brand and design today are two fundamental tools in the construction of the meaning of clothes. They shape the symbolic affordance of clothing: in a world full of sophisticated, fashionable, and branded garments, impersonal clothing inevitably communicates a certain meaning, which can range from indifference to sloppiness. When this happens out of necessity and not choice, it is a source of frustration. Hence poor-quality design is perceived as a form of scarcity of supply, as the following anecdote about shopping for a prom dress illustrates:

> I had never shopped for a fancy dress before, and I didn't know that my size would be a hindrance. All of the dresses we found at the malls seemed made for tiny girls only. The few beautiful and sophisticated dresses I did see were made in sizes 3–7. Ugly flowered tents were made in my size. (Derry 2017: 47)

Poor-quality designs frequently go hand in hand with poor-quality fabrics and manufacture, given that plus-size garments typically occupy the mass market segment. The fact that plus-size clothes make frequent use of stretch fabric and polyester (Adam 2001: 46–7), refraining from the finest and richest fabrics, is perceived by consumers as an additional limitation and source of discrimination.

Faced with all these reasons for dissatisfaction, the permanently unresolved problem of poor fit when it comes to plus-size clothes—a critical issue often mentioned by consumers—is merely the final obstacle. As we saw in Chapter 2, how clothes fit concerns the relationship between the clothes-body complex and the social world in which it is staged. As Degher and Hughes (1999: 18) point out, ill-fitting clothing is one of the most frequently cited indicators of being fat. Indeed, Catherine Derry's anecdote regarding her experience shopping for prom dress continues like this:

> While I hadn't often thought of myself as "fat" before that day, I certainly felt fat
> after shopping for a prom dress. Being big breasted and larger than a size 7, it
> was hard for me to find a dress in these young girls' stores. I started to hate my
> body for not fitting into the cute little dress. (Derry 2004: 47)

Awareness of possessing an unsuitable body can arise from passive cues, as in
the case mentioned here, or from active cues, such as when the inadequacy
of one's body in relation to what the fashion market offers is made explicit by
other people: relatives, friends, or shop assistants (Degher and Hughes 1999:
14). The most interesting aspect highlighted by Degher and Hughes, and also
evidenced by Derry's story, is that the awareness of being fat produced by the
shopping experience is immediately accompanied by the stigmatization or self-
stigmatization of the body. Clothing that does not fit is an indicator of a devalued
condition and triggers hatred not of the dress that does not fit the body, but of
the body that does not fit into the dress.

We can better understand the significance of this observation if we consider
the intermediate sizes that bridge the gap between the regular and the plus
world: sizes twelve and fourteen. The point is that body measurements are not a
discrete variable, and individuals may fall anywhere on the body size continuum.
Many women can wear a size twelve and fourteen depending on the moment,
brand or design. They are neither "regular" nor "plus-size": they are simply who
they are. But the purchase of clothes inevitably places them within a definite
size, and thus into a category. Being led by the clerk to the plus-size section of
a department store means being placed into a category of women stigmatized
and marginalized by the fashion system: it implies having little choice and
is equivalent to being escorted away from the realm of fashion. "Despite the
fact that [women] may place themselves at any point on the fat continuum,
the fashion industry only discerns between standard and plus-size with little
accounting for bodily variations" (Peters 2014: 64). Bodies that fail to conform
to these rigid standards, which we might term "bridge bodies," are those that
most strongly experience the violence that the system exerts on them through
practices and discourse.

While the discomfort experienced by overweight consumers is usually
expressed through criticism of the quality of clothing, it is actually a
discomfort that stems from the anticipation of the "lived experience" while
wearing those clothes. A dress that appears inadequate in the mirror appears
so not only with respect to the body wearing it, but also and above all with
respect to the social contexts which it will have to "face." It is not the "one

fold too many" that stops it from being worn, but the awareness of how that fold will be "read" by others in situations of daily life. This implies that the inadequate range of available plus-size clothing is not so much a technical or economic issue that can be tackled with skill and talent as it is a social issue related to the clothing practices that guide us in our daily choices. Poorly fitting plus-size clothing is more the outcome of the segregation of non-thin bodies from fashion than the latter is the outcome of the plus-size clothing difficulty of fitting.

Spaces of Segregation

Los Angeles—based fashion journalist Amy Lamare wrote in 2018:

> Out of the 25 largest clothing retailers by revenue, all but four offer a minimal line of plus-size options. [. . .] The thing is, those options are much more limited than the ones offered in sizes 0–12. At J.C. Penney, 16% of the dresses on the website are plus size. At Nordstrom.com, only 8.5% of the dresses are plus sized. When it comes to a retailer's brick and mortar store, plus sizes can be even harder to find. Physical stores stock fewer items and have less variety. [. . .] For decades, brands have shied away from plus sizes in the belief that they are bad for the brand. On the retailer side, stores think of plus size as an add-on to their businesses along with petite-sized and maternity lines. Stores often hide their plus-size offerings in corners of their stores, making the shopping experience uncomfortable and even embarrassing. Meanwhile, designs are often concealing rather than fashionable and colorful. Still, other stores ignore the category all together. (Lamare 2018)

In this passage, the Californian journalist draws attention to the fact that the segregation of non-thin bodies from fashion takes place in multiple physical and social spaces, particularly in production, design, and distribution. In the following sections, I will analyze and describe these spaces in more detail, as well as the equally important area of fashion communication.

Segregation among Market Players

Segregation arises from the very structure of the clothing market, with its clear division into a mainstream market of regular sizes and a separate plus-size market niche. To explain this division, it might be tempting to see fashion as a field of cultural production, as suggested by Bourdieu and Delsaut (1975).

Fashion would then be "the structured set of the manifestation of the social agents involved in the field" (Bourdieu 1993: 30), a space of fashion position-takings. The separation between the plus-size market segment and high fashion could be interpreted as the contrast between two subfields characterized by a marked asymmetry of symbolic capital. High fashion would occupy the dominant position in the field, plus-size the dominated one. However, I think that this way of understanding the division tends to overlook the extent of the divide and its power of segregation. After all, if they constituted two positions within the same social field, they would have to struggle for the same stakes, as the Bourdieusian theory assumes. The struggle itself is already a form of recognition of the legitimacy of the dominated part. But this does not happen, except for a limited number of plus-size brands that implement such strategies as staging fashion shows, belonging to institutional associations, and using fashion professionals: all policies aimed at acquiring a central role in the fashion field. The vast majority of the plus-size sector neither recognizes the specific capital of the fashion field nor struggles to accumulate it. Exclusion from the fashion system coincides with segregation from the fashion field of cultural production, although this does not mean that the plus-size sector is not responsible for the production of a significant part of the clothing landscape that surrounds us.[4]

The most striking aspect of this segregation, and the one that gives rise to the paradox of fashion which is the subject of this book, is the fact that fashion brands limit their scope to small sizes, that is to say, the fact that fashion brands do not market sizes larger than twelve. Table 1 evidences this point in relation to high fashion.[5]

Table 1 shows that the preclusion of larger sizes from the fashion system is wholesale and blatant, and goes far beyond the mere separation of two market segments, given that in most cases the upper bound for available products is around sizes six and eight. Only three brands have a significant assortment of sizes larger than ten, and the availability of single garments in sizes larger than twelve is a very rare exception. The evidence for the paradox of fashion could hardly be clearer.

This segregation is further fueled by other policies practiced by fashion companies. Not only do they sell a range of very small sizes within high fashion brands and lines, but they also do not retail secondary brands or lines that include plus sizes. There are very few exceptions to this rule, such as Marina Rinaldi, the Max Mara brand that represents one of the top players in the plus-size market. Interestingly, Marina Rinaldi maintains a very low public profile, avoiding fashion shows, focusing on the technical quality of the product and maintaining a sober

Table 1 Maximum Size of Garments (Dresses) Available on Fashion Brands' Official Websites

Brand	Largest size available for the greatest number of designs	Largest size available overall
A.P.C.	10	10
Agnès b.	10	12
Alexander McQueen	8	10
Altuzarra	10	12
Andrew Gn	8	10
Ann Demeulemeester	6	10
Anrealage	6	6
ATLEIN	8	10
Balenciaga	8	8
Balmain	6	10
Celine	10	12
Chloé	8	10
Christian Dior	8	10
Christian Wijnants	10	10
Courreges	10	14
Each other	8	12
Givenchy	8	12
Hermès	10	12
Isabel Marant	8	10
Kimhekim	8	8
Koché	8	8
Lacoste	14	14
Lanvin	10	14
Lemaire	8	8
Leonard Paris	16	16
Loewe	8	12
Louis Vuitton	8	10
Lutz Huelle	6	6
Maison Margiela	8	8
Manish Arora	10	10
miu miu	8	10
Olivier Theyskens	6	12
Paco Rabanne	6	12
Saint Laurent	6	10
Shiatzy Chen	10	10
Stella McCartney	6	10
Thom Browne	6	12
Valentino	6	12
Vivienne Westwood	12	14

For a description of the table contents and sources, see note 5, p. 194.

communication strategy, almost as if to feign not belonging to the fashion system. Conversely, high fashion brands seek to avoid being "contaminated" by plus-size brands, fearing that this might undermine their appeal and exclusivity. In light of the thin ideal, "it is not uncommon for more high-end fashion designers to claim that fat women are 'not their market.' They fear that these undesirable customers would taint the brand's image and, therefore, scare away their customer base" (Czerniawski 2015: 135). This was already clear in the nineteen-eighties, as Susan Kaiser remarked: "Many companies that manufacture misses and juniors sizes do not want their name affiliated with large sizes, so if they do manufacture in this market, they have a different label for it" (Kaiser 1997: 137). Today the divide is even more marked and it is very rare for companies that market high fashion to have plus-size brands too. The segregation of large sizes from the fashion system results in a segregation of the brands that manufacture them. The dearth of fashion choices for plus-size garments is rooted in the segregation of the plus-size clothing industry from the fashion system.

Segregation within Design

The separation of plus-size manufacturing processes from those used in regular fashion production has led to a parallel separation of their respective design processes, with the consequence that plus-size design is similarly relegated to a separate niche dominated by stylistic solutions designed to hide rather than exalt the female body (Bertola 2014; Colls 2004: 591, 2006: 537). This is not only the feeling of plus-size consumers but is also evidenced by a stylistic analysis of plus-size brand collections. Types of garments that seek to conceal the underlying body forms are often prevailing in those collections: palazzo pants, baggy shirts, caftans, knee-length tube skirts, sack dresses—in general, loose-fitting garments with soft silhouettes that do not set off the waist or breast line, a paucity of vents, soft colors, and continuous patterns as opposed to placed pattern prints. Lower-end brands tend to repeat products with few variations over the years. Other brands try to adjust their lines to follow seasonal trends, while at the same time keeping an eye on the disguising function of clothing. Very few brands favor a design strategy similar to luxury ready-to-wear, developing homogeneous, original seasonal collections based on a unifying idea.

The strategy of hiding the fat body through the design of clothes has ancient origins, dating back to the industrialization of apparel production and the rise of stoutwear (Keist 2017 and 2018). Stoutwear manufacturers used the formal characteristics of clothes to alter the appearance of the body and make it conform to the fashionable silhouette. Peters (2019a) has shown that stoutwear designs, which were particularly flattering to the figure, actually consisted mainly of devices to slenderize the silhouette, in accordance with the already dominant thin ideal. This "figure flattery," which continues to be a goal of fashion design for plus sizes today, maintains the objective of eliciting a slimming effect. This implies that clothing prevails over the body in the clothes-body complex, leading to a dissimulation of the physical body, and in particular of body shapes that are non-compliant with the thin ideal, concealing them behind an artificial silhouette. To flatter the body does not only mean wearing garments that fit the body but also giving shape to make the wearer fit well with the common body ideal:

> In the case of fashion, to flatter the body, or to show it to the "best advantage," is [...] to shape it, either by physical or optical means, in the image of the prevailing or fashionable silhouette. Thus, garments that flatter the body both fit the body as the designer intended—that is, absent the real, fleshy body—and help the wearer to embody or inch closer to the prevailing corporeal norm. Conversely, garments that do not flatter share a tendency to exacerbate the degree to which the natural, unencumbered body strays from that which is elevated in any given era as the ideal. (Peters 2019a: 187)

This policy has been adopted over the last hundred years not only by fashion designers, but also by anyone involved in styling looks on catwalks, in images and on people. Klepp (2011) has investigated the publications that provide advice for women on how to dress the body in order to achieve a fashionable figure and show that they are largely focused, today as in the 1960s, on recommendations and standards to create a slimming effect through clothes. She identifies four different, very common principles on which advice about appearing slender is normally based. Optical illusions, obtained for example by using vertical lines and avoiding horizontal lines, and erasing contours, allow the perceived silhouette to be made different from the real one. Analogously works the principle of diverting the attention away from that which is considered big and directing the observer's eyes toward more appropriate parts of the body. A third principle is that of physically shaping the body through the use of shapewear such as push-up jeans or bras, and corsets. Finally, some suggestions expressly leverage the principle of concealment, suggesting that the body be hidden under loose-fitting clothes.

The success of this strategy is related to the fact that plus-size design does not form part of the vocabulary of major fashion designers and falls outside their interests and practices (cf. Connolly 2009; Gunn 2016). I am not aware of cases of influential fashion designers who have designed collections for plus-size bodies. On the contrary, I am aware of at least one case of a mainstream fashion designer who agreed to design the collection of a plus-size brand only as long as it was not made publicly known.[6] The exclusion of larger sizes from designer fashion originates from the fashion schools, which have incorporated it into training courses, and affects fashion's cultural heritage, given that clothes for fat bodies hardly ever survive destruction and are rarely included in fashion and costume collections, as evidenced by Kevin Almond (2013: 203).[7] As cultural heritage is not independent of the power of discourse and practice, being a space where dominant social values reproduce and establish themselves, as Laurajane Smith (2006) thoroughly argued in addressing archaeology, it is no surprise that "the material record of large-size women's dress is scanty at best, and non-existent at worst," since plus-size garments simply have not been collected or conserved over time (Peters 2018b).

Trainee designers do not learn the techniques of plus-size design and pattern construction, being encouraged instead to develop their creativity on basic sizes (zero to four). Research carried out in 2015 by Jeffrey Mayer, professor of Fashion Design at Syracuse University and founder of Fashion Without Limits, failed to identify a single design course for plus-size clothing at a single fashion school anywhere in the world (Pipia 2015). Almond (2013) reports on a survey which he conducted in a large university fashion and costume department interviewing students and academics, according to which

> few fashion design students choose to design for the more voluptuous or fuller-sized market and fashion education fails to incorporate it into their curriculums. When they do design this type of clothing it may be less fashionable, less attractive, of low quality fabrication, and not suitable for all occasions. (Almond 2013: 201)

An aspect closely linked to this situation is the absence of textbooks teaching the design of plus-size clothing. Existing textbooks pay lip services to plus-size design, mostly focusing only on the specificity of size grading when dealing with a special population such as the plus-size demographic (Christel 2016: 2). The only known textbook specifically dedicated to plus-size fashion, authored by Frances Leto Zangrillo, dates back to 1990 and has long been out of print. Interestingly, even in this textbook the strategy of concealment is taught.

Consider Figures 8–11, which are taken from Zangrillo (1990: 23–4). They visually exemplify the designer's effort to mask the shape of the physical body behind a cover that broadly reproduces an ideal female silhouette borrowed from smaller sizes. The four figures show how to work on the four basic shapes of plus-size bodies to hide their peculiarities and bring them back to the ideal hourglass shape. The captions accompanying them make this goal explicit, explaining how the proposed solutions "slim and flatter the average, rectangular-8 body type," "elongate and balance pear-shape figures," and "work to camouflage stockiness in the average box-shape figure" (Figures 8–11).

Christel (2014) has gone further, showing that fashion design students hold negative stereotypes toward obese women, holding them responsible for their weight and considering obesity the effect of a number of negative attitudes: lack of willpower, lack of education, poor eating habits, and addiction to

Figure 8 Figure-flattering garments for a rectangular-eight shaped body type, in F. L. Zangrillo, *Fashion Design for the Plus-Size*, New York: Fairchild Publications 1990, p. 23.

Figure 9 Figure-flattering garments for a pear-shaped body type, in F. L. Zangrillo, *Fashion Design for the Plus-Size*, New York: Fairchild Publications 1990, p. 23.

Figure 10 Figure-flattering garments for a barrel-shaped body type, in F. L. Zangrillo, *Fashion Design for the Plus-Size*, New York: Fairchild Publications 1990, p. 24.

Figure 11 Figure-flattering garments for a box-shaped body type, in F. L. Zangrillo, *Fashion Design for the Plus-Size*, New York: Fairchild Publications 1990, p. 24.

food. Admittedly, her investigation (as well as that of Rudd et al. 2015, which produced similar results) specifically concerns obesity, that is the extreme range of very fat bodies. However, it is significant that respondents showed a hostile attitude toward obese people, confessing to feeling anger toward fat bodies and believing that obese women are to blame for their weight. Although this tells us nothing about the propensity of future fashion system professionals to ostracize fat bodies, it nevertheless shows a hostile disposition that is unlikely to spur them to apply their creativity for the benefit of those bodies.

Segregation in Retail Spaces

The segregation of non-thin bodies from fashion also surfaces in retail, albeit with its own specific characteristics. The dissatisfaction of plus-size women does not stem solely from the fact that fashion brands do not actually market their garments in sizes larger than eight or ten, nor from the fact that the long-term trend among clothing stores is to stock smaller and smaller sizes (Seid 1989: 110). It is also produced by the geographical distribution and physical arrangement of retail spaces. I am referring to three aspects in particular: the geographical distribution of bricks-and-mortar plus-size stores, the arrangement of departments within stores that sell regular and plus sizes, and the visibility these stores give to plus sizes.

The geographical distribution of plus-size retailers, whether they are chain stores or independent boutiques, is different from that of fashion stores. While the latter usually crowd into big-city downtowns and places dedicated to luxury consumption (grand hotels, airports, etc.), establishing exclusive urban clusters, plus-size stores are more evenly distributed in suburban areas and malls, and in the high streets of country towns. The map featured in Figure 12 compares the geographical distribution in the United States of shop locations of large straight-size and plus-size fast-fashion chains, and makes the different arrangement visually intuitive. While straight-size retailers gather in large urban areas, particularly those in New England, Texas, and California, plus-size retailers are widely scattered across rural areas, particularly those in the Mid-West and West.

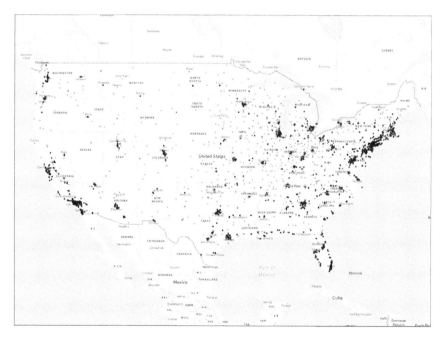

Figure 12 Straight-size (black) versus plus-size (grey) store locations in the United States. Adapted from Lamare (2018).

At first glance, one might conclude that the plus-size population actually enjoys greater choice, since the network of plus-size stores seems to be more evenly spread. However, this map does not reflect the distribution of all clothing stores. What the map shows is rather that plus-size stores are distributed in such a way that they are not concentrated in the same streets or malls and compete directly with each other. This is related to the low investment that plus-size retailers make in fashion. Most plus-size stores base their marketing power on local exclusivity rather than branding or product policies (Gruys 2012: 489). In the plus-size market niche, customer service—in this case the geographical proximity of the store—is a greater asset than the semantic value of the product for the clothes-body idiom. The poor symbolic affordance of the range of items on offer induces consumers to attach greater value to geographical convenience.

Regular-size fashion brands that do make plus-size lines to sell in their own stores, such as international retail chain H&M and Italian retail chain OVS, never display plus sizes in their windows and may end up shunting them to low-visibility nooks, with little in the way of signage and where stocks may not be replenished often. The survey by Otieno et al. (2005: 306) showed that in the United Kingdom it is very common for plus-size women to find that their sizes are displayed at the back of the store. Alison Adam (2001: 48) has called this typical arrangement a "shop within a shop," and noted that it is sometimes replaced by a separate shop around the corner. An analysis of brick-and-mortar stores in Milan reveals a similar situation, in which multiple hidden strategies are deployed. Milan H&M stores include a small, hidden and barely visible section for H&M+ plus sizes (Figure 13). The OVS retail chain markets the OVS Curvyglam brand but distributes it only in some of its Milan-based OVS stores, locating it in interstitial spaces such as the wall facing the staircase (Figure 14). In its Milan store, the Siste's brand relegates its plus-size second line, More by Siste's, to a corner of the basement corridor. In many other stores, such as Zara, there is no plus-size section and larger sizes (and in any case only up to XXL) are offered for just a few items: one has to ask the salesperson. Plus sizes are there but are in a sense hidden from the consumers' view.

The consequence of this policy in retail spaces is the rejection of overweight consumers, who in brick-and-mortar stores are forced to expose the nonconformity of their body in order to access clothes of their size. The effect has been well described by Alison Adam (2001: 45): "Alas, having made it into the shop I find a notice proclaiming that customers should ask the salesperson for the ranges that go up to [UK size] 18. I freeze, then head for the door. If I ask a salesperson then I will be exposed as a fraud: a big woman in a thin

Figure 13 H&M+ department at the H&M department store in Milan. Photo by the author.

Figure 14 Curvy department at the OVS department store in Milan. Photo by the author.

woman's shop." In general, the tendency of fashion retailers to stock only small sizes in store, requiring larger women to have to ask for larger sizes, "causes embarrassment" (Borland and Akram 2007: 326). Plus-size customers do not like entering straight-size shops, not even to look around, because they are embarrassed when the shop assistant sends them away or directs them to the plus-size section (Gruys 2012).

Overall, the way retail spaces are organized produces a segregation of non-thin bodies that Bishop, Gruys and Evans, in drawing conclusions from their investigation, describe as follows:

> The retailers we studied reinforce narrow cultural body ideals by segregating larger clothing and clothing for purportedly uncommon proportions either in designated sections within individual stores or across stores. The inaccessibility of extended size ranges beyond these spaces stigmatize particular body types, as evidenced by many women's interpretations of "having to" shop in specialty stores as an indicator of their failure to meet body ideals. (Bishop et al. 2018: 197)

As these authors maintain, being unable to access one's clothing size via the most common channels, that is, shopping in fashionable urban locations, brands outsized bodies as being outside body norms (Bishop et al. 2018: 190). The physical marginality of plus-size shops and departments provides visible evidence of the marginality of their products with respect to fashion, which has the privilege of serving bodies considered "beautiful" and "regular." Segregation of stores and stigmatization of bodies are connected phenomena.

Segregation and Concealment in Fashion Communication

Finally, communication requires analysis on its own terms. Klepp has convincingly argued that

> The undesirability of the large body is evident in books and magazines in several ways: first, by not representing the large body visually except when it is the explicit point at issue—and often not even then; second, by talking about the bodies as if they were small, but have something in addition—something loose, temporary or extra; and third, by having stricter clothes norms for the big than for the slender. (Klepp 2011: 476)

Yet it is fair to say that, in fashion communication, non-thin bodies are not merely segregated or classified as "undesirable," but actually concealed. Advertising of plus-size clothing brands is very rare in mainstream magazines, and often uses models who are smaller than the actual size range of the brand being advertised. Fat and average bodies are similarly hidden from view in the fashion press.

A glance at the major mainstream fashion magazines is enough to realize the extent of this concealment. To validate this idea I resorted to the opinion of the experts. I asked them to analyze two international mainstream fashion magazines, *L'Officiel Paris* and *Vogue* (American edition), and appraise the size of the female bodies featured.[8] Table 2 shows the results.

In both magazines, the range of featured bodies is extremely homogeneous and limited to smaller sizes. More than two-thirds of all featured bodies wear very small or anorexic sizes (zero to four), while sizes over eight, that is sizes that in all non-Asian countries cover the vast majority of the female population, are the exception. In the world represented by fashion magazines, non-thin bodies do not exist. Moreover, the few average and fat bodies featured in fashion magazines never appear in fashion advertisements or editorials (unless they portray celebrities), but only in advertisements for non-fashion products and articles devoted to current events, where concealing actual bodies is more difficult. Nevertheless, even in these spaces fashion magazines conceal fat bodies, especially weekly fashion magazines, which usually feature several sections devoted to current events.

Occasionally, mainstream fashion magazines do dedicate special issues to nonstandard bodies or curvy models. I will discuss this point in detail in Chapter 7. However, I should point out here that in doing so they do not substantially modify the geography of female body sizes featured in the fashion press, but rather confirm and reinforce it, as the exceptional nature of such issues itself conveys the idea that non-thin bodies are the exception to the standard of beauty based on the thin ideal. So-called independent or alternative, niche fashion magazines constitute a different case. Lynge-Jorlén (2017: 52–3) observes that these magazines, being image-driven, tend to promote visual creativity as opposed to the representation of an ideal of bodily beauty. They favor a

Table 2 Apparent Size of Female Bodies Featured in Fashion Magazines

	Total female bodies	Total assessable female bodies	S	M	L
Vogue, May 2019	206	178	123 (69.1%)	39 (21.9%)	16 (9.0%)
L'Officiel Paris, April 2019	116	94	73 (77.7%)	20 (21.2%)	1 (1.1%)

For a description of the table contents and sources see note 10, p. 195.

hyperrealistic photographic style, in which the image is rendered unrealistically perfect thanks to postproduction digital manipulation. The featured body, as a result, does not claim to represent an accessible ideal. Consequently, it is not so unusual for this kind of magazine to feature non-compliant bodies, that is bodies that are fat, old, or with physical imperfections. Nevertheless, even in niche fashion magazines, the geography of featured bodies remains distant from that of real ones and strongly biased toward thin bodies.[9]

Expert consensus concerned the size assessment of featured bodies. To be sure that this kind of magazine actually has the effect of segregating and concealing fat bodies it would be necessary to survey consumers. I, therefore, embarked on an exploratory investigation of a typical target of fashion magazines, namely fashion course college students. I presented them with the same fashion magazines used for the focus group and asked them to identify figures that most closely matched their idea of thin, regular, and fat bodies.[10] Despite the essentially subjective nature of this survey, the result was consistent with the consensus. According to the respondents' perception, 65.7 percent of the images of female bodies published by *L'Officiel Paris* feature thin bodies, 33.6 percent regular bodies, and 0.7 percent fat bodies. Likewise, the results for *Vogue* were 55.2 percent thin bodies, 40.7 percent regular bodies, and 4.1 percent fat bodies. The issue merits more detailed research; nonetheless, the extent of the phenomenon is already clear from these initial findings.[11] They show that fashion magazines relegate body types that are prevalent in the real world to the status of exceptions, producing what could be considered a typical agenda-setting effect: what does not appear in the media remains hidden from people's awareness. As Eugene Shaw has argued (1979: 96), "people are aware or not aware, pay attention to or neglect, play up or downgrade specific features of the public scene. People tend to include or exclude from their cognitions what the media include or exclude from their content." Through typical content selection mechanisms, such as gatekeeping, fashion media in fact conceal the fat body and exclude it from the social imaginary and cultural landscape that they contribute to building.

The concealment of fat bodies in the fashion press leads specialist plus-size companies to resort to specialized communication channels, which however remain "closed off" from the general public. Often these are magazines expressly dedicated to overweight or obese women, in which, unlike the mainstream fashion press, unequivocally fat bodies appear almost exclusively. They target a very limited audience, are often published at irregular intervals, are sometimes the creations of a brand or an e-commerce website, do not have wide public circulation, and "fly under the radar" of the fashion system and the average consumer.[12]

The advent of Web 2.0 initially offered a space for the emancipation of fat bodies, one in which they could finally be free of the intermediation of mainstream fashion's "gatekeepers." Internet technology and the increased power of networks and computers had enabled the development of a media environment in which nonprofessional individuals could produce and circulate various types of content (Hewitt 2006). In the field of fashion, the blogosphere is a realm whereby actors that have been "othered" by the fashion system can find a space to express themselves and meet an audience:

> Bodies excluded from a fashion visual landscape dominated by white, Western, young, thin bodies are rendered visible, their practices of fashionable and stylish adornment encouraged and supported, hopefully supporting them in carving out for themselves positive spaces of expression offline too. (Mora and Rocamora 2015: 153)[13]

Among the several minority subgenres in the blogosphere, one of the first, richest, and most recognizable was what became known as the fatshion style blog genre.[14] This phenomenon has often been considered an exemplary case of how digital media can free individuals from the power of media corporations and the unidirectionality of mass media. Fatshion blogs, in fact, flourished as a sort of revenge against the fashion world by a category of consumers previously excluded from its realm. Findlay (2017: 33) observes that

> [w]hile fatshion bloggers employ the conventions of personal style blogging on their blogs—publishing outfit posts and writing in a conversational tone about fashion—they have traditionally written their blogs as alternative spaces, a response to their exclusion from the mainstream fashion industry.

Fatshion bloggers and their readers were initially consumers animated by the desire to read and write the kinds of stories that they were not seeing in other fashion media, and fatshion blogs gave visibility to types of bodies that mainstream fashion media concealed. This, at least, was the refrain when the blogosphere was frenetically expanding between 2009 and 2010. It is exemplified by a well-known article in which Catherine Connell (2013) summarizes her case study of the blog Fa(t)shion February for Femmes and Friends, concluding that the blog "offers users a respite and a place of belonging in the context of the exclusive, elitist, and oppressive confines of mainstream fashion. It also empowers users to critique hegemonic fashion discourses and to publicly imagine more egalitarian and radical alternatives" (Connell 2013: 221). In general terms, for Connell "fashion blogging has diluted the power of mainstream fashion tastemakers and created a symbiotic relationship between mainstream and virtual fashion communities," so much so that in her opinion "the possibility of disrupting normative fashion discourse through online fashion projects is a real one" (Connell 2013: 210).

Has the evolution of the blogosphere met these expectations? The answer can only be complex. Simply exposing fat bodies within a communicative environment dedicated to fashion does not suffice to overcome their segregation. It is also necessary to consider how one talks about those bodies and they are represented. The end of concealment does not instantly mean the end of segregation. In fact, investigations of this phenomenon have tended to conclude that while fatshion bloggers "have been the privileged spokespersons for the battle against discrimination" and "have played a vital role in the popularity of the curvy phenomenon" by playing a counter-hegemonic role, in many cases their blogs "are not significantly different to 'classical' female outfit blogs, where an audience is commodified as a source of material income and symbolic capital" (Pedroni and Pofi 2018: 6–7). In other words, in many cases focusing on fat fashion primarily serves to gather a target of consumers with whom to promote products of fashion and cosmetics industries, without this translating into pressure for the fashion industry to become more inclusive toward nonstandard bodies.

A common feature of plus-size fashion blogs is their commitment to making fashion accessible for all sizes, thus countering the segregation of fat bodies. However, they go about this in very different ways, with different results. Harju and Huovinen (2015) identify a number of "performative practices" through which fatshion bloggers resist existing cultural discourses surrounding female beauty. Some of them underscore the diversity of fat bodies from hegemonic representations and enact either destigmatization of fat, rejecting demands for bodily change and promoting acceptance of diversity, or reappropriation of a legitimate social space, demanding social visibility and cultural prominence for fat people. Others emphasize similarity and affiliation with hegemonic conceptions of the body and pursue strategies of inclusion in the realm of fashion that can leverage either the communal empowerment gained by participating in the blogging community or the mimicking of existing fashion practices and discourses, which positions fatshion bloggers closer to hegemonic ideals. Although Harju and Huovinen, in sharing Connell's optimistic view, claim that these are "resistant practices" that empower plus-sized consumers, I feel that some of them do not help build counter-market resistance any more than they help confirm and reinforce the normative ideal of fashion discourse. Indeed, resistant practices that strive to assimilate the resistant individual to the hegemonic culture end up reinforcing such hegemony at a social level.

Navigating the fatshion blogosphere reveals different rhetorical registers. Some verbal or visual statements can be classified as anti-hegemonic discourses aimed at unmasking the tyranny of slenderness. Examples of this type are abundant, for instance, in the "Body Image" section of the blog TheCurvyFashionista,[15] or can be found scattered in many comments illustrating posts of plus-sized Instagrammers, such as when GabiFresh writes: "My favorite thing is going into designer/luxury stores that don't make my size and making everyone visibly uncomfortable while I touch everything and then proceed to take fire mirror selfies," to which a follower responds: "Or taking an item, changing in the fitting room and buying it just to see the questioning in their eyes when I'm about to pay and how they detail my body" (Figure 15). Yet, the effect that fatshion blogs can have on common clothing culture often depends more on other factors than on explicit claims. Although some blogs promote practices of valorization, exhibition, and appreciation of the body regardless of its size, many of them explicitly address the *problem* of dressing fat bodies, such as TrendyCurvy stating in the "About Me" section: "While it has sometimes been difficult, I have

Figure 15 GabiFresh's Instagram post from December 9, 2019. Courtesy of GabiFresh.

learned throughout the years how to dress my frame in the most flattering ways possible."¹⁶ Although the blogger Kristine writes this with the intent of liberating overweight consumers from fat shame, the statement implicitly reiterates the idea that being overweight is an aesthetic flaw that makes it more difficult to find adequate looks. The power of hegemonic discourse also lies in being able to legitimize itself even through ostensibly counter-hegemonic statements. Another rhetoric that can be found on fatshion blogs involves the establishment of minority communities. TheCurvyFashionista, among others, presents itself as "the curvy and plus-size commentary designed to help you get your life and be your fabulous self," that is, designed for curvy women. The formation of minority communities is an important step in the struggle for the emancipation and acceptance of diversity. However, it can sometimes lead to the ghettoization of these communities. The fact that comments below fatshion bloggers' posts come mostly from plus-sized women (see, e.g., Figure 15) is an indication of the weakness of this movement in making itself visible in the realm of fashion at large. In addition, it is not uncommon to encounter in fatshion blogs—especially microblogs—the rhetoric of assimilation to the dominant body ideal. It inhabits diet and lifestyle advice, styling suggestions aimed at slimming down the figure, poses designed to hide the parts of the body considered problematic. While these expressions reflect the need for the emancipation of the individual blogger, in general, they simply affirm the thin ideal and the need for plus-size consumers to subject their body to discipline and manipulation if they want to access the opportunities to articulate the clothes-body complex offered by the fashion system.

In more general terms, what limits the counter-hegemonic force of the fatshion blogosphere is, as Pedroni and Pofi (2018) have observed, the fact that it is populated by bloggers whose main objective is not at all counter-hegemonic, but to gain a personal space that offers them visibility in fashion thanks to the opportunities offered by Web 2.0. This new visibility of fat bodies in the realm of fashion imagery does not necessarily translate as legitimization, since often it is subject to acceptance of hegemonic discourse or self-segregation of those same bodies in a ghettoized social space. It is therefore not surprising that the fatshion blogging movement has had a marginal impact on the dominant ideal of female beauty. In most cases, it has not moved beyond its original function as a counseling and self-help service for overweight or obese consumers, and has not been able to undermine the tyranny of slenderness and segregation of fat bodies in the fashion system.

In the last few years, fashion blogs have rapidly turned into inactive image repositories, while the activity of bloggers has moved to social media, particularly Instagram. This recent evolution of the fashion blogosphere into the movement of fashion influencers does not seem to have substantially changed the situation. On the contrary, the affordances of social media seem to have abetted the standardization of clothing culture. The architecture of Instagram places images in the spotlight, with limited space for text. This obviously penalizes critical reasoning, analyses, and distinctions, and favors clichés and stereotypes. In terms of imagery, the homogeneity that characterizes print media is replicated on social media, where the incessant flow of images published by slim influencers submerges the few images featuring plus-sized women. A scroll through Instagram images hashtagged #fashionblogger throws up overwhelmingly young and slender women. This is even more striking when referring to aspects that are typical of the fashion system. Rocamora's research into the myth of the Parisian woman, which I have reported in Chapter 3, has shown how curvy women are "sized out" of the idea of fashionable femininity. Instagrammers that exploit the idea of *Parisienne* are normally slim and, above all, do not disclose how they attain and maintain this bodily size, which appears to be an effortlessly thin one (Rocamora 2019: 179).

The Many Facets of Segregation

The fashion system variously restricts its scope to slim bodies, while neglecting, segregating, or concealing the world of non-thin, overweight, and obese bodies. This has led to the development of a separate, autonomous market for plus sizes, characterized primarily by *low aesthetic commitment*: garments are often anonymous, merely covering the body, and do not enhance the figure but rather attempt to blend it into the background of the visual landscape. Moreover, it is a market with *low semantic commitment*: advertising is scant and of poor quality, often hidden away in niche channels; products are retailed through peripheral multi-brand stores and marketed by means of unappealing brands, whose corporate claims often insist on body size as their most salient feature (H&M+, ASOS Curve, etc.). This parallel market does work, since in reality, it serves the overweight population. However, it works through deprivation, since it sacrifices the symbolic and relational aspects of attire. I have used the concept of "segregation" to describe this situation because it highlights some fundamental characteristics of the marginalization of fat bodies from fashion, namely exclusion, confinement, and concealment.

Segregation of a social group implies its *exclusion* from the dominant social sphere and from the benefits it grants. The segregated class or ethnic group is often excluded, de facto or de jure, from fundamental rights, such as land tenure, the exercise of institutionalized professions, freedom of marriage, and political participation. Often the group discriminated against cannot access the same facilities that "included" groups enjoy in education, health, housing, or burial. Something analogous happens, in due proportion, to fat bodies in our society, especially with regard to the clothes-body complex, which as we saw in Chapter 2 is a fundamental element of social life. In this case, exclusion concerns the symbolic sphere, meaning that it is about reduced opportunities to access the tools of clothed-bodily communication. Due to the segmentation of the regular-size and plus-size apparel markets, and the fashion system's refusal to manufacture and retail plus sizes, fat bodies are excluded from the benefits of fashion as a means of articulating the clothes-body idiom. The tyranny of slenderness in fashion deprives nonstandard bodies of social opportunities because it reduces the range of expressive tools available to them.

As a consequence of social exclusion, segregation often implies the *confinement* of the social group that is discriminated against to delimited spaces (such as the ghetto), thus restricting the range of possible actions and choices available to members of that group. Not only does exclusion from the benefits of the dominant class imply, in many cases, the need to create separate physical spaces (restrained schools, deputy hospitals, reservations). It also very often translates as residential segregation even when segregationist policies do not exist, as the Chicago School demonstrated almost a century ago (Park et al. 1925). The segregation of fat bodies from fashion, too, is characterized by a geographical dimension. It excludes fat bodies from the physical places of fashion, leaving them out of straight-size shops and trendy neighborhoods, confining them to rural malls, suburban neighborhoods, stores dedicated to them, or even confining them to their homes to shop online. The feeling of discomfort that women who do not conform to the thin ideal say they experience on entering a straight-size store recalls the typical feeling of discomfort that minorities subject to discrimination experience when passing through privileged neighborhoods.

Finally, segregation frequently also involves forms of *concealment* of those who are segregated, whose presence is removed from public space and hidden from the majority. Especially smaller or politically "troublesome" minorities may—in the absence of specific protection policies—be the object of denial within legislation or social behavior (for instance in the media) which removes them from the social geography of the country. This is what happens to fat bodies in the fashion system, too. They are removed not only from the imagery that circulates in traditional media and in the blogosphere, but also from the main events around which the system revolves (such as fashion shows), the objects it uses (such as dummies), the practices it performs (such as fashion design education). The exclusion of fat bodies from fashion is often accompanied by the concealment of their existence.

The segregation of non-thin bodies from the fashion system is not just an unwanted effect of its dominant discourse, practices, and technologies. It is a policy that actors in the field proactively enact in order to adapt to those discourse, practices, and technologies. Companies deliberately do not manufacture clothes and lines for larger sizes, designers work on the basis that their creations will not be worn by bodies that are less than thin, stores deliberately hide their plus departments in the basement, magazines exclude fat bodies even when they have to select photographs to illustrate a news article. And the list could go on. Since fashion practices are so viscous, fashion discourse is so pervasive, and the size grading technique so effective, subjects participating in this great game have no choice but to implement proactive strategies that allow them to adapt to the system's expectations. These are policies of discrimination against nonconforming bodies. This also depends on the fact that the segregation of nonconforming bodies from the fashion system does not result in mere impoverishment of consumption opportunities, it is not something analogous to the impossibility for less well-off people to have a private pool or sleep in a luxury hotel. Instead, it touches an essential aspect of people's lives, such as the full capacity to unfold meaningful social relationships, and therefore is rather equivalent to such inclusion issues as unequal access to education, the limitation of people's mobility due to architectural barriers or the digital divide. Hence, I am arguing that the segregation of non-thin bodies from the fashion system is a political issue, which concerns citizens' fundamental rights in democratic regimes—with all due respect to those who think that fashion is a frivolous topic.

Outlook

How We Should Expect Fashion's
Appreciation for Thinness to Evolve

The overview that I have provided in previous chapters describes a fashion system totally focused on the thin ideal, which has become a major element of fashion practice. This unilateral vision of female beauty leads the fashion system first to stigmatize and then to segregate fat bodies, closing them off within a market niche that is not only *separate* from the mainstream fashion industry but also *excluded* from the institutional sphere of fashion, to the point that it tends in turn to renounce to enhance its products through fashion contents. The segregation of fat bodies produces a paradox in which the fashion system is ensnared, and which it struggles to escape because it is held back by the inherent inertia of fashion practice and fashion discourse, which are incorporated in technologies, bodies, doings, and sayings. By "paradox," I mean the fact that fashion relinquishes a part of the potential market which—following the population's tendency to become fatter and the democratization of consumption—has now reached vast proportions, comparable to those of the market for slim bodies.

Two questions arise naturally at this point. The first is whether the situation is really as extreme as I have described it: are there no countertrends, that is, areas of the fashion system that avoid subscribing to the thin ideal and segregation of fat bodies? The second asks where we are going: What are the current developments? Is the tyranny of slenderness still tightening its grip or is it loosening instead? Can we expect significant changes over the coming years? Such questions are made urgent by a series of signals emanating from the fashion system that seem to indicate increasing sensitivity to the issue of fat fashion and growing inclusion of non-thin bodies. I do not intend to venture into forecasts about the future, which are bound to be proven wrong. However,

I wish to make some considerations about the limits of the overview that I have provided here and the reasonableness of certain expectations about the future evolution of fashion discourse.

In Search of Countertrends

Almost twenty years ago, at the beginning of the new millennium, Kathleen LeBesco wrote:

> For many years, the fat woman was indeed the forgotten woman, invisible in advertising and strictly limited to comic or tragic roles in fictional media depictions. In the late 1990s, though, fat women have emerged as all-too-eager consumers. While growth in retail clothing sales is essentially flat, plus-size segment growth ranks at 10 to 11 percent annually and has shown consistent increases. (LeBesco 2004: 66)

For LeBesco, fashion was finally emerging from a long period of plus-size clothing ghettoization, and fashions for large-size women were becoming mainstream. She believed that the policy of segregation of fat bodies had been replaced by a policy of domestication of the threat they pose to the mainstream beauty ideal based on their inclusion in the fashion system.

In support of this statement, the American scholar cited a number of examples drawn from the fashion system: the growth of plus-size brands such as Girlfriends and Lane Bryant; the spread of *MODE* magazine, based on female body acceptance and the rejection of mainstream ultra-thin models; and the success of decidedly overweight celebrities, such as Camryn Manheim. LeBesco claimed that it is not necessary to detest fashion in order to be feminist. In support of her claim, she argued that the fashion system was shifting toward a greater acceptance of body diversity.

In the following years, the mainstream fashion press seemed to confirm the trend, dedicating sometimes sensational initiatives to the representation of so-called "curvy" bodies. In 2010 and 2011, some magazines devoted special issues to fashion editorials and covers representing plus-size models framed in the rhetoric usually reserved for "normal" fashion editorials with regard to poses, clothing, and locations. *V Magazine* kick-started 2010 with a January issue titled "The size issue," which featured models whose dress sizes hit double digits, photographed by Solve Sundsbo in poses and looks that did nothing to hide their body shape (Inbar 2010). In a fashion editorial, a standard model

(Jacquelyn Jablonski) and a plus-size model (Crystal Renn) were portrayed wearing identical outfits and striking similar poses. In April of the same year, the French monthly *Elle* published an editorial of eighteen photographs of the plus-size model Tara Lynn wearing both specialist brands and high-fashion brands that had created a feature piece for the shoot. The fashion editorial was strengthened by references to French plus-size fashion bloggers. The following year, it was the turn of *Vogue Italia* to publish, in the June issue, the fashion editorial and cover story "Sogno di donna" ("Dream woman") photographed by Steven Meisel and styled by Edward Enninful. The eighteen-page editorial featured plus-size models Tara Lynn, Candice Huffine, and Robyn Lawley dressed in lingerie and posing sexually in a luxurious interior (The Towers of the Waldorf Astoria, New York), mimicking a late nineteenth-century brothel. An image of the editorial was featured on the cover with the title "Belle Vere" ("True Beauties").

Considering a number of events that made the news, the process of body diversification within the fashion system seems to have continued in the subsequent decade. In 2016, for example, the French government introduced legislation to combat the anorexia epidemic, requiring fashion show and photoshoot models to have a medical certificate of general physical well-being, based, among other things, on their BMI. A law known as the *"loi mannequin"* was introduced on October 1, 2017, making it compulsory for digitally altered photographs for commercial use to bear the disclaimer "digitally enhanced photo." High-end magazines, for their part, are showing signs of change, the most important of which is perhaps the new direction given to *Vogue Italia* by its new director, Emanuele Farneti, after the untimely death of previous director Franca Sozzani in late 2016. With the shift in the magazine's focus from high-fashion images to articles discussing general (albeit still fashion-related) issues, it now publishes real-life photographs featuring more or less real bodies, thus weakening the fashion beauty ideal. The second decade of this century has also seen certain fatshion blogs establish an online presence, gaining huge numbers of followers worldwide. The best-known plus-size models, who are also the most established plus-size influencers, now boast millions of followers on Instagram, and can hence be considered outright celebrities according to Pedroni's classification (2016).[1] In addition, some scholars argue that positive forms of body talk are spreading in the public sphere, weakening the hegemony of the ultra-thin ideal (Webb et al. 2013).

There is a widespread perception, therefore, that things are changing, and rapidly at that. Must we conclude, then, that the paradox of fashion is short-lived? That we are discussing an outdated issue? Consider this advertorial from the American edition of *Vogue*:

> Something exciting is happening. A new woman is stepping into the fashion spotlight. She is active and intelligent, fabulous and fascinating, demanding and discriminating. She is proud of herself and her accomplishments.
>
> She does not, however, look like a mannikin. Yet she, too, has chosen to be beautiful.
>
> Now, perhaps for the first time in her life, fashion is catching up to her.
>
> Who is she? She is one of the 40 million American women who wear size 14 and over.
>
> Suddenly, it seems, leading fashion names, traditional fashion houses, and a whole new breed of designers are creating up-to-the-minute ready-to-wear clothes for the large-size woman. Theirs is an important new message: you can be fashionable and look attractive no matter what size you wear. (Quoted in Peters 2017: 176)

Yes, it seems that things are changing very quickly. However, this text appeared in the March 1986 issue, twenty years before LeBesco's book. If things are changing, they are not changing rapidly. The same period saw Roberta Pollack Seid (1989: 304–6) claim that resistance to the thin ideal was mounting. She brought the birth of *Big Beautiful Woman* magazine as evidence, as well as the introduction of plus-size sections in department stores, the opening of agencies for curvy models, the publication in a mainstream magazine such as *Cosmopolitan* (1987) of an article titled "The voluptuous girl: She's bouncing back." Wisely, Seid argued that it would be foolish to draw, from these examples, the conclusion that a bigger body ideal was about to be accepted. In fact, echoing what we have seen throughout this book, *Big Beautiful Woman* closed in 1996, the plus-size sections in the department stores are at best reservations, "shops within a shop," curvy models who parade in the main fashion weeks are exotic exceptions, and the 1980s and 1990s were decades of further slimming of the body ideal. During the 1990s, several Italian haute-couture houses tried to develop plus-size fashion lines or brands: Valentino with Carisma, Versace with GV Versatile, and Gianfranco Ferré with Ferré Forma (Mathras et al. 2012: 391). They were short-lived undertakings with the exception of the brand Per Te by Krizia, which still survives because, although created by fashion designer Krizia, it was placed directly in the hands of the manufacturing company Miroglio, which specializes in plus-size garments through brands such as Elena Mirò and Luisa Viola.

In short, the claims of the *Vogue* advertorial were contradicted by subsequent events. Will LeBesco's optimism meet the same fate? It might be argued that the history of fashion spans several centuries, and that the tyranny of slenderness must therefore be placed in the right historical context. The thin ideal flourished at the beginning of the twentieth century, becoming gradually more entrenched for a hundred years or so, as we saw in Chapter 1. But then—according to this narrative—events began to take a turn, the effects of which were anticipated in the *Vogue* advertorial, observed upon their initial appearance by LeBesco in 2004, and are becoming conspicuous now. In response to this argument, I shall adduce another advertisement dating to 1923, that is, the very beginnings of the tyranny of slenderness a 100 years ago:

> Time was when the woman of fuller proportions had to be content with almost anything that would go on at all. Her choice was limited. Her size was difficult to find, and never was found in the newest styles—until Lane Bryant solved her garment problem for her. (Quoted in Keist 2018: 34)

What conclusions can we draw? The perception that the tyranny of slenderness is loosening its grip on power is as old as the tyranny of slenderness itself. However, this perception has never been reflected in any tangible decline. The examples just cited (to which others could be added)[2] show that caution is necessary in interpreting the current situation as a turn. In fact, the fashion system has propounded messages promoting the inclusion of larger sizes since the onset of the tyranny of slenderness, just as it was actually molding the segregation of fat bodies and the creation of a separate market niche for them. The suspicion arises that controlled forms of questioning the thin ideal are a strategic part of a fashion discourse which nevertheless includes body thinness as a standard to be pursued.

Further elements reinforce this suspicion. Comparing today's styling tips for fat women with those contained in the publications of the mid-twentieth century, Klepp (2011: 477) has observed that although the language has changed significantly to accommodate greater sensitivity to all forms of discrimination, the substance of the advice has not changed, and consists of tricks to make the body appear thinner than it is. Things are no longer presented as norms but as personal choices. Still, they are communicated as the ideal to follow in order to attain bodily beauty.

Moreover, the use of average or fat bodies in brand communication is not always reflected in an expansion of the range of sizes marketed by the brand. Peters (2018c), who has described this phenomenon, calls it an example of size appropriation, thus stigmatizing behavior that commercially exploits specific features of a social group whose members do not have the power to protect their cultural heritage. Brands that behave in this way take advantage of widespread sensitivity to the protection of minorities, the increased awareness of plus-size women elicited by fatshion bloggers, and the growth in popularity of the fat acceptance movement in order to increase their profit which is entirely based on the thin ideal and disregards fat bodies.

I, therefore, suspect that the various recent cases of fashion "opening up" to fat bodies should rather be regarded as marketing episodes in a fairly stable cultural context. Special issues of mainstream magazines devoted to curvy fashion, governments introducing legislation to limit the use of ultra-thin bodies in fashion photography and fashion shows, straight-size fashion brands that choose slightly overweight women as testimonials (like Kim Kardashian for Balmain), and increasing numbers of plus-size models featured in the New York Fashion Week are weak and contradictory signals. They are "explorations" mostly restricted to the sphere of communication, and which do not affect the structure of fashion production, distribution, and consumption. Moreover, in many cases these explorations do not call into question, but rather reinforce the thin ideal, as we have seen in the case of fatshion blogs actually reinforcing the idea that fat bodies are "irregular" bodies that have to be dissimulated. Consecrating a special issue of a straight-fashion magazine to curvy fashion is a way of confirming the segregation of plus sizes by presenting them as exceptions that prove the rule.

The increased "buzz" around fat bodies in fashion, therefore, does not seem to correspond to a paradigm shift in the fashion system, still dominated by traditional fashion discourse. Other events will have to signal a change, other forces are required.

The Resilience of Fashion Discourse

Discourses, in any context, have the ability to adapt to changing circumstances. They are camouflaging. Discourses have this characteristic, first of all, because they do not belong to the linguistic frame, but to that of practices. As such, they are resistant to change. Foucault observed that, as it is a "practice that has its own forms of sequence and succession" ([1969] 2002: 187), discourse has an inertia that is difficult to modify, it has "its own particular index of temporal 'viscosity'" ([1969] 2002: 193). In simpler terms, this means that the statements that make up a discourse (e.g., Karl Lagerfeld's infamous statement of 2009: "No one wants to see curvy women on the catwalk") tend to repeat themselves over time (for example Kirstie Clements' in 2013: "I see no problem in presenting a healthy, toned size 6"), precisely because the discourse is what makes them possible and plausible. Yet, discourses also have another characteristic: resilience. I mean that they have the ability to adapt to changing external conditions without altering their core meanings. Let us consider in more detail Klepp's comparison between styling tips from the 1960s and today. She cites the following two, from 1961 and 2007, respectively: "Avoid long trousers when you can if your bum is a little on the big side" (Klepp 2011: 465); "For those of you who prefer to cover your butt and tummy" (Klepp 2011: 461). There is a substantial difference between the statements: the first is imperative, defines the fat bum as an anti-aesthetic condition and establishes the norm that it should be concealed, while the second is conditional, gives advice for those who are not comfortable with their butt, leaving them the choice. Yet, both statements convey the same message: a body ideal exists, and is thin. As such, the common message stigmatizes fat butts and secludes them in the realm of what is ugly. This makes it clear that in the course of fifty years hegemonic fashion discourse has adapted to a transformation of the dominant culture, thanks to which open discrimination toward those who are different is less and less tolerated. Yet in doing so it has not dismissed the thin ideal. On the contrary, *fashion discourse has made it now possible to articulate thoughts and statements that actually reaffirm the thin ideal while using linguistic formulations that respect the need not to stigmatize fat bodies.*

Regarding imagery, a similar example is constituted by special issues of fashion magazines dedicated to curvy models or plus-size fashion, as previously mentioned. They confirm fashion discourse about thinness, not only because they enclose large-sized bodies within a separate section of a text that otherwise does not include fat bodies—framing it with titles and descriptions that leverage the dimensions of the bodies that it features and not concepts related to fashion trends, designs or looks—but also because the bodies featured are not just any fat bodies. They are bodies that reproduce in larger forms the dominant ideal of female beauty: young, toned, moderately overweight, in dynamic or erotic poses. Their being non-thin is not a neutral characteristic (such as hair color) but the permissible error, the exception in a representation that otherwise confirms hegemonic fashion discourse.

The explanation for the growing but "tokenistic" use of larger bodies in fashion communication (Arnold 2001: 93), therefore, should be less optimistic than is usually held. This trend—I suspect—does not signal a paradigm shift, but a strategy inherent to the paradigm centered on the thin ideal. This strategy is based on the "logic of wrong" (Mackinney-Valentin 2017: 35–6), that is, on the principle of enhancing what could be considered ugly, reversing the status symbol of thinness. In this view, emphasizing something "wrong," such as the fat body, is seized upon by creatives (be they designers, photographers, stylists, or art directors) as a tool for strengthening their personal image in a fashion system in which the time gap between the introduction of the novelty and its adoption by the general public has been reduced to the point that the traditional distinction between innovators and early adopters is no longer evident. Innovators are thus forced to make themselves more original, hence more intriguing, by assuming attitudes and behaviors which are apparently contradictory to the system, such as celebrating overweight women. According to Haller (2018: 246), hype about diversity has evolved into a fashionable trend. Mackinney-Valentin identified the logic of wrong at work in the case of old bodies, commenting on two related phenomena: the use of models aged above sixty for fashion editorials, and the trend of dying one's hair gray before it loses its pigmentation naturally. Cases like these suggest

> a form of cultural appropriation where fashion borrows from an imagined senior culture—older women—that it is simultaneously oppressing through a dogma of youth. [. . .] Within this context, the promotion of age diversity is foregrounded to achieve commercial gain rather than furthering social or cultural tolerance as the main objective. (Mackinney-Valentin 2017: 35)

Mackinney-Valentin's claims about age can certainly be extended to size issues, as Peters's idea of size appropriation also implies (Peters 2018c). In general, the concept of appropriation should be used with caution, because as an evaluative concept it attaches negative connotations to the act of using cultural expressions of other populations or social groups, running the risk of stigmatizing any form of cultural exchange. However, its use is suitable if members of a dominant culture appropriate from disadvantaged minority cultures, when it is not part of a policy to foster cultural pluralism or ordinary intercultural exchange but rather a case of exploitation of the minority's cultural traditions that contributes to their submission to the dominant culture. This is the case when protagonists of the fashion system resort to images of fat bodies to strengthen a message which, overall, confirms and reinforces the thin ideal and the segregation that it involves. In this case, in fact, cultural appropriation increases inequality rather than reducing it, as Haller notes:

> Diversity as vogue also means that these bodies that do not conform to the norm are further marginalized in fashion and do not find suitable clothing for their physical dispositions. Therefore, diversity as vogue should currently

be considered first and foremost a marketing strategy within the attention economy that can be located in Reckwitz's society of singularities, for which what is special has become the linchpin. (Haller 2018: 247)[3]

Instances of fat bodies in fashion that do not weaken but strengthen their segregation and the seclusion of plus-size clothing in a separate market niche should therefore be understood as expressions of the resilience of hegemonic fashion discourse and its ability to survive through cultural changes by adapting to new and apparently incompatible values.

The fashion system, which is part of the dominant culture in Western societies, contributes to domesticating what infringes hegemonic fashion discourse and threatens its power to set out the clothing landscape. It does so by employing some specific strategies. One of these strategies is to reject, segregate, and conceal instances of anti-fashion—that is, what has occurred to plus-size clothing in the last 100 years. The "other," that which is eccentric with respect to dominant styles and body ideal, is not even mentioned by the system, but excluded from shops and concealed in magazines: partly because hegemonic fashion discourse does not equip fashion professionals and consumers with the resources to make it thinkable, and partly because addressing the eccentric is dangerous, as it questions fashion hegemony. A second strategy is the deliberate use of references to instances of anti-fashion as a "status ploy" (Mackinney-Valentin 2017: 31), which does not weaken but reinforces the mainstream fashion culture. This is the case, as described in this chapter, when we see fat or old bodies used as marketing tools in contexts that actually confirm the ideal of youthfulness and slenderness currently dominating Western fashion. It goes without saying that such a ploy can only work to the extent that hegemonic fashion discourse establishes a conceptual framework that is solid enough not to be endangered by the reference to anti-fashion. Finally, there is the strategy of assimilation, which fashion has often used to domesticate subcultures and street styles, as well as alternative voices such as those of fashion bloggers. It consists of transforming and adapting practices, styles, rules, and ideals of mainstream fashion to make room for occurrences of anti-fashion, assimilate them, and thus subject them to the rules of fashion discourse and the economic power of the fashion industry. Accordingly, it happens that high-fashion brands create outfits full of safety pins to domesticate punk (such as the Versace Safety Pin Dress, Spring/ Summer 1994), or that companies pay fashion bloggers to make them not forget to celebrate a certain brand in their "independent" commentaries (Pedroni 2015; Rocamora and Pedroni 2021). This last policy of normalization of the abnormal has not yet been employed significantly in the case of fat fashion, but we can expect that sooner or later the fashion system will also pursue this path.

However, the assimilation of fat bodies in fashion would not automatically mean their emancipation from the tyranny of slenderness. The inclusion of abnormal bodies could result in yet another body technique through which these bodies, too, are regimented, disciplined, and made compliant. Scholars who have studied the issue of fashion for older people have already encountered this scenario, since the aging of generations accustomed to fashion consumption seems to have freed the elderly from the obligation to adopt "frumpy" age-related styles and the ensuing invisibility. While on the one hand, this certainly constitutes a form of emancipation of social groups previously marginalized by fashion, on the other hand, it can easily result in a new form of segregation: you can play the game, but only if you cease being yourself and become an imitation of authentic protagonists of the game. Julia Twigg observes:

> As the culture extends new opportunities, it also imposes new demands, new requirements—that [older women] be fashionable. Dress can be part of a wider process of governmentality in relation to women's bodies in which they are increasingly subject to disciplinary demands regarding appearance. We are familiar with these pressures in terms of younger women, with widespread regimes of slimming, exercise and cosmetic surgery through which they are required to discipline and control their bodies [. . .]. Increasingly these demands are spreading to older women too [. . .]. The requirement to be fashionable, to avoid age-stigmatized clothing, can thus be seen as part of the wider set of Foucauldian techniques of the self, through which the bodies of older people are disciplined, ordered, and made subject to cultural norms. (Twigg 2013b: 83–4)

Very similar considerations can be made regarding the case of fat bodies. Being assimilated by a fashion system that does not relinquish its idealization of slim bodies can mean, for large-sized women, an additional pressure to discipline their body in order to adapt it to the ideal. Melanie Haller observed this pressure in her study on plus-size blogs (2018), in which she identified a number of bodily practices implemented by fatshion bloggers to adapt to the canons imposed by the fashion system, such as outfitting (the use of concealing outfits and accessories), shaping (the use of designs that give the body the desired shape), and posing (never get caught in frontal and static positions and mimic the fashionable poses usual in fashion photography). Through such practices, fatshion bloggers make visible the nonstandard bodies that fashion discourse normally conceals. However, they can only do so by applying similar self-concealing tactics to the nonstandard body that is made "visible," thus manipulating its "visibility," or appearance. Considered from this point of view, the liberation of fat bodies made possible by social media has paradoxically also meant that they are now free to submit to fashion norms, including the thin ideal.

For all these reasons, one should be cautious about making any assumptions with regard to the direction in which the fashion system is moving in relation to the female body ideal. This is not to say that the resilience of the fashion discourse I have described so far excludes any alternative form of behavior. The field of cultural studies has taught us to identify the forms of resistance to hegemonic discourse present in society's subcultural groups. These also exist in the field of fashion. Although they are not strong enough to change the discourse, they do signal that our destiny is not locked up in the opposition of segregation and assimilation. Fashion discourse cannot prevent what Stuart Hall (1992: 137–8) called oppositional reading: the ability to decode a hegemonic message *as hegemonic*, that is to say as an expression of the interests or culture of dominant social groups.

The blogosphere, having diluted the power of mainstream fashion tastemakers, is clearly the area within which this occurs more frequently. As we saw in Chapter 6, it created the media space to make counter-hegemonic statements about fashion possible. Connell (2013) and Harju and Huovinen (2015) hypothesized that thanks to the blogosphere, and in particular some of its subsets such as fatshion blogs and blogs focusing on fashion for queer people, fashion could serve as a site of resistance against systems of privilege and inequality. This implies that situations at the edge of the fashion system can favor the formation of so-called counter-discourses (Deleuze and Foucault 1977) that disrupt the politics of body size that Western fashion as a whole pursues through fashion discourse. Their argument is that fashion, while producing and upholding hegemonic discourses of beauty that maintain oppressive hierarchies, can become a vehicle of empowerment for marginalized communities that strive for more egalitarian alternatives. The blog Fa(t)shion February for Femmes and Friends investigated by Connell

> goes beyond simply displaying fat bodies and fashions, a radical act in and of itself, but in fact engages in a direct reversal of typical fashion discourse in its written content. For instance, users rarely used the language of "flattering" to describe their fashion, which would imply that fat fashion should disguise or minimize fatness. Rather, users complement each other on how their outfits highlighted fatness; comments regularly included direct references to visible fatness as cute, sexy, and enviable. (Connell 2013: 213)

In experiences of this type, fashion discourse is recognized as hegemonic and actually adverse to one's own predisposition, and therefore replaced with statements and practices that make sense within the framework of a different discourse, opposite to the hegemonic one. Hegemonic discourse expressions (e.g., photographs of ultra-thin models) are then read and understood through an oppositional code that reverses their meaning (from symbol of beauty to symbol of oppression).

Looking for Structural Change Factors

The oppositional reading of the thin ideal is a form of resistance to hegemonic fashion discourse. However, it does not seem to be enough on its own to promote a paradigm shift in the ideal of female beauty cultivated by fashion. Oppositional readings of the thin ideal have always existed over the last 100 years. However, they have been unable to challenge hegemonic fashion discourse. Therefore, I conclude that the forces for potential change must lie elsewhere, and I assume that they lie in social changes and dynamics of a more general nature. This conviction also underpins the analysis proposed by Seid in the 1980s, although the Californian scholar evidently overestimated certain social phenomena of that time. She claimed that the very circumstances that helped the establishment of the thin ideal were changing, and discussed a number of them (in a North American context) which are worth mentioning here. Demographically speaking, the generation that ushered in the radicalism of the 1960s were now middle-aged, an age at which identifying with the slim body becomes arduous. A return to family values and childcare seemed to erode the masculinized ideal which, as seen in Chapter 3, constitutes one of the main drivers of the thin ideal. The waning emphasis on sexual promiscuity and the role of sex in life after the excitement of the 1960s and 1970s reduced the pressures that had made women focus so intensely on their bodies. The fashion industry had failed to universally impose body-baring styles like the miniskirt. And, as a general consideration, fashionable beauty cannot stay long at one extreme: "Fashions change in response to large historical developments, but they also evolve in accord with their own internal dynamics" (Seid 1989: 308).

Apparently, such social changes have not been able to trouble the thin ideal. Despite this, we can adopt the same approach and inquire into current social and cultural transformations. If we reflect on the most recent social changes, what factors might plausibly undermine the ideal of beauty that is dominant in the fashion system? Let us try to identify some of them.

The most pressing factor for overcoming the thin ideal is undoubtedly the fact that the world population is getting fatter. The increase in average weight in all Western countries in recent decades is putting growing pressure on the fashion industry to revise the beauty standards that are dominant within it. When over half of potential customers are overweight, as is the case in the United States and the United Kingdom, the prospect of manufacturing clothing sizes and shapes suitable for dressing overweight bodies may become appealing even for high-fashion houses. The paradox of fashion—as is the nature of all paradoxes—will probably evolve toward a new balance. The inertia of the practice of fashion supports the persistence of the thin ideal and has prevented economic interests from prevailing in past decades. Yet economic interest does not cease to exert pressure, and the constant growth in the share of overweight or obese population increases such pressure as time passes.

As noted by Seid, demographic changes can also play an important role, albeit not in the way she posited. Putting aside the cultural trends to which she referred, the aging of Western populations progressively reduces the rate of young people, while shifting the entry thresholds into adulthood and old age upward. The increasing participation of elderly people in active social life is gradually legitimizing the idea that there must be something like a true fashion for elderly bodies. The bodies of older people "have increasingly been colonized by the concept of fashionability" (Twigg 2013a: 6). While this can result, as we have seen above, in the usual pressures on women to lose weight, it can also result, conversely, in the gradual acceptance of non-thin bodies on the part of fashion. The reason is that population aging in Western countries may have the effect of weakening the youthful norm, and accordingly the thin ideal. Older and fat bodies seem to share a common fate in the field of fashion.

Fashion, too, is moving in a direction that, in the long run, may help to weaken the tyranny of slenderness. For more than a century, fashion has been experiencing a slow but steady process of democratization (Kidwell and Christman 1974; Silla 2020), which has gradually included increasingly broad social strata in fashion consumption. Since the proportion of overweight individuals is higher among the working class than it is among the more affluent classes, we can expect fashion democratization to go hand in hand with the growth of BMI in the world population and further increase the pressure that economic interests exert on the fashion system to extend the range of manufactured and marketed sizes upward. The fashion industry is gradually realizing that today's fat consumers often have considerable disposable income (LeBesco 2004: 67). If once fat women were not deemed potential customers of fashion and luxury brands due to lack of economic resources, there is no longer any reason for such exclusion.

Furthermore, current worldwide migration flows, which involve the displacement of masses of people from Africa, Asia, and South America, have the potential to bring about substantial changes within their new host societies, mainly in the West, where the fashion system has its roots. This is likely to impact Europe more than the United States, where the ethnic diversity of bodies is not new. In Europe, immigration from other continents may legitimize body and weight variety as a result of the increasing number of "ethnic" bodies in the visual landscape. Of course, immigration will have to combine with a further democratization of fashion and progressive social inclusion to overcome the current ghettoization of many immigrants in cultural clusters that are excluded from fashion. Similarly, in the United States fashion democratization and the inclusion of disadvantaged social classes in fashion consumption imply the progressive inclusion of African American consumers, who are prevalent among those classes and often have larger bodies than Caucasians. If democratization of fashion and ethnic diversification continue hand in hand, the clothing landscape is destined to change gradually and, with it, maybe also the common perception of standards of beauty and elegance.

A final factor that may play a part in loosening the thin ideal's grip on fashion is technology. In Chapter 5, I discussed the expectations elicited by body scanners, although these have not led to any appreciable change in fashion so far. However, looking beyond body scanners to digital technology as a whole, which has its place in both fashion manufacturing and retail, it is not difficult to imagine that in the long run it might help foster the transformations outlined here. Indeed, digital technologies support the current trend toward customization in many ways (Ricchetti and Volonté 2018), such as by promoting anthropometric data surveys based on image processing technologies, by developing 3D printing technologies, digital textile printing and peer-to-peer production, and by fostering the gradual expansion of open manufacturing processes (Anderson 2012). Although customization has always been an aspect of fashion, it has been severely restricted as a result of the transition to mass production and the related split in the clothes-body complex. As this fracture facilitated the spread of body standards in fashion, the return to custom manufacture by the same token should facilitate the loosening of standards. Overall, digital technologies help to loosen restrictions due to standardization, thereby undermining the constraint imposed by the sizing technique in fashion.

The world population getting fatter, demographic changes, fashion dynamics in the long run, worldwide migration flows, and technological innovation: all these trends are very general social changes that do not concern the fashion system alone, not to mention individual actors within the fashion system. They have a bearing on the social structure and the basics of mainstream culture. Yet this is exactly what makes them relevant to our topic. My point is, that if the general framework of society changes, the resilience of hegemonic fashion discourse may be challenged. I am not claiming that I expect these five factors to vanquish the tyranny of slenderness in fashion or to undermine the thin ideal in Western cultures, but I suggest that if they are to be vanquished, it will more likely be due to such kinds of general social change than to the actions and behavior of individuals and organizations within the fashion system itself.

Notes

Chapter 1

1 I am referring here to the established definition of social action proposed by Max Weber in *Economy and Society* ([1921/22] 1978: 22–4).

2 Taylor (2002: 64–89). See also Calefato and Breward (2018); Bethke and Keigel (2019).

3 For example, Simmel (1905), Veblen (1899), and Flügel (1930), but also Hollander (1994), Wilson ([1985] 2003), and Lipovetsky ([1987] 1994).

4 We tend to forget that even vocal sounds, and any case of mediated communication, need a body in order to take shape.

5 See Wykes and Gunter (2005: 2–6) and the extensive literature to which they refer.

6 See Rudofsky (1972: 93–124) and Fallon (1990: 96–106).

7 Sources on this topic include Cassidy (1991), Malcolm (1925), Rudofsky (1972: 99–100), Rothblum (1990), and Seid (1989: 45).

8 See Bordo (1993: 102); Craik (2009: 168); Wilson ([1985] 2003: 115); Wykes and Gunter (2005: 7). As an example of the shift in non-Western bodily ideals resulting from the introduction of Western culture, see Becker (1995).

9 On this point see Fallon (1990: 84–92), Gordon (1990: 77), Keist (2017), Mennell (1991) and Walden (1985).

10 Thin-internalization is the "extent to which an individual cognitively 'buys into' socially defined ideas of attractiveness and engages in behaviors designed to produce an approximation of these ideals" (Thompson and Stice 2001: 181, following Thompson et al. 1999). It is, therefore, about the internalization of a normalizing gaze that disciplines individual practices leading them to the pursuit of a body ideal characterized by thinness.

11 Here, I am summarizing, very briefly, a topic that I will expand upon in Chapter 2.

12 Any comparison between bodies promoted by fashion and real bodies based on sizes is problematic due to inconsistent size standards. As we shall see in Chapter 5, size systems are approximate and change significantly not only between countries but also between brands. Yet, clothing sizes are a convenient indicator of the relationship between body and clothing measurements and are reliable to the extent that they are not drawn from heterogeneous sources.

13 I will consistently refer to US size numbering, from which the corresponding size in various European countries can easily be derived (see the Size Conversion Table).

14 These figures are merely indicative, not only because I do not have access to an analytical report of the research results, but also because the company which commissioned the report, an e-commerce site, has an evident conflict of interest on the subject.

15 These data are not completely reliable because the methods used to collect them are controversial and not comparable. Moreover, the very idea of a BMI is disputed (see, e.g., Flegal et al. 2010; Poulain 2002: 95–128; Volonté and Pedroni 2014), especially because it is not weighted to take account of ethnic differences, as different standards of "normality" apply to the weight-to-height ratio for different ethnic groups. Even more questionable is the suspiciously round number (25) that marks the threshold between normal weight and overweight. However, despite these inherent limitations and because of the congruence between BMI 25 and size twelve, the BMI indicator offers a useful way of highlighting the discrepancy between the clothing offered by the fashion "system" and the (potential) demand on the part of consumers.

16 For data and a more detailed discussion of this issue see Chapter 6.

17 In 2017 the *Wall Street Journal* valued the female plus-size market in the United States at $21 billion (Westervelt 2017), reporting data from major market research companies. However, this is a valuation of the *current* plus-size market, that is, a market that suffers from a low level of "aesthetic investment" on the part of manufacturers.

18 More about this in Chapter 6.

19 Those interested in reconstructing the evolution of the phenomenon over time can enjoy the works of Lauren Downing Peters and Carmen Keist listed in the bibliography or forthcoming.

Chapter 2

1 As Elizabeth Wilson (1992: 15) has noted, a mere visit to a fashion exhibition where clothes are displayed on mannequins (or worse, on hangers, or enclosed in a display case) makes it clear that the body is crucial for clothes to fully exist.

2 I use this expression to stress that the human body becomes socially relevant only through the interpretation provided by culture. However, I do not share a radical constructivist idea of the body, according to which the human body is entirely the result of a social construction (see e.g., Synnott 1993). I feel that the complexity of this phenomenon is accounted for more fully by the position of those who, like Shilling ([1993] 2012), maintain that emphasizing the social dimension of the body, while making the naive naturalistic view untenable, does not imply reducing the

body to a cultural construct as ephemeral as any other product of culture, although it enables an awareness that the human body is always modified by culture.

3 Experiences such as nudism can be considered exceptions in today's society.

4 On this topic see Shilling ([1993] 2012: 103–34).

5 For an overview of the psychological theory of embodied cognition, see Wilson (2002). Evidence of the enclothed cognition is reported, among others, in Civile and Obhi (2017), Kraus and Mendes (2014), and López-Pérez et al. (2016).

6 That walking is gendered, for instance, is shown by innumerable cases of cultural representations (e.g., films like *Tootsie*) in which walking determines the effectiveness or ineffectiveness of a disguise. Based on his research into the Kabyle people, Bourdieu states: "The opposition between male and female is realized in posture, in the gestures and movements of the body, in the form of the opposition between the straight and the bent, between firmness, uprightness and directness (a man faces forward, looking and striking directly at his adversary), and restraint, reserve and flexibility" (Bourdieu [1980] 1990: 70). See also Iris Marion Young's essay "Throwing like a girl" (2005: 27–45).

7 See, for example: Black et al. (2013: 97–56); Entwistle ([2000] 2015); Finkelstein (1991); González and Bovone (2007); Mackinney-Valentin (2017); Paulicelli and Clark (2009).

8 Erving Goffman (1983: 3) argues that there are two fundamental forms of identification: "the *categoric* kind involving placing [the] other in one or more social categories, and the *individual* kind, whereby the subject under observation is locked to a uniquely distinguishing identity through appearance, tone of voice, mention of name or other person-differentiating device." Scholars who highlight the role of clothing in the construction of the individual's social identity tend to favor the categoric form of identification and disregard the individual one.

9 It is probably superfluous to point out that such identification of clothing communication with a language has nothing to do with the role played by verbal language in Barthes's idea of the fashion system (see Barthes [1967] 1983).

10 I am elaborating here on some suggestions made by Barthes himself ([1957] 2013: 17–18).

11 See for instance the works of Austin (1962), Lewis (1969), Levinson (1983), and Grice (1989).

12 A significant exception is represented by quantitative psychological studies on the inferences that clothes elicit about their wearers (see, e.g., Damhorst 1990; Hebl et al. 2004; Lennon et al. 2014). It goes without saying that these studies apply an inferential theoretical framework. Because of their methodological characteristics (e.g., their adoption of a quantitative approach and extremely limited research questions), however, they actually take for granted what it means to "infer" a

meaning from an experience and do not discuss the mechanisms of clothed-bodily communication.

13 On the meaning given to hoodies in the UK in recent decades, see, for example, Rahman (2016) and Turney (2018).

14 The thesis of the agency of objects has been developed with sometimes rather different traits by various authors (see Gell 1988; Latour 2005; Miller 1987). Common to all of their arguments, however, is the idea that the presence of material things in a given situation produces effects in social interactions that are not entirely related to the intentions and actions of human participants, nor to the laws of physical nature, so that they have to be ascribed to the objects themselves. I have discussed the differences between these theories in Volonté (2017). For a convincing application of the agency of objects to the field of fashion, see Haller (2015).

15 For example, Tseëlon (1995: 59), based on Cox (1993), argues that in dressing women give more importance than men to the sense of self-worth and self-confidence that clothes can convey.

16 In certain specific situations, such as telephone conversations, the mediation of the body can exclude physical form and clothing and be limited to the sound of the voice. However, in such situations interaction is so impoverished (Thompson 1995: 82–7) that in delicate circumstances we may need to switch to face-to-face interaction, which by allowing the use of the five senses provides a wider spectrum of information than mediated interaction.

17 See Enninger (1985: 107); Kaiser (1997: 308–11); Stone ([1962] 1995: 21).

18 As is well known, sumptuary laws are rules established by a political authority that prescribe or prohibit certain types of clothing for certain categories of the population. They have often been used in the past as markers of class or profession, or to limit luxury consumption on the part of the wealthier classes. However, one should not assume that this phenomenon is exclusive to pre-modern or non-Western societies. Regulations of this type are present in the legislation of all countries in the form of principles of decency and modesty in specific situations (e.g., at school, on the beach, etc.).

19 See Lisberg Jensen and Elahi (2017).

20 Barnard (1996: 59–70); Enninger (1985: 96–100); Roach and Eicher ([1979] 2007).

21 Clearly, I am not talking about the class differentiation which Simmel (1905) considers a driving force in fashion, nor about the distinction that Bourdieu ([1979] 1984) describes as the effect of the individual's social trajectories. I am focusing, instead, on actors' ability to partially distance themselves from the dressing habits of their own milieu to highlight their unique individualities.

22 See for instance Entwistle ([2000] 2015: 16–26); Peters (2018a: 54–64); Rocamora (2009: 54–62).

Chapter 3

1 See for example Mazur (1986: 284), Myers and Biocca (1992), Silverstein et al. (1986: 520–1), Wolf (1991: 61–80).

2 Wykes and Gunter (2005: 156–8). On these issues see also Ahern et al. (2008), L. L. Davis (1985), Myers and Biocca (1992).

3 It is also worth noting that the interpretation of these phenomena is complex and not linear. Hebl et al. (2009) observed that Black women, due to their physical structure, typically find it more difficult to adapt to the thin ideal, and that this generates an attitude of disidentification and disengagement from it. The authors suggest that such disengagement could be a reason for the lower exposure of Black women to eating disorders, as these have a clear correlation with body image concerns.

4 In 2006, the Spanish Association of Fashion Designers decided to exclude underweight models with a BMI of less than eighteen from the Madrid fashion show. Italy banned ultra-thin models from the 2007 Milan Fashion Week in a bid to tackle anorexia among models. A law banning the hiring of ultra-thin models in France came into effect in October 2017. Similar initiatives have also been launched in Israel (Sykes 2017) and Argentina (Lebesco 2004: 67). In other countries (e.g., the United States, the United Kingdom, and Denmark), by contrast, institutional authorities have promulgated ethical guidelines aimed at promoting awareness about how to recognize the early signs of eating disorders and helping models with eating disorders to seek professional help and stop modeling until they obtain a doctor's approval (see, e.g., Model Health Inquiry 2007).

5 Wykes and Gunter (2005). Most notably, in 2018, the Health Initiative of the Council of Fashion Designers of America became the Initiative for Health, Safety, and Diversity to improve diversity in fashion and tackle sexual harassment and abuse at work (see the CFDA website at https://bit.ly/31OQkwe. Accessed October 26, 2019).

6 After a thorough investigation of 312 female international runway models from 2012 to 2018, Jestratijevic et al. (2020: 12) concluded that "extreme thinness in the modeling industry represents a universal and normative occupational standard, regardless of age. All female models in the sample fell below the severely underweight BMI cutoff (BMI > 16)."

7 Among others, Sarah Watkins, director of the 12+ UK Model Management Agency, has confirmed this in commenting on the London initiative *All Walks Beyond the Catwalk* (www.allwalks.org). See Bourne et al. (2011: 6).

8 Maria Angela Polesana (2017) has made the same observation regarding the influencer Chiara Ferragni.

9 This section is substantially based on contributions by Lauren Downing Peters (2018a; 2018b; 2019a; 2019b) and Carmen Keist (2017; 2018; Keist and Marcketti 2013). See also Banner (1983), Kidwell and Christman (1974: 105–11), Seid (1989: 81–102), Stearns (1997: 11–17), Thesander (1997), and Vester (2010).

10 Wray and Deery (2008) argue that the media promulgates a popularized biomedical knowledge that encourages women to connect health to appearance, thus contributing to the circulation of a gendered discourse which currently dominates attitudes toward body shapes and sizes and promotes thinness under the rhetoric of health.

11 It has been shown that there is an inverse correlation between a woman's body weight and quality of employment (Rothblum et al. 1990).

12 Although Barthes was concerned with the short utterances describing clothes within captions, Agnès Rocamora (2009: 59–62) has aptly argued that written fashion includes all forms of fashion writings.

13 More about this in Chapter 6.

Chapter 4

1 Interestingly, this thesis is at odds with the opinion of many fashion photographers, who ascribe the responsibility for nonintrusive model bodies to fashion designers. For more on this, see the next section.

2 In most European countries, including the UK, Italy, and France, until the middle of the twentieth century, civilian clothing for everyday use continued to be largely home-made or produced by local tailors and seamstresses. It was only at the beginning of the 1950s that industrial mass production came to predominate (Aldrich 2007; Jeacle 2003; Lipovetsky [1987] 1994; Paris 2006).

3 See also Keist (2018: 32) and Wissinger (2015: 108–40).

4 Some examples can be easily retrieved on the web, such as statements by Coco Rocha (2015), Jess Cole, quoted in Friedman (2018), and Grace Han interviewed in Zhang (2019). For an explicit example of the rhetoric of hanger models, see Byrnes (2018).

5 On the relationship between discourse and practice, cf. Nicolini (2012: 189–212).

6 For example, Andreas Reckwitz (2002), Theodore Schatzki (1996; 2002), Elizabeth Shove (Shove et al. 2012; Shove and Trentmann 2019), and Alan Warde (2005).

7 See Dant (1999) on windsurfing; Nicolini and Monteiro (2016) on skiing; Shove and Pantzar (2005) on Nordic walking.

8 Proponents of the practice approach have taken the accusation seriously and discussed it from different points of view. See, for example, Hui et al. (2017), Schatzki (2002: 189–264) and Warde (2014).

9 See Entwistle and Wissinger (2012b); Godart and Mears (2009); Mears (2011).

10 See also Jennifer Craik's (1993: 62–4) analysis of the book *The Princess of Wales Fashion Handbook* (James 1984).

11 Czerniawski (2015: 63) describes this "circle of blame," where models are thin because the samples are designed and made in sizes from zero to four, but the samples are made in those sizes because it is only for those dimensions that the agencies are able to supply a sufficient number of models.

12 LeBesco (2004: 71–2) observes: "The fashion industry won't feature fat models because the public apparently won't accept them, but the public stands little chance of being able to accept fat models until the fashion industry portrays them in the same flattering light they shine on their slimmer sisters."

13 As we will see in the next chapter, the size grading systems are based on incremental grading concepts that are no longer functional above size twelve.

Chapter 5

1 The fact that there is generally a correlation between wealth and the Body Mass Index, in the sense that overweight and obese individuals are more commonly found among the poorer classes (Goldblatt et al. 1965), implies that ultimately the social strata affected by this new form of exclusion are largely the same as before.

2 The first large-scale anthropometric survey was carried out in the United States by the Bureau of Home Economics at the request of the clothing industries between 1939 and 1941 (O'Brien and Shelton 1985). In the UK, very similar research was carried out in the 1950s and published in 1957 (Board of Trade 1957). In Germany, anthropometric surveys have been conducted regularly every decade since 1963 (DOB-Verband 1994). In Italy, the first study not attributable to a single company was only performed in the 1970s (Eim 1979). In other countries, such as Australia, similar surveys were limited to the validation of foreign anthropometric research data (Hackett and Rall 2018).

3 The issue of comparability of the size systems adopted by different countries is awkward for the various reasons discussed in this chapter. In fact, although companies in a country generally adopt a single size labeling system (2, 4, 6 in the United States, 38, 40, 42 in Italy), the measures of the clothes labeled with those sizes can vary significantly from one manufacturer or brand to another. Even if we consider exclusively the measurements provided by national standards bodies, comparisons are highly approximate, as the measurements underlying two equivalent sizes differ (Lee 2014). For example, although American size six corresponds broadly to Italian size forty-two, the height, breast, waist, and hip measurements do not match. Nevertheless, there is a broad comparability between

size systems, both in the numbering (numerical, increasing by two units), and in the progression from one size to another. Therefore, for the purposes of this book, I have deemed it appropriate to refer to a single size numbering system (the American one) as displayed in the Size Conversion Table.

4 The publication of a European standard for labeling clothes sizes (EN 13402) by the Comité Européen de Normalization (CEN) in 2007 to date has not produced any significant alignment between the sizing systems used in different European countries. On the variability of sizing systems, see, for example, Bogusławską-Bączek (2010).

5 An interesting step in this direction was made by Charming Shoppes. Having identified three distinct lower body shapes based on a body scan survey of over 50,000 women, they were also able to find three fit models for those shapes. By means of a body scanner, they subsequently recorded the body measurements of the fit models and then used them as virtual models in creating new garments (Borody 2014: 158).

6 Armies exclude "eccentric" (e.g., fat) bodies from recruitment not only because they are less suitable for fighting, but also because they do not meet the standards imposed by clothing, equipment, and weapons. See Jeacle (2003: 361).

7 An example in this regard is the explicit opinion of Mike Jeffries, then CEO of Abercrombie & Fitch, who in a 2006 interview said: "Candidly, we go after the cool kids. We go after the attractive all-American kid with a great attitude and a lot of friends. A lot of people don't belong [in our clothes], and they can't belong. Are we exclusionary? Absolutely. Those companies that are in trouble are trying to target everybody: young, old, fat, skinny. But then you become totally vanilla" (quoted in Denizet-Lewis 2006).

8 As for plus-size clothing, see Zangrillo (1990), which is the most renowned and perhaps only textbook on fashion design for the plus sized and is based on the identification of four female full-figure body shapes: the rectangular-eight shape, the pear shape, the barrel shape and the box shape (1990: 4–7).

9 In a well-known case, Wiebe Bijker (1995) showed in detail how the standard modern safety bicycle which established itself at the beginning of the twentieth century and which we still consider a successful design, was not "more advanced" than the high-wheel "ordinary" bicycle of the 1870s and 1880s. Rather, it responded to different needs expressed by different social groups. Of course, it was more stable, secure, faster, and easier to use than its predecessor. Yet these are not intrinsic qualities of technology; they are merely ways in which technology responds to the expectations of social groups—in this case to the idea that the bicycle is a means of transport. Young cyclists who had found the ordinary bicycle perfectly suited to their needs (having fun, athletic challenge, competition) considered the safety bicycle a case of design involution that sacrificed the elegance, style, and exclusivity of the ordinary bicycle to safety and stability.

10 Market data are not easy to obtain and are often reported very briefly and without reference to sources and methods. Wang (2007: 9–10) reports the results of several market studies which showed strong growth in the US plus-size market between 1996 and 2006, in contrast with the women's clothing market as a whole which is essentially saturated and experiencing very slow growth (see also LeBesco 2004: 66). Statista (2019) reports a growth in sales in the US plus-size apparel market of 2.4 percent in 2013, 8.6 percent in 2014, 4.8 percent in 2015, and 3 percent in 2016 (sources: Bloomberg and NPD Group), and forecasts consistent growth in the worldwide plus-size apparel market over the next few years (source: Credence Research). PwC (2017) reports that in the period 2012–17 the plus-size segment in the UK outperformed the overall womenswear and menswear clothing market, and forecasts growth of about 5–6 percent between 2017 and 2022.

11 These data are available on the Statista website (2019) and refer to a report from the market research firm The NPD Group. Based on the same report, Weinswig (2018) cites a women's plus-size clothing market value of $21.4 billion, or around 17.5 percent of the total market. In general, the figures provided by market research are not always reliable. However, they do provide an indication of current trends.

12 Nadia Boujarwah is CEO of the e-commerce website Dia&Co, a sales service for plus-size apparel based on a try-on-at-home model.

13 For a brief but informative account of *MODE*, which was forced to close following the events of 9/11, see Lubitz (2017).

14 Sixty-two out of the sixty-six models featured on the Curve Model Management agency website in November 2019 were between size ten and size sixteen. Similarly, forty out of the fifty-nine models on the Bridge Agency website were between size ten and size fourteen, the others being of a smaller size. On the size of plus-size models, see Czerniawski (2015: 9–10, 28–9).

15 There are obviously exceptions, such as the American fashion designer Christian Siriano, a member of the Council of Fashion Designers of America who also produces large sizes and features models of various sizes at the New York Fashion Week.

Chapter 6

1 "Those who do not comply with such beauty constituents are placed outside of the discourse of feminine identity represented in much of our culture. For them, there is an exclusion to the dark zone of nonconformity or an expensive or even painful search for ways of fitting the femininity on offer" (Wykes and Gunter 2005: 50). See also Christel (2014: 305–7), Harju and Huovinen (2015: 1614), Keist (2018: 26), and Peters (2014: 49–50).

2 I should remind the reader that fashion standards size out (i.e., regard as fat) bodies that are statistically average and medically on the line between a "healthy" weight and overweight. In other words, almost all non-thin bodies are outsized.

3 Starting with Holverson (1952), several scholars have addressed this issue based on empirical investigations, including Chowdhary and Beale (1988), Adam (2001), Klepp and Storm-Mathisen (2005), Otieno et al. (2005), and Gruys (2012). Gruys (2019) demonstrates that the lack of well-fitting plus-size clothing trickles down to nonprofit organizations supporting the poor, in particular those that help unemployed women to put together business attire to wear during job interviews.

4 I think that Bourdieu's attempt to apply his theory of social fields to the field of fashion is not successful on the whole, above all because he fails to acknowledge the radical change that fashion underwent in the shift from the regime dominated by haute couture, that is, what Lipovetsky ([1987] 1994) has called the Hundred-Year Fashion, to the regime dominated by luxury ready-to-wear fashion. I have discussed this criticism in Volonté (2008). The idea of interpreting the contrast between plus-size and high fashion in Bourdieu's terms is supported by Scaraboto and Fischer (2013).

5 Table 1 shows the data collected in November 2019 from the websites of the brands included in the official calendar of the Paris Fashion Week, which was held from September 23 to October 1, 2019 (Women's Fashion, Spring-Summer 2020). Only brands which at the time of the survey were selling their products on their official websites were considered. For each brand, the products in the "dresses" category (sometimes "dresses and gowns") were counted, furthermore limiting the information to the products actually available for purchase. The "Largest size available overall" column indicates the largest size that can be purchased for all products. The "Largest size available for the greatest number of designs" column indicates the largest available size for the largest number of marketed designs. In fact, the absolute maximum size is often only available for one or two designs, while most designs are sold in smaller sizes. French sizes have been converted to American ones.

6 Mauro Davico, personal communication.

7 According to Almond (2013: 203), Miles Lambert, costume curator of the Gallery of English Costume, "attributed this to the fact that fuller-sized clothes were difficult to exhibit in a way that made them appear aesthetically pleasing."

8 Expert opinions were gathered in July 2019 through a focus group based on the consensus approach. Participants (laboratory technicians and clothing store assistants) were asked to agree on the presumed size of each female body featured by the magazines, classifying it in a very simple scale made up of three large groups of sizes: S (sizes up to four) , M (sizes from six to eight), and L (sizes ten and plus). The assessment regarded the featured body, not the real person, so that it could

have varied from photograph to photograph even if the person was the same. Accordingly, the size assessment was independent of the actual measurements of featured models or celebrities. Bodies of which it was impossible to infer the size were excluded.

9 This depends both on the presence of fashion advertising, which replicates in these magazines the very same stylistic elements used in mainstream magazines (for example, in the Spring and Summer 2019 issue of *The Gentlewoman*, on a total of 306 pages, 70 were occupied by advertisements of women fashion brands, all featuring very skinny models), and on the fact that also in "stylist-driven" editorials there prevail the use of professional models, which are expressions of the beauty ideal promoted by the model industry.

10 In summer 2019, I carried out an exploratory survey among students attending the Politecnico di Milano's fashion courses. They were asked to browse the May 2019 issue of American *Vogue* and April 2019 issue of *L'Officiel Paris* and say which images of female bodies they perceived as being fat, thin, or regular. The subject of the investigation was therefore not the size of featured bodies, but the reader's perception of that size. The actual size of the individuals featured is not significant because it does not contribute to forming the social imaginary related to the female body. Instead, what matters is readers' perception: a photoshopped image of a size forty-two model featured in plastic poses can appear much thinner than one of a size forty model featured in order to enhance its curves. Assignment of the "thin," "regular" and "fat" labels is arbitrary, and only serves to organize female body representations into discrete categories. 149 students participated in the survey. They were required to only count the number of images of recognizably fat, regular, and thin female bodies. Data were normalized excluding questionnaires (about 10 percent) in which the total sum of images considered assessable deviated significantly ($+/-$ 20 percent) from the average, assuming that in these cases there was a bias in the evaluation of assessibility.

11 Some scholars have sought to investigate the public perception of female body images featured in magazines, but there is no agreement on what approach needs to be taken. The various methods used (see Wykes and Gunter 2005: 187–8) identify the reader's body image rather than his or her perception of featured figures. For the same reason, the widely used Contour Drawing Rating Scale (Thompson and Gray 1995) and the similar Figure Rating Scale (Stunkard et al. 1983) do not serve our purpose (see also Borland and Akram 2007; Greenleaf et al. 2020; Sypeck et al. 2004). Almond (2013: 212–13) analyzed the August 2011 issue of British *Vogue* with a nonstandard approach, finding that the models were extremely thin and "only one advert hinted at a level of voluptuousness," while there were "only two images of more voluptuous figures in the whole magazine."

12 See, for example, *Slink*, a bi-monthly magazine published in the UK but sold in different countries, *Love U Magazine*, published quarterly in the United States, *Dare*, published quarterly in Canada, *The Curvy Magazine*, published quarterly in Germany, and *Be Plus*, published quarterly in Puerto Rico. See also Gaddi (2014: 104).

13 See also Pham (2011) and Rocamora (2013).

14 On this subject, see Andrew and Fairclough (2015); Haller (2018); Harju and Huovinen (2015); Pedroni and Pofi (2018); Scaraboto and Fischer (2013). Although a census of fatshion blogs is impossible, it is no exaggeration to estimate several thousand world fashion blogs and Instagram profiles owned by curvy influencers. Adopting the distinction proposed by Pedroni (2016) between outright celebrities, meso-celebrities, and micro-celebrities, the smaller number of outright celebrities who are curvy are famous plus-size models with their own blog and/or Instagram profile (Ashley Graham, Tess Holliday, and Ashley Alexiss). Then there is a large group of meso-celebrities with tens and hundreds of thousands of followers on Instagram (easily extending into the dozens, the most famous of them likewise being plus-size models such as Nadia Aboulhosn, Denise Bidot, and Candice Huffine). This group also includes influencers with the first wave of fatshion blogs between 2006 and 2008 (e.g., Gabi Gregg with GabiFresh, Marie Denee with TheCurvyFashionista, Nicolette Mason, and Elisa d'Ospina with their homonymous blogs). The plethora of curvy micro-bloggers, often with few followers and of local interest, is difficult to quantify.

15 https://bit.ly/34Nn0JT. Accessed October 10, 2020.

16 https://bit.ly/2SKMmmb. Accessed October 10, 2020.

Chapter 7

1 As of late 2019, Ashley Graham has 9.7 million followers on Instagram, Tess Holliday 2 million, and Ashley Alexiss 1.9 million. A sizeable group of plus-size models and bloggers, including Nadia Aboulhosn, Denise Bidot, Gabi Gregg (GabiFresh), Tara Lynn, and Hunter McGrady, can count between half a million and a million followers. For an overview see also above, Chapter 6, note 15.

2 Czerniawski (2015: 139) argues, for instance, that "[w]ith the effort of the [Plus Size Designers] council and independent plus-size designers entering the field, plus-size apparel offerings boomed in the 1990s, and new challenges emerged to appease a hungry demographic that had purchasing power."

3 Haller refers here to Reckwitz (2017) and, as regards the attention economy, to Franck (2007).

References

Adam, Alison (2001), "Big girls' blouses: Learning to live with polyester," in A. Guy, E. Green and M. Banim (eds.), *Through the Wardrobe: Women's Relationships with Their Clothes*, 39–52, Oxford and New York: Berg.

Adam, Hajo, and Galinsky, Adam D. (2012), "Enclothed Cognition," *Journal of Experimental Social Psychology*, 48 (4): 918–25.

Ahern, Amy L., Bennett, Kate M. and Hertherington, Marion M. (2008), "Internalization of the ultra-thin ideal: Positive implicit associations with underweight fashion models are associated with drive for thinness in young women," *Eating Disorders: The Journal of Treatment and Prevention*, 16 (4): 294–307.

Alexander, M., Connell, L. J. and Presley, A. B. (2005), "Clothing fit preferences of young female adult consumers," *International Journal of Clothing Science and Technology*, 17 (1): 52–64.

Aldrich, W. (2007), "History of sizing systems and ready-to-wear garments," in S.P. Ashdown (ed.), *Sizing in Clothing: Developing Effective Sizing Systems for Ready-to-Wear Clothing*, 1–56, Cambridge: Woodhead.

Ålgars, Monica, Santtila, Pekka, Varjonen, Markus, Witting, Katarina, Johansson, Ada, Jern, Patrick and Sandnabba, N. Kenneth. (2009), "The adult body: How age, gender, and body mass index are related to body image," *Journal of Aging and Health*, 21 (8): 1112–32.

Almond, Kevin (2013), "Fashionably voluptuous: Repackaging the fuller-sized figure," *Fashion Theory*, 17 (2): 197–222.

Anderson, Chris (2012), *Makers: The New Industrial Revolution*, New York: Crown.

Andrew, Jill and Fairclough, Aisha (2015), "Plus-size fashion blogging for a 'size' of our Own," in C. Smallwood (ed.), *Women, Work, and the Web: How the Web Creates Entrepreneurial Opportunities*, 89–98, Lanham, MD: Rowman & Littlefield.

Apeagyei, Phoebe R. (2008), "Significance of body image among UK female fashion consumers: The cult of size zero, the skinny trend," *International Journal of Fashion Design*, 1 (1): 3–11.

Argyle, Michael (1975), "The syntaxes of body communication," in J. Benthall and T. Polhemus (eds.), *The Body as a Medium of Expression*, 143–61, London: Allen Lane.

Arnold, Rebecca (2001), *Fashion, Desire and Anxiety: Image and Morality in the 20th Century*, New Brunswick, NJ: Rutgers University Press.

Ashdown, Susan (2014), "Creation of ready-made clothing: The development and future of sizing systems," in M.-E. Faust and S. Carrier (eds.), *Designing Apparel for Consumers: The Impact of Body Shape and Size*, 17–34, Cambridge: Woodhead.

Austin, John L. (1962), *How to Do Things with Words*, Oxford: Oxford University Press.

Banner, Lois (1983), *American Beauty*, Chicago: University of Chicago Press.

Barnard, Malcolm (1996), *Fashion as Communication*, London: Routledge.

Barnard, Malcolm (2007), "Fashion statements: Communication and culture," in M. Barnard (ed.), *Fashion Theory: A Reader*, 170–81, London: Routledge.

Barnes, Barry (2001), "Practice as collective action," in T. Schatzki, K. Knorr Cetina and E. von Savigny (eds.), *The Practice Turn in Contemporary Theory*, 17–28, London and New York: Routledge.

Barthes, Roland ([1957] 2013), "History and sociology of clothing: Some methodological observations," in *The Language of Fashion*, 3–19, London: Bloomsbury [original edition: "Histoire et sociologie du vêtement," *Les Annales*, n. 3: 430–41].

Barthes, Roland ([1960] 1993), "'Le bleu est à la mode cette année'. Note sur la recherche des unités signifiantes dans le vêtement de mode," *Revue française de sociologie*, 1 (2): 147–62. Reprinted in *Œuvres Complètes*, I, 1023–38, Paris: Editions du seuil 1993.

Barthes, Roland ([1967] 1983), *The Fashion System*, Berkeley, CA and Los Angeles: University of California Press [original edition: *Système de la Mode*, Paris: Éditions du Seuil].

Bartky, Sandra (1988), "Foucault, femininity, and the modernization of patriarchal power," in R. Weitz (ed.), *The Politics of Women's Bodies: Sexuality, Appearance, and Behavior*, 93–111, New York: Oxford University Press.

Bauman, Zygmunt (1998), "On glocalization: Or globalization for some, localization for some others," *Thesis Eleven*, 54: 37–49.

BBC (2000), "Models link to teenage anorexia," *BBC News*, May 30. Available online: https://bbc.in/2WgBtZ9 (accessed March 23, 2019).

Becker, Anne (1995), *Body, Self, and Society: The View from Fiji*, Philadelphia: University of Pennsylvania Press.

Becker, Howard (1982), *Art Worlds*, Berkeley: University of California Press.

Bellafante, Ginia (2010), "Plus-Size Wars," *The New York Times Magazine*, July 28. Available online: https://nyti.ms/2ZrfN1B (accessed August 25, 2019).

Bentley, Mary K. (1999), "The body of evidence: Dangerous intersections between development and culture in the lives of adolescent girls," in S.R. Mazzarella and N.O. Pecora (eds.), *Growing Up Girls: Popular Culture and the Construction of Identity*, 209–23, New York: Peter Lang.

Bertola, Paola (2014), "La ricerca progettuale oltre la frontiera della taglia," in M. Canina and P. Volonté (eds.), *Overfashion: Nuove prospettive per la moda nella società che ingrassa*, 117–32, Milano: FrancoAngeli.

Bethke, Svenja and Keigel, Nathalie (2019), "Fashion and history: There is no doubt that clothes matter," *International Journal of Fashion Studies*, 6 (2): 183–91.

Bhuiyan, Johana (2017), "Nadia Boujarwah, CEO of Dia&Co: Plus-size shoppers were first movers on buying clothing online," *Vox*, September 13. Available online: https://bit.ly/2p4qx60 (accessed November 7, 2019).

Bijker, Wiebe E. (1995), *Of Bicycles, Bakelites, and Bulbs*, Cambridge, MA: The MIT Press.

Bijker, Wiebe E., Hughes, Thomas P. and Pinch, Trevor eds. (1987), *The Social Construction of Technological Systems: New Directions in the Sociology and History of Technology*, Cambridge, MA: The MIT Press.

Bishop, Katelynn, Gruys, Kjerstin and Evans, Maddie (2018), "Sized out: Women, clothing size, and inequality," *Gender & Society*, 32 (2): 180–203.

Black, Sandy, de la Haye, Amy, Entwistle, Joanne, Rocamora, Agnès, Root, Regina A. and Thomas, Helen eds. (2013), *The Handbook of Fashion Studies*, London: Bloomsbury.

Board of Trade (1957), *Women's Measurements and Sizes: A Study Sponsored by the Joint Clothing Council Limited*, London: Her Majesty's Stationery Office.

Bogusławską-Bączek, Monika (2010), "Analysis of the contemporary problem of garment sizes," 7th International Conference on Textile Science (TEXSCI 2010), Liberec, Czech Republic.

Boorady, Lynn M. (2014), "Overweight and obese consumers: Shape and sizing to design apparel that fits this specific market," in M.E. Faust and S. Carrier (eds.), *Designing Apparel for Consumers: The Impact of Body Shape and Size*, 153–68, Cambridge: Woodhead.

Bordo, Susan (1993), *Unbearable Weight: Feminism, Western Culture, and the Body*, Berkeley: University of California Press.

Bordo, Susan (2003), "In the empire of images: Preface to the tenth anniversary edition," in S. Bordo, *Unbearable Weight: Feminism, Western Culture, and the Body*, xiii–xxxvi, Berkeley: University of California Press.

Borland, Helen and Akram, Selina (2007), "Age is no barrier to wanting to look good: Women on body image, age and advertising," *Qualitative Market Research*, 10 (3): 310–33.

Bougourd, Jennifer (2007), "Sizing systems, fit models and target markets," in S.P. Ashdown (ed.), *Sizing in Clothing: Developing Effective Sizing Systems for Ready-to-Wear Clothing*, 108–51, Cambridge: Woodhead.

Bourdieu, Pierre ([1979] 1984), *Distinction: A Social Critique of the Judgment of Taste*, Cambridge, MA: Harvard University Press [original edition: *La distinction: critique sociale du jugement*, Paris: Les éditions de minuit].

Bourdieu, Pierre ([1980] 1990), *The Logic of Practice*, Cambridge, UK: Polity Press [original edition: *Le sens pratique*, Paris: Les éditions de minuit].

Bourdieu, Pierre (1993), *The Field of Cultural Production: Essays on Art and Literature*, Cambridge, UK: Polity Press.

Bourdieu, Pierre ([1997] 2000), *Pascalian Meditations*, Stanford, CA: Stanford University Press [original edition: *Méditations pascaliennes*, Paris: Éditions du Seuil].

Bourdieu, Pierre and Delsaut, Yvette (1975), "Le couturier et sa griffe: contribution à une théorie de la magie," *Actes de la recherché en sciences sociales*, 1: 7–36.

Bourne, Debra, Franklin, Caryn, O'Connor, Erin and Ringwood, Susan (2011), *All Walks beyond the Catwalk*, London: All Walks beyond the Catwalk.

Boselli, Mario (2012), "Fashion and anorexia," in A. Michelini (ed.), *Food Nutrition Agriculture: The Challenges of the New Millenium*, 169–73, Roma: 'L'Erma' di Bretschneider.

Brady, Martha (2005), *Letting Girls Play: Using Sport to Create Safe Spaces and Build Social Assets*, New York: Population Council.

Brantley, Aquiashala Shavon, Jackson, Vanessa and Lee, M.-Y. (2012), "A quantitative study of females: Ethnicity and its influence on body image, thin-internalization, and social comparison," in K. A. Miller-Spillman, A. Reilly and P. Hunt-Hurst (eds.), *The Meanings of Dress*, 164–70, New York and London: Fairchild Books.

Brar, Falth (2019), "Victoria's Secret added a slightly more size-inclusive Angel to their roster," Shape, March. Available online: http://bit.ly/2KlQ4iT (accessed August 7, 2019).

Breward, Christopher (2004), *Fashioning London: Clothing and the Modern*, Metropolis, Oxford: Berg.

Bruch, Hilde (1974), *Eating Disorders: Obesity, Anorexia Nervosa, and the Person Within*, New York: Basic Books.

Brumberg, Joan Jacobs (1997), *The Body Project: An Intimate History of American Girls*, New York: Random House.

Buote, Vanessa M., Wilson, Anne E., Strahan, Erin J., Gazzola, Stephanie B. and Papps, Fiona (2011), "Setting the bar: Divergent sociocultural norms for women's and men's ideal appearance in real-world contexts," *Body Image*, 8 (4): 322–34.

Buss, David M. (1989), "Sex differences in human mate preferences: Evolutionary hypotheses tested in 37 cultures," *Behavioral and Brain Sciences*, 12 (1): 1–14.

Butler, Judith (1990), *Gender Trouble: Feminism and the Subversion of Identity*, New York: Routledge.

Butler, Judith (2004), *Undoing Gender*, New York: Routledge.

Bye, Elizabeth and McKinney, Ellen (2007), "Sizing up the wardrobe – Why we keep clothes that do not fit," *Fashion Theory*, 11 (4): 483–98.

Byrnes, Callie (2018), "Why are models tall?," *The Hub*, September 14. Available online: http://bit.ly/2TZUgrx (accessed August 24, 2019).

Calefato, Patrizia (1986), *Il corpo rivestito*, Bari: Edizioni dal sud.

Calefato, Patrizia and Breward, Christopher (2018), "Reflections on Three Decades of Studies in Fashion Theory," *International Journal of Fashion Studies*, 5 (1): 247–53.

Campbell, Colin ([1997] 2007), "When the meaning is not a message: A critique of the consumption as communication thesis," in M. Barnard (ed.), *Fashion Theory: A Reader*, 159–69, London: Routledge [original edition: M. Nava et al. (eds.), *Buy This Book: Studies in Advertising and Consumption*, 340–51, London: Routledge].

Cash, Thomas F. (1990), "The psychology of physical appearance: Aesthetics, attributes, and images," in T. F. Cash and T. Pruzinsky (eds.), *Body Images: Development, Deviance and Change*, 51–79, New York: Guilford Press.

Cash, Thomas F. and Pruzinsky, T. eds. (1990), *Body Images: Development, Deviance and Change*, New York: Guilford Press.

Cassidy, Claire M. (1991), "The good body: When big is better," *Medical Anthropology*, 13 (3): 181–213.

Cavallaro, Dani and Warwick, Alexandra (1998), *Fashioning the Frame: Boundaries, Dress and the Body*, Oxford and New York: Berg.

Cheang, Sarah and Kramer, Elizabeth (2017), "Fashion and East Asia: Cultural translations and East Asian perspectives," *International Journal of Fashion Studies*, 4 (2): 145–55.

Chernin, Kim (1981), *The Obsession: Reflections on The Tyranny of Slenderness*, New York: Harper and Row.

Chowdhary, Usha and Beale, Nadine V. (1988), "Plus-size women's clothing interest, satisfactions and dissatisfactions with ready-to-wear apparel," *Perceptual and Motor Skills*, 66: 783–88.

Christel, Deborah (2014), "It's your fault you're fat: Judgements of responsibility and social conduct in the fashion industry," Clothing Cultures, 3 (1): 303–20.

Christel, Deborah A. (2016), "The efficacy of problem-based learning of plus-size design in the fashion curriculum," *International Journal of Fashion Design, Technology and Education*, 9 (1): 1–8.

Christel, Deborah A. and Dunn, Susan C. (2017), "Average American women's clothing size: Comparing National Health and Nutritional Examination Surveys (1988–2010) to ASTM international misses and women's plus size clothing," *International Journal of Fashion Design, Technology and Education*, 10 (2): 129–36.

Christel, Deborah and O'Donnell, Nicole (2016), "Assessment of plus-size women's swimwear for industry applications," *Fashion Practice*, 8 (2): 257–78.

Civile, Ciro and Obhi, Sukhvinder (2017), "Students wearing police uniforms exhibit biased attention towards individuals wearing hoodies," *Frontiers in Psychology*, 8: 62.

Clark, Kenneth (1980), *Feminine Beauty*, New York: Rizzoli International.

Clements, Kirstie (2014), *The Vogue Factor: The Inside Story of Fashion's Most Illustrious Magazine*, San Francisco, CA: Chronicle Books.

ClicknDress (2016), "Tailles de vetements et tailles des françaises: une offre adaptée à la réalité?," *ClicknDress* website. Available online: http://bit.ly/2RCA4eb (accessed June 24, 2019).

Cogan, Jeanine C. (1999), "Re-evaluating the wight-centered approach toward health: The need for a paradigm shift," in J. Sobal and D. Maurer (eds.), *Interpreting Weight: The Social Management of Fatness and Thinness*, 229–53, New York: Aldine de Gruyter.

Colls, Rachel (2004), "'Looking alright, feeling alright': Emotion, sizing, and the geographies of women's experiences of clothing consumption," *Social and Cultural Geography*, 5 (4): 583–96.

Colls, Rachel (2006), "Outsize/outside: Bodily bignesses and the emotional experiences of British women shopping for clothes," *Gender, Place & Culture*, 13 (5): 529–45.

Conley, Dalton and Glauber, Rebecca (2007), "Gender, body mass, and economic status: New evidence from the PSID," *Advances in Health Economics and Health Services Research*, 17: 253–75.

Connell, Catherine (2013), "Fashionable resistance: Queer 'fa(t)shion' blogging as counterdiscourse," *WSQ: Women's Studies Quarterly*, 41 (1–2): 209–24.

Connolly, Kate (2009), "Karl Lagerfeld says only 'fat mummies' object to thin models," *The Guardian*, October 12. Available online: http://bit.ly/31z8CSn (accessed August 12, 2019).

Conti, Giovanni (2014), "L'esclusione del plus-size dall'immaginario del made in Italy," in M. Canina and P. Volonté (eds.), *Overfashion: Nuove prospettive per la moda nella società che ingrassa*, 85–96, Milano: FrancoAngeli.

Corrigan, Peter (1997), *The Sociology of Consumption: An Introduction*, London: Sage.

Cox, J. (1993), "The Functions of Clothing and Clothing Deprivation: A Gender Analysis among Students," BA (Hons) thesis, University of Sussex.

Craik, Jennifer (1993), *The Face of Fashion: Cultural Studies in Fashion*, London: Routledge.

Craik, Jennifer (2005), *Uniforms Exposed: From Conformity to Transgression*, Oxford: Berg.

Craik, Jennifer (2009), *Fashion: The Key Concepts*, Oxford: Berg.

Czerniawski, Amanda M. (2012), "Disciplining corpulence: The case of plus-size fashion models," *Journal of Contemporary Ethnography*, 41 (2): 127–153.

Czerniawski, Amanda M. (2015), *Fashioning Fat: Inside Plus-Size Modeling*, New York and London: New York University Press.

Damhorst, Mary Lynn (1990), "In search of a common thread: Classification of information communicated through dress," *Clothing and Textiles Research Journal*, 8 (2): 1–12.

Dant, Tim (1999), *Material Culture in the Social World: Values, Activities, Lifestyles*, Buckingham and PA: Open University Press.

Davis, Fred (1985), "Clothing and fashion as communication," in M.R. Solomon (ed.), *The Psychology of Fashion*, 15–27, Lexington, MA: Lexington Books.

Davis, Fred (1992), *Fashion, Culture and Identity*, Chicago, IL: The University of Chicago Press.

Davis, Leslie L. (1985), "Perceived somatotype, body-cathexis, and attitudes toward clothing among college females," *Perceptual and Motor Skills*, 61: 1199–205.

de Beauvoir, Simone ([1949] 1997), *The Second Sex*, London: Vintage [original edition: *Le deuxième sexe*, Paris: Gallimard].

Degher, Douglas and Hughes, Gerald (1999), "The adoption and management of a 'fat' identity," in J. Sobal and D. Maurer (eds.), *Interpreting Weight: The Social Management of Fatness and Thinness*, 11–27, New York: Aldine de Gruyter.

Deleuze, Gilles and Foucault, Michel (1977), "Intellectuals and power," in M. Foucault, *Language, Counter-Memory, and Practice: Selected Essays and Interviews*, 205–17, Ithaca, NY: Cornell University Press.

Denizet-Lewis, Benoit (2006), "The man behind Abercrombie & Fitch," *Salon*, January 24. Available online: https://bit.ly/32zO78s (accessed November 8, 2019).

de Perthuis, Karen (2008), "Beyond perfection: The fashion model in the age of digital manipulation," in E. Shinkle (ed.), *Fashion as Photograph: Viewing and Reviewing Images of Fashion*, 168–81, London: I.B. Tauris.

de Perthuis, Karen (2016), "People in fashionable clothes: Street style blogs and the ontology of the fashion photograph," *Fashion Theory*, 20 (5): 523–43.

Derry, Catherine (2004), "'I'll never find a dress': Shopping for the prom" in S. Weber and C. Mitchell (eds.), *Not Just Any Dress: Narratives of Memory, Body and Identity*, 45–55, New York: Peter Lang.

DOB-Verband (1994), *DOB Size Charts Germany 1994: Body Dimension Charts, Market Share Charts and Garment Construction Dimensions for Ladies' Outerwear*, Köln: DOBVerband.

Eco, Umberto (1973), "Social life as sign system," in D. Robey (ed.), *Structuralism: An Introduction. Wolfson College Lectures 1972*, 57–72, Oxford: Oxford University Press.

Eco, Umberto (1975), *Trattato di semiotica generale*, Milano: Bompiani.

Eco, Umberto (1979), *The Role of the Reader: Explorations in the Semiotics of Texts*, Bloomington: Indiana University Press.

Eco, Umberto ([1998] 2007), "Lumbar thought," reprinted in M. Barnard (ed.), *Fashion Theory: A Reader*, 315–17, London: Routledge, 2007.

Eim (1979), *Le misure antropometriche della popolazione adulta italiana: l'abbigliamento delle classi giovani dai 6 ai 19 anni*, Milano: FrancoAngeli.

Eisenstadt, Shmuel N. (2000), *Multiple Modernities*, Milton Park: Taylor and Francis.

Emberly, Julia (1987), "The fashion apparatus and the deconstruction of postmodern subjectivity," *Canadian Journal of Political and Social Theory*, 11 (1–2): 38–50.

Enninger, W. (1985), "The design features of clothing codes: The functions of clothing displays in interaction," *Kodikas/Code*, 8 (1–2): 81–110.

Entwistle, Joanne ([2000] 2015), *The Fashioned Body: Fashion, Dress and Modern Social Theory*, 2nd ed., Cambridge, UK: Polity Press.

Entwistle, Joanne (2001), "The dressed body," in J. Entwistle and E. Wilson (eds.), *Body Dressing*, 33–58, Oxford: Berg.

Entwistle, Joanne (2009), *The Aesthetic Economy of Fashion: Markets and Value in Clothing and Modelling*, Oxford: Berg.

Entwistle, Joanne and Slater, Don (2012), "Models as brands: Critical thinking about bodies and images," in J. Entwistle and E. Wissinger (eds.), *Fashioning Models: Image, Text and Industry*, 15–33, London and New York: Berg.

Entwistle, Joanne and Wissinger, Elizabeth, eds. (2012a), *Fashioning Models: Image, Text and Industry*, London and New York: Berg.

Entwistle, Joanne and Wissinger, Elizabeth (2012b), "Introduction," in J. Entwistle and E. Wissinger (eds.), *Fashioning Models: Image, Text and Industry*, 1–14, London and New York: Berg.

Fallon, April (1990), "Culture in the mirror: Sociocultural determinants of body image," in T. F. Cash and T. Pruzinsky (eds.), *Body Images: Development, Deviance and Change*, 80–109, New York: Guilford Press.

Featherstone, Mike (1991), "The body in consumer culture," in M. Featherstone, M. Hepworth and B. Turner (eds.), *The Body: Social Process and Cultural Theory*, 170–97, London: Sage.

Findlay, Rosie (2017), *Personal Style Blogs: Appearances that Fascinate*, Bristol and Chicago, IL: Intellect.

Finkelstein, Joanne (1991), *The Fashioned Self*, Cambridge, UK: Polity Press.

Flegal, Katherine M., Carroll, Margaret D., Ogden, Cynthia L. and Curtin, Lester R. (2010), "Prevalence and trends in obesity among US adults, 1999–2008," *Journal of the American Medical Association*, 303 (3): 235–41.

Flichy, Patrice ([1995] 2007), *Understanding Technological Innovation: A Socio-Technical Approach*, Northampton, MA: Edward Elgar [original edition: *L'innovation technique*, Paris: Éditions La Découverte].

Flügel, John Carl (1930), *The Psychology of Clothes*, London: The Hogarth Press.

Ford, Clellan S. and Beach, Frank A. ([1952] 1970), *Patterns of Sexual Behaviour*, London: Methuen.

Foucault, Michel ([1969] 2002), *The Archaeology of Knowledge*, London: Routledge [original edition: *L'archéologie du savoir*, Paris: Gallimard].

Foucault, Michel (1971), *L'ordre du discours*, Paris: Gallimard.

Foucault, Michel ([1975] 1995), *Discipline and Punish: The Birth of the Prison*, New York: Vintage Books [original edition: *Surveiller et punir: Naissance de la prison*, Paris: Gallimard].

Foucault, Michel ([1975] 1980), "Body/power," in *Power/Knowledge: Selected Interviews and Other Writings 1972–1977*, 55–62, New York: Pantheon Books [original edition: "Pouvoir et Corps," *Quel Corps?*, September/October].

Foucault, Michel ([1977] 1980), "The confession of the flesh," in *Power/Knowledge: Selected Interviews and Other Writings 1972–1977*, 194–228, New York: Pantheon Books [original edition: "Le jeu de Michel Foucault," *Ornicar?*, July 10].

Franck, Georg (2007), *Ökonomie der Aufmerksamkeit. Ein Entwurf*, München: Hanser.

Fredrickson, Barbara and Roberts, Tomi-Ann (1997), "Objectification theory: Toward understanding women's lived experiences and mental health risks," *Psychology of Women Quarterly*, 21: 173–206.

Friedman, Vanessa (2018), "Modeling in the #TimesUp era," *The New York Times*, September 6. Available online: https://nyti.ms/2zkKnLO (accessed August 24, 2019).

Gaddi, Rossana (2014), "Strategie comunicative della moda per le taglie forti," in M. Canina and P. Volonté (eds.), *Overfashion: Nuove prospettive per la moda nella società che ingrassa*, 97–113, Milano: FrancoAngeli.

Gagnard, A. (1986), "From feast to famine: Depiction of ideal body type in magazine advertising, 1950–1984," *Proceedings of the American Academy of Advertising, USA*, 41: 451–9.

Garner, David M., Garfinkel, Paul E., Schwartz, Donald and Thompson, Michael (1980), "Cultural expectations of thinness in women," *Psychological Reports*, 47: 483–91.

Gell, Alfred (1998), *Art and Agency: An Anthropological Theory*, Oxford: Clarendon Press.

Gilbert, David (2000), "Urban outfitting: The city and the spaces of fashion culture," in S. Bruzzi and P. Church Gibson (eds.), *Fashion Cultures: Theories, Explorations and Analysis*, 7–24, London: Routledge.

Gilman, Sander L. (2011), "Introduzione all'edizione italiana," in *La strana storia dell'obesità*, 7–26, Bologna: il Mulino.

Gimlin, Debra L. (2002), *Body Work: Beauty and Self-Image in American Culture*, Berkeley and Los Angeles: University of California Press.

Gimlin, Debra L. (2007), "What is body work? A review of the literature," *Sociology Compass*, 1 (1): 353–70.

Giovanelli, Dina, and Ostertag, Stephen (2009), "Controlling the body: Meda representations, body size, and self-discipline," in E. Rothblum and S. Solvay (eds.), *The Fat Studies Reader*, 289–96, New York and London: New York University Press.

Godart, Frédéric and Mears, Ashley (2009), "How do cultural producers make creative decisions? Lessons from the catwalk," *Social Forces*, 88 (2): 671–92.

Godley, Andrew (1997), "The development of the clothing industry: Technology and fashion," *Textile History*, 28 (1): 3–10.

Goffman, Erving (1959), *The Presentation of Self in Everyday Life*, Garden City, NY: Doubleday.

Goffman, Erving (1961), *Encounters: Two Studies in the Sociology of Interaction*, Indianapolis, IN: Bobbs-Merrill.

Goffman, Erving (1963), *Behavior in Public Places: Notes on the Social Organization of Gatherings*, Glecoe: Free Press.

Goffman, Erving (1974), *Frame Analysis: An Essay on the Organization of Experience*, Cambridge, MA: Harvard University Press.

Goffman, Erving (1983), "The interaction order: American Sociological Association, 1982 presidential address," *American Sociological Review*, 48 (1): 1–17.

Goldblatt, Phillip B., Moore, Mary E. and Stunkard, Albert J. (1965), "Social factors in obesity," *JAMA: The Journal of the American Medical Association*, 192 (12): 1039–44.

González, Ana Marta and Bovone, Laura eds. (2007), *Fashion and Identity: A Multidisciplinary Approach*, New York and Barcelona: Social Trends Institute.

Goodman, W. Charisse (1995), *The Invisible Woman: Confronting Weight Prejudice in America*, Los Angeles: Gürze.

Gordon, Richard A. (1990), *Anorexia and Bulimia: Anatomy of a Social Epidemic*, London: Blackwell.

Gramsci, Antonio ([1948–1951] 2011), *Prison Notebooks*, New York: Columbia University Press [original edition: *Quaderni del carcere*, Torino: Einaudi].

Grana, Cosetta and Bellinello, Angela (2004), *Modellistica integrata e fondamenti di confezione*, Trescore Balneario: San Marco.

Greenleaf, Christy, Hauff, Caitlyn, Klos, Lori and Serafin, Gabriel (2020), "'Fat people exercise too!': Perceptions and realities of shopping for women's plu-size exercise apparel," *Clothing and Textiles Research Journal*, 38 (2): 75–89.

Grice, Paul (1989), *Studies in the Way of Words*, Cambridge, MA: Harvard University Press.

Gruys, Kjerstin (2012), "Does this make me look fat? Aesthetic labor and fat talk as emotional labor in a women's plus-size clothing store," *Social Problems*, 59 (4): 481–500.

Gruys, Kjerstin (2019), "'Making over' poor women: Gender, race, class, & body size in a welfare-to-work nonprofit organization," *Sociological Forum*, 34 (1): 47–70.

Gunn, Tim (2016), "Designers refuse to make clothes to fit American women," *The Washington Post*, September 8. Available online: https://wapo.st/37IwdUF (accessed November 25, 2019).

Hackett, Lisa J. and Rall, Denise N. (2018), "The size of the problem with the problem of sizing: How clothing measurement systems have misrepresented women's bodies, from the 1920s to today," *Clothing Cultures*, 5 (2): 263–83.

Hall, Stuart (1992), "Encoding/decoding," in S. Hall, D. Hobson, A. Lowe and P. Willis (eds.), *Culture, Media, Language: Working Papers in Cultural Studies, 1972–79*, 128–38, London: Routledge.

Hall, Stuart (2013), "The work of representation," in S. Hall, J. Evans and S. Nixon (eds.), *Representation*, 1–47, Los Angeles: SAGE.

Haller, Melanie (2015), "Mode Macht Körper – Wie sich Mode-Körper-Hybride materialisieren," *Body Politics*, 3 (6): 187–211.

Haller, Melanie (2018), "Plus-Size-Blogs als Diversität von Mode? Zu Praktiken visueller Repräsentationen von Körpern und der Infragestellung weiblicher Normkörper in der Mode," in E. Grittmann, K. Lobinger, I. Neverla and M. Pater (eds.), *Körperbilder – Körperpraktiken. Visuelle Repräsentationen, Regulationen und Aneignungen vergeschlechtlichter Körper und Identitäten in Medienkulturen*, 245–60, Köln: Halem.

Hannerz, Ulf (1992), *Cultural Complexity*, New York: Columbia University Press.

Hansen, Karen Tranberg (2004), "The world in dress: Anthropological perspectives on clothing, fashion, and culture," *Annual Review of Anthropology*, 33: 369–92.

Harju, Anu A. and Huovinen, Annamari (2015), "Fashionably voluptuous: Normative femininity and resistant performative tactics in fatshion blogs," *Journal of Marketing Management*, 31 (15–16): 1602–25.

Haswell, Natasha Sian (2010), "Analysis and Conceptualization of Plus Size Fashion Online Shopping Motivations," PhD Thesis, The University of Manchester, Manchester.

Hebdige, Dick (1979), *Subculture: The Meaning of Style*, London: Methuen.

Hebl, Michelle R., King, Eden B. and Lin, Jean (2004), "The swimsuit becomes us all: Ethnicity, gender and vulnerability to self-objectification," *Personality and Social Psychology Bulletin*, 30 (10): 1322–31.

Hebl, Michelle R., King, Eden B. and Perkins, Andrew (2009), "Ethnic differences in the stigma of obesity: Identification and engagement with a thin ideal," *Journal of Experimental Social Psychology*, 45 (6): 1165–72.

Heckel, Francis (1911), *Les grandes et petites obésités. Cure radicale*, Paris: Masson et C^{le}.

Hegel, Georg Wilhelm Friedrich (1970), *Vorlesungen über die Ästhetik II*, Frankfurt a.M.: Suhrkamp (Werke 14).

Hesse-Biber, Sharlene (1996), *Am I Thin Enough Yet?: The Cult of Thinness and the Commercialization of Identity*, Oxford: Oxford University Press.

Hesse-Biber, Sharlene (2007), *The Cult of Thinness*, New York: Oxford University Press.

Hesselbein, Chris (2019), "Walking the catwalk: From dressed body to dressed embodiment," *Fashion Theory*: 1–27.

Hewitt, Hugh (2006), *Blog: Understanding the Information Reformation That's Changing Your World*, Nashville, TN: Thomas Nelson.

Hillestad, R. (1980), "The underlying structure of appearance," *Dress*, 5: 117–25.

Hochschield, Arlie Russell (1983), *The Managed Heart: Commercialization of Human Feeling*, Berkeley: University of California Press.

Hollander, Anne ([1975] 1993), *Seeing through Clothes*, Berkeley: University of California Press.

Hollander, Anne (1994), *Sex and Suits*, New York: Knopf.

Hollander, Anne (1999), *Feeding the Eye: Essays*, Berkeley: University of California Press.

Holliday, Ruth ([1999] 2007), "The comfort of identity," in M. Barnard (ed.), *Fashion Theory: A Reader*, 318–32, London: Routledge [original edition: *Sexualities*, 2 (4): 475–91].

Holliday, Ruth (2001), "Fashioning the queer self," in J. Entwistle and E. Wilson (eds.), *Body Dressing*, 215–31, Oxford: Berg.

Holverson, Dorothy A. (1952), "Clothing preferences of stout women," *Journal of Home Economics*, 44: 774–5.

Hui, Allison, Schatzki, Theodore and Shove, Elizabeth eds. (2017), *The Nexus of Practices: Connections, Constellations, Practitioners*, London and New York: Routledge.

Iannello, A. (2006), "Le signore sopra la 46 sono il 58% della popolazione," MF *fashion*, February 14. Available online: https://goo.gl/22JAHN (accessed October 12, 2017).

Inbar, Michael (2010), "Plus-size models buck thin trend in V magazine," *Today*, January 8. Available online: https://on.today.com/34h5L1v (accessed December 12, 2019).

Jakobson, Roman ([1968] 1971), "Language in relation to other communication systems," in *Languages in Society and in Technique*, Milano: Olivetti. Reprinted in *Selected Writings*, vol. 2, *Word and Language*, 697–708, The Hague, Mouton.

Jasanoff, Sheila (2004), "Ordering knowledge, ordering society," in S. Jasanoff (ed.), *States of Knowledge: The Co-production of Science and Social Order*, 13–45, London: Routledge.

Jeacle, Ingrid (2003), "Accounting and the construction of the standard body," *Accounting, Organizations and Society*, 28 (1): 357–77.

Jestratijevic, Iva, Rudd, Nancy A. and Ilic. Sanja (2020), "A body to die for: Body measurements and BMI values among female and male runway models," *Clothing and Textiles Research Journal*, OnlineFirst: 1–17.

Joanisse, Leanne and Synnott, Anthony (1999), "Fighting back: Reactions and resistance to the stigma of obesity," in J. Sobal and D. Maurer (eds.), *Interpreting Weight: The Social Management of Fatness and Thinness*, 49–70, New York: Aldine de Gruyter.

Kaiser, Susan B. (1997), *The Social Psychology of Clothing: Symbolic Appearances in Context*, 2nd edn revised, New York: Fairchild.

Kaiser, Susan B. (2012), *Fashion and Cultural Studies*, London: Berg.

Karazsia, Bryan T., Murnen, Sarah K., and Tylka, Tracy L. (2017), "Is body dissatisfaction changing across time? A cross-temporal meta-analysis," *Psychological Bulletin*, 143 (3): 293–320.

Kawamura, Yuniya (2005), *Fashion-ology: An Introduction to Fashion Studies*, Oxford: Berg.

Keist, Carmen N. (2017), "'Stout women can now be stylish': Stout women's fashions, 1910–1919," *Dress*, 43 (2): 99–117.

Keist, Carmen N. (2018), "How stout women were left out of high fashion: An early twentieth-century perspective," *Fashion, Style and Popular Culture*, 5 (1): 25–40.

Keist, Carmen N. and Marcketti, Sara B. (2013), "'The new costumes of odd sizes': Plus-sized women's fashions, 1920–1929," *Clothing and Textiles Research Journal*, 31 (4): 259–74.

Khaled, Salma M., Shockley, Bethany, Qutteina, Yara, Kimmel, Linda and Le, Kien T. (2018), "Testing Western media icons influence on Arab women's body size and shape ideals: An experimental approach," *Social Sciences*, 7 (9): 142.

Kidwell, Claudia B. and Christman, Marget C. (1974), *Suiting Everyone: The Democratization of Clothing in America*, Washington, DC: Smithsonian Institution Press.

Klepp, Ingun Grimstad (2011), "Slimming lines," *Fashion Theory*, 15 (4): 451–80.

Klepp, Ingun Grimstad and Storm-Mathisen, Ardis (2005), "Reading fashion as age: Teenage girls' and grown women's accounts of clothing as body and social status," *Fashion Theory*, 9 (3): 323–42.

Koda, Harold and Yohannan, Kohle (2009), *The Model as Muse: Embodying Fashion*, New York: Yale University Press.

Kraus, Michael W. and Mendes, Wendy Berry (2014), "Sartorial symbols of social class elicit class-consistent behavioral and physiological responses: A dyadic approach," *Journal of Experimental Psychology: General*, 143 (6), n. 2330: 1–42.

LaBat, Karen L. (2007), "Sizing standardization," in S.P. Ashdown (ed.), *Sizing in Clothing: Developing Effective Sizing Systems for Ready-to-Wear Clothing*, 88–107, Cambridge: Woodhead.

Lamare, Amy (2018), "The $20-billion plus-size fashion market is a missed opportunity," *Thinknum Alternative Data*, May 29. Available online: https://bit.ly /3jOCd3K (accessed September 27, 2020).

Latour, Bruno (1992), "Where are the missing masses? The sociology of a few mundane artifacts," in W. E. Bijker and J. Law (eds.), *Shaping Technology/Building Society: Studies in Sociotechnical Change*, 225–58, Cambridge, MA: The MIT Press.

Latour, Bruno (2005), *Reassembling the Social: An Introduction to Actor-Network-Theory*, Oxford and New York: Oxford University Press.

Lee, Jungtaek (2017), "The birth of modern fashion in Korea: Sartorial transition between *hanbok* and *yangbok* through production, mediation and consumption," *International Journal of Fashion Studies*, 4 (2): 183–209.

Lee, Y.-S. (2014), "Developing apparel sizing systems for particular groups," in D. Gupta and N. Zakaria (eds.), *Anthropometry, Apparel Sizing and Design*, 197–254, Cambridge: Woodhead.

Lemoine-Luccioni, Eugénie (1983), *La robe. Essai psychanalytique sur le vêtement*, Paris: Éditions du Seuil.

Leopold, Ellen (1992), "The manufacture of the fashion system," in J. Ash and E. Wilson (eds.), *Chic Thrills*, 101–17, Berkeley and Los Angeles: University of California Press.

Levinson, Stephen C. (1983), *Pragmatics*, Cambridge, UK: Cambridge University Press.

Lévi-Strauss, Claude ([1971] 1981), *The Naked Man*, Chicago: The University of Chicago Press [original edition: *Mythologique IV, L'homme nu*, Paris: Plon].

Lewis, David (1969), *Convention: A Philosophical Study*, Cambridge, MA: Harvard University Press.

Lewis, Van Dyk (2007), "Sizing and clothing aesthetics," in S. P. Ashdown (ed.), *Sizing in Clothing: Developing Effective Sizing Systems for Ready-to-Wear Clothing*, 309–27, Cambridge: Woodhead.

LeBesco, Kathleen (2004), *Revolting Bodies? The Struggle to Redefine Fat Identity*, Amherst: Massachussetts University Press.

Lennon, Sharron J., Johnson, Kim K. P., Noh, Mijeong, Zheng, Zhiying, Chae, Yoori and Kim, Yumin (2014), "In search of a common thread revisited: What content does fashion communicate?," *International Journal of Fashion Design, Technology and Education*, 7 (3): 170–8.

Lipovetsky, Gilles ([1987] 1994), *The Empire of Fashion: Dressing Modern Democracy*, Princeton, NJ: Princeton University Press [original edition: *L'empire de l'éphémère. La mode et son destin dans les sociétés modernes*. Paris: Gallimard].

Lisberg Jensen, Ebba and Elahi, Babak (2017), "Conspicuous conservation: The green clothing of Swedish environmentalists," *International Journal of Fashion Studies*, 4 (1): 7–34.

Liu, Yung (2017), "Westernization and the consistent popularity of the Republican *qipao*," *International Journal of Fashion Studies*, 4 (2): 211–24.

Lomrantz, Tracey (2009), "10 easy ways to make swimsuit season less scary," *Glamour*, May 18. Available online: http://bit.ly/2KuZRmM (accessed August 12, 2019).

López-Pérez, Belén, Ambrona, Tamara, Wilson, Ellie and Khalil, Marina (2016), "The effect of enclothed cognition on empathic responses and helping behavior," *Social Psychology*, 47 (4): 223–31.

Lottersberger, Anna and Pradel, Patrick (2014), "Il processo produttivo nella moda plus-size," in M. Canina and P. Volonté (eds.), *Overfashion: Nuove prospettive per la moda nella società che ingrassa*, 97–113, Milano: FrancoAngeli.

Lubitz, Rachel (2017), "The untold story behind 'Mode' magazine, the 'Vogue' for plus-size women in the '90s," *mic.com*, October 10. Available online: https://bit.ly /2Coq9SL (accessed November 7, 2019).

Lurie, Alison (1981), *The Language of Clothes*, New York: Random House.

Lynge-Jorlén, Ane (2017), *Niche Fashion Magazines: Changing the Shape of Fashion*, London and New York: I.B. Tauris.

Mackinney-Valentin, Maria (2017), *Fashioning Identity: Status Ambivalence in Contemporary Fashion*, London: Bloomsbury.

Malcolm, L. W. G. (1925), "Note on the seclusion of girls among the Efik at Old Calabar," *Man*, 25 (8): 113–14.

Mason, Katherine (2012), "The unequal weight of discrimination: Gender, body size, and income inequality," *Social Problems*, 59 (3): 411–35.

Mathras, Daniele, Loveland, Katherine E. and Mandel, Naomi (2012), "Media image effects on the self," in R. Belk and A. Ruvio (eds.), *The Routledge Companion to Identity and Consumption*, 387–95, New York: Routledge.

Mauss, Marcel (1936), "Les techniques du corps," *Journal de psychologie* 32 (3–4): 271–93. [English: "Techniques of the body," *Economy and Society* 2: 1 (1973).]

Mazur, Allan (1986), "US trends in feminine beauty and overadaption," *Journal of Sex Research*, 22: 281–303.

McCracken, Grant (1990), *Culture and Consumption: New Approaches to the Symbolic Character of Consumer Goods and Activities*, Bloomington: Indiana University Press.

McReaddy, Y. (1988), "The forgotten woman: Large-size profits," *Women's Wear Daily*, January 2: 20.

Mead, George Herbert (1934), *Mind, Self and Society*, Chicago: The University of Chicago Press.

Mears, Ashley (2010), "Size zero high-end ethnic: Cultural production and the reproduction of culture in fashion modeling," *Poetics*, 38 (1): 21–46.

Mears, Ashley (2011), *Pricing Beauty: The Making of a Fashion Model*, Los Angeles: University of California Press.

Mennell, Stephen (1991), "On the civilizing of appetite," in M. Featherstone, M. Hepworth and B. Turner (eds.), *The Body: Social Process and Cultural Theory*, 126–56, London: Sage.

Miller, Daniel (1987), *Material Culture and Mass Consumption*, Oxford: Blackwell.

Millman, Marcia (1980), *Such a Pretty Face: Being Fat in America*, New York: W.W. Norton & Co.

Model Health Inquiry (2007), "Fashioning a healthy future: The report of the model health inquiry," September 2007. Available online: https://bit.ly/2BHd8mW (accessed October 26, 2019).

Moeran, Brian (2015), *The Magic of Fashion: Ritual, Commodity, Glamour*, London: Routledge.

Moi, Toril (2005), *Sex, Gender, and the Body*, Oxford: Oxford University Press.

Moore, Carolyn L., Mullet, Kathy K. and Young, Margaret Prevatt (2001), *Concepts of Pattern Grading: Techniques for Manual and Computer Grading*, New York: Fairchild.

Mora, Emanuela and Rocamora, Agnès (2015), "Letter from the editors: Analyzing fashion blogs – Further avenues for research," *Fashion Theory*, 19 (2): 149–56.

Morley, Janine (2017), "Technologies within and beyond practices," in A. Hui, T. Schatzki and E. Shove (eds.), *The Nexus of Practices: Connections, Constellations, Practitioners*, 81–97, London and New York: Routledge.

Morris, Abigail, Cooper, Troy and Cooper, Peter J. (1989), "The changing shape of female fashion models," *International Journal of Eating Disorders*, 8 (5): 593–6.

Myers, Philip N. and Biocca, Frank A. (1992), "The elastic body image," *Journal of Communication* 42 (3): 108–33.

Nicolini, Davide (2012), *Practice Theory, Work, and Organization: An Introduction*, Oxford: Oxford University Press.

Nicolini, Davide and Monteiro, Pedro (2016), "The practice approach in organizational and management studies," in A. Langley and H. Tsoukas (eds.), *The SAGE Handbook of Process Organization Studies*, 110–26, London: Sage.

O'Brien, Ruth and Shelton, William Chastain (1985), *Women's Measurements for Garment and Pattern Construction*, Washington, DC: US Department of Agriculture, Miscellaneous Publication 454.

Orbach, Susie ([1978] 2016), *Fat Is a Feminist Issue*, London: Arrow Books.

Otieno, Rose, Harrow, Chris and Lea-Greenwood, Gaynor (2005), "The unhappy shopper, a retail experience: Exploring fashion, fit and affordability," *International Journal of Retail and Distribution Management*, 33 (4): 298–309.

Paris, Ivan (2006), *Oggetti cuciti. L'abbigliamento pronto in Italia dal primo dopoguerra agli anni Settanta*. Milano: FrancoAngeli.

Park, Robert E., Burgess, Ernest W. and McKenzie, Roderick D. (1925), *The City*, Chicago, IL: The University of Chicago Press.

Parsons, Talcott (1951), *The Social System*, Glencoe: Free Press.

Paulicelli, Eugenia and Clark, Hazel, eds. (2009), *The Fabric of Cultures: Fashion, Identity, and Globalization*, London: Routledge.

Pedroni, Marco (2015), "'Stumbling on the heels of my blog': Career, forms of capital and strategies in the (sub)field of fashion blogging," *Fashion Theory*, 19 (2): 179–99.

Pedroni, Marco (2016), "Meso-celebrities, fashion and the media: How digital influencers struggle for visibility," *Film, Fashion & Consumption*, 5 (1): 103–21.

Pedroni, Marco and Pofi, Maria Paola (2018), "Commodifying the followers or challenging the mainstream? The two-sided potential of curvy fashion bloggers," *Observatorio*, 12 (spe1): 5–27.

Peters, Lauren Downing (2014), "You are what you wear: How plus-size fashion figures in fat-identity formation," *Fashion Theory*, 18 (1): 45–72.

Peters, Lauren Downing (2017), "Fashion plus: Pose and the plus-size body in *Vogue*, 1986–1988," *Fashion Theory*, 21 (2): 175–99.

Peters, Lauren Downing (2018a), "Stoutwear and the discourses of disorder: Constructing the fat, female body in American fashion in the age of standardization, 1915–1930," PhD Dissertation, Stockholm University.

Peters, Lauren Downing (2018b), "Reinserting the fat body into fashion history—A reading list," *AHTR*, November 30. Available online: http://arthistoryteachingresou rces.org/2018/11/reinserting-the-fat-body-into-fashion-history-a-reading-list (accessed July 6, 2019).

Peters, Lauren Downing (2018c), "When brands use plus-size models and don't make plus-size clothes: 'Size appropriation' gets brands the brownie points without doing the work," *Vox*, June 5. Available online: https://bit.ly/2Pk2lXF (accessed December 12, 2019).

Peters, Lauren Downing (2019a), "Flattering the figure, fitting in: The design discourses of stoutwear, 1915–1930," *Fashion Theory*, 23 (2): 167–94.

Peters, Lauren Downing (2019b) (Accepted for Publication), "A history of fashion without fashion: Recovering the stout body in the digital archive," *Critical Studies in Fashion and Beauty*.

Petrova, Adriana (2007), "Creating sizing systems," in S.P. Ashdown (ed.), *Sizing in Clothing: Developing Effective Sizing Systems for Ready-to-Wear Clothing*, 57–87, Cambridge: Woodhead.

Pham, Minh-Ha T. (2011), "Blog ambition: Fashion, feelings, and the political economy of the digital raced body," *Camera Obscura*, 26 (1): 1–36.

Pipia, Alexa (2015), "The push for plus: How a small part of the fashion industry hopes to make big changes to the plus-size women's fashion market," *CUNY Academic Works*, Fall, December 31. Available online: https://bit.ly/2pgeUJ2 (accessed October 19, 2019).

Polesana, Maria Angela (2017), "Chiara Ferragni: il corpo simulacro," *Mediascapes Journal*, 9: 194–210.

Polhemus, Ted (1975), "Social bodies," in J. Benthall and T. Polhemus (eds.), *The Body as a Medium of Expression*, 13–35, London: Allen Lane.

Polhemus, Ted (2011), *Fashion and Anti-Fashion: Exploring Adornment and Dress from an Anthropological Perspective*, Great Britain: Amazon.

Polivy, Janet, Garner, David M. and Garfinkel, Paul E. (1986), "Causes and consequences of the current preference for thin female physiques," in C. P. Herman, M. P. Zanna and E. T. Higgins (eds.), *Physical Appearance, Stigma and Social*

Behaviour: The Ontario Symposium, Vol. 3, 89–112, Hillsdale, NJ: Lawrence Erlbaum Associates.

Pomarico, Nicole (2018), "How the average US woman compares to a Victoria's Secret Angel," *Insider*, November 30. Available online: http://bit.ly/31rgFAS (accessed August 7, 2019).

Poulain, Jean-Pierre (2002), *Sociologies de l'alimentation*, Paris: PUF.

Puhl, Rebecca M., Andreyeva, Tatiana and Brownell, Kelly D. (2008), "Percetions of weight discriminations: Prevalence and comparison to race and gender discrimination in America, *International Journal of Obesity*, 32: 992–1000.

PwC (2017), "The UK plus size clothing market review," *PwC UK*. Available online: https://pwc.to/2Utdg4v (accessed October 23, 2019).

Rahman, Osmud (2016), "The hoodie: Consumer choice, fashion style and symbolic meaning," *International Journal of Fashion Studies*, 3 (1): 111–33.

Rathner, Günther (2001), "Post-communism and the marketing of the thin ideal," in M. Nasser, M. A. Katzman and R. A. Gordon (eds.), *Eating Disorders and Cultures in Transitions*, 93–104, Hove, UK: Brunner-Routledge.

Reckwitz, Andreas (2002), "Toward a theory of social practices: A development in culturalist theorizing," *European Journal of Social Theory*, 5 (2): 243–63.

Reckwitz, Andreas (2017), *Die Gesellschaft der Singularitäten – Zum Strukturwandel der Moderne*, Frankfurt a.M.: Suhrkamp.

Ricchetti, Marco and Volonté, Paolo (2018), "Il sistema della moda in Italia: cambiamenti strutturali e profili professionali | The fashion system in Italy: structural changes and professional profiles," in *White Book: Imparare la moda in Italia | Fashion Education in Italy*, 55–83, Venezia: Marsilio.

Ritenbaugh, Cheryl (1982), "Obesity as a culture-bound syndrome," *Culture, Medicine, and Psychiatry*, 6: 347–61.

Roach, Mary Ellen and Eicher, Joanne Bubolz ([1979] 2007), "The language of personal adornment," in M. Barnard (ed.), *Fashion Theory: A Reader*, 109–21, London: Routledge [original edition: J. M. Cordwell and R. A. Schwartz (eds.), *The Fabrics of Culture: The Anthropology of Clothing and Adornment*, 7–22, The Hague, Paris and New York: Mouton de Gruyter].

Roberts, Alan, Cash, Thomas F., Feingold, Alan and Johnson, Blair T. (2006), "Are black–white differences in females' body dissatisfaction decreasing? A meta-analytic review," *Journal of Consulting & Clinical Psychology*, 74 (6): 1121–31.

Rocamora, Agnès (2009), *Fashioning the City: Paris, Fashion and the Media*, London and New York: I.B. Tauris.

Rocamora, Agnès (2013), "How new are new media? The case of fashion blogs," in D. Bartlett, S. Cole and A. Rocamora (eds.), *Fashion Media: Past and Present*, 155–64, London and New York: Bloomsbury.

Rocamora, Agnès (2019), "#parisienne: Social media stratification in visions of Parisian women," in V. Steele (ed.), *Paris, Capital of Fashion*, 164–81, London: Bloomsbury.

Rocamora, Agnès and Pedroni, Marco (2021) (forthcoming), *Fashion in the Age of Social Media: The Cultural Economy of Influence*, London: Routledge.

Rocha, Coco (2015), "Five myths about modeling," *The Washington Post*, February 6. Available online: https://wapo.st/30u1qad (accessed August 24, 2019).

Rogers, Everett M. (2003), *Diffusion of Innovations*, 5th ed., New York: Free Press.

Rothblum, Esther D. (1990), "Women and weight: Fad and fiction," *Journal of Psychology*, 122 (4): 5–24.

Rothblum, Esther D., Brand, Pamela A., Miller, Carol T. and Oetjen, Helen A. (1990), "The relationship between obesity, employment discrimination, and employment related victimization," *Journal of Vocational Behavior*, 37 (3): 251–66.

Rouse, Elizabeth (1989), *Understanding Fashion*, Oxford: Blackwell.

Rouse, Joseph (2007), "Practice theory," in S. Turner and M. Risjrod (eds.), *Handbook of the Philosophy of Science: Philosophy of Anthropology and Sociology*, vol. 15, 639–81, Amsterdam: Elsevier.

Rudd, Nancy A., Harmon, Jennifer, Heiss, Valerie and Buckworth, Janet (2015), "Obesity bias and body image: How do fashion and retail students compare to other personal service majors?," *International Journal of Fashion Design Technology and Education*, 8 (1): 30–8.

Rudofsky, Bernard (1972), *The Unfashionable Human Body*, New York: Doubleday.

Ruggerone, Lucia (2006), "The simulated (fictitious) body: The production of women's images in fashion photography," *Poetics*, 34 (6): 354–69.

Ruggerone, Lucia (2017), "The feeling of being dressed: Affect studies and the clothed body," *Fashion Theory*, 21 (5): 573–93.

Russ, Terri L. (2008), *Bitchin' Bodies: Young Women Talk about Body Dissatisfaction*, Chicago: StepSister Press.

Sandre-Orafai, Stephanie (2016), "Recasting fashion image production: An ethnographic and practice-based approach to investigating bodies as media," in H. Jenss (ed.), *Fashion Studies: Research Methods, Sites and Practices*, 101–16, London: Bloomsbury.

Saraceni, Reana and Russell-Mayhew, Shelly (2007), "Cultural expectations of thinness in women: A partial replication and update of magazine content," *Eating and Weight Disorders*, 12 (3): e68–74.

Sarbin, Deborah (2005), "The short, happy life of plus-size women's fashion magazines," *Feminist Media Studies*, 5 (2): 241–3.

Saussure, Ferdinand de ([1916] 2011), *Course in General Linguistics*, eds. Charles Bally and Albert Sechehaye, trans. Wade Baskin, New York: Columbia University Press [original edition: *Cours de linguistique générale*, Paris: Payot].

Scaraboto, Daiane and Fischer, Eileen (2013), "Frustrated fatshionistas: An institutional theory perspective on consumer quests for greater choice in mainstream markets," *Journal of Consumer Research*, 39 (6): 1234–57.

Schatzki, Theodore (1996), *Social Practices: A Wittgensteinian Approach to Human Activity and the Social*, New York and Cambridge: Cambridge University Press.

Schatzki, Theodore (2001), "Introduction: Practice theory," in T. Schatzki, K. Knorr Cetina and E. von Savigny (eds.), *The Practice Turn in Contemporary Theory*, 1–14, London and New York: Routledge.

Schatzki, Theodore (2002), *The Site of the Social: A Philosophical Account of the Constitution of Social Life and Change*, University Park: The Pennsylvania State University Press.

Schooler, D., Ward, M., Merriweather, A. and Caruthers, A. (2004), "Who's that girl: Television's roles in the body image development of young White and Black women," *Psychology of Women's Quarterly*, 28: 38–47.

Schütz, Alfred ([1932] 1967), *The Phenomenology of the Social World*, Evanston, IL: Northwestern University Press [original edition: *Der sinnhafte Aufbau der sozialen Welt*, Wien: Julius Springer].

Schütz, Alfred ([1955] 1973), "Symbol, reality and society," in Maurice Natanson (ed.), *Collected Papers I: The Problem of Social Reality*, 287–356, The Hague: Martinus Nijhoff.

Schwartz, Hillel (1986), *Never Satisfied: A Cultural History of Diets, Fantasies, and Fat*, New York: Free Press.

Seegers, Lu (2019), "Germany's next Topmodel: On the historical contexts of a talent show," *International Journal of Fashion Studies*, 6 (2): 283–90.

Seid, Roberta Pollack (1989), *Never Too Thin: Why Women Are at War with Their Bodies*, New York: Prentice Hall.

Seifert, Tim (2005), "Anthromorphic characteristics of centrefold models: Trends towards slender figures over time," *International Journal of Eating Disorders*, 37 (3): 271–4.

Sender, Katherine, and Sullivan, Margaret (2008), "Epidemics of will, failures of self-esteem: Responding to fat bodies in The Biggest Loser and What Not to Wear," *Continuum*, 22 (4): 573–84.

Shah, Bhumika, Sucher, Kathryn and Hollenbeck, Clarie B. (2006), "Comparison of ideal body weight equations and published height-weight tables with body mass index tables for healthy adults in the United States," *Nutrition in Clinical Practice*, 21 (3): 312–19.

Shannon, Claude E. and Weaver, Warren (1949), *The Mathematical Theory of Communication*, Urbana: University of Illinois Press.

Shaw, Eugene F. (1979), "Agenda-setting and mass communication theory," *Gazette (International Journal for Mass Communication Studies*, 25) (2): 96–105.

Shilling, Chris ([1993] 2012), *The Body and Social Theory*, 3rd edn, London: Sage.

Shilling, Chris and Bunsell, Tanya (2009), "The female body builder as a gender outlaw," *Qualitative Research in Sport and Exercise*, 1 (2): 141–59.

Shinkle, Eugénie, ed. (2008), *Fashion as Photograph: Viewing and Reviewing Images of Fashion*, London: I.B. Tauris.

Shove, Elizabeth and Pantzar, Mika (2005), "Consumers, producers and practices: Understanding the invention and reinvention of Nordic walking," *Journal of Consumer Culture*, 5 (1): 43–64.

Shove, Elizabeth and Trentmann, Frank (2019), *Infrastructures in Practice: The Dynamics of Demand in Networked Societies*, London and New York: Routledge.

Shove, Elizabeth, Pantzar, Mika and Watson, Matt (2012), *The Dynamics of Social Practice: Everyday Life and How It Changes*, London: Sage.

Silla, Cesare (2020), "Marketing lifestyles in American consumer capitalism: Ready-to-wear industry, 'democratization' of fashion and the genesis of the consumer (1880–1930)," *International Journal of Fashion Studies*, 7 (1): 3–23.

Silverstein, Brett, Perdue, Lauren, Peterson, Barbara and Kelly, Eileen (1986), "The role of the mass media in promoting a thin standard of body attractiveness for women," *Sex Roles*, 14 (9–10): 519–32.

Simmel, Georg (1905), *Philosophie der Mode*, Berlin: Pan Verlag.

Singh, Devendra (1993), "Body shape and female attractiveness: The critical role of waist-to-hip ratio (WHR)," *Human Nature*, 4: 297–321.

Sismondo, Sergio (2010), *An Introduction to Science and Technology Studies*, 2nd edn, Chichester, UK: Blackwell.

Smith, Laurajane (2006), *Uses of Heritage*, London: Routledge.

Soley-Beltran, Patricia (2004), "Modelling femininity," *European Journal of Women Studies*, 11 (3): 309–26.

Soper, Kate (2001), "Dress needs: Reflection on the clothed body, selfhood and consumption," in J. Entwistle and E. Wilson (eds.), *Body Dressing*, 13–32, Oxford: Berg.

Sperber, Dan and Wilson, Deirdre (1986), *Relevance: Communication and Cognition*, Oxford: Blackwell.

Statista (2019), "Women's plus size apparel market in the U.S.," webpage. Available online: https://bit.ly/2Jgpzul (accessed October 23, 2019).

Stearns, Peter N. (1997), *Fat History: Bodies and Beauty in the Modern West*, New York: New York University Press.

Steele, Valerie (2003), *The Corset: A Cultural History*, New Haven, CT: Yale University Press.

Stewart, Mary Lynn and Janovicek, Nancy (2001), "Slimming the female body?: Re-evaluating dress, corsets, and physical culture in France, 1890s–1930s," *Fashion Theory*, 5 (2): 173–93.

Stone, Gregory P. ([1962] 1995), "Appearance and the self," in M. E. Roach-Higgins, J. B. Eicher and K. K. P. Johnson (eds.), *Dress and Identity*, 19–39, New York: Fairchild 1995 [original edition: A. M. Rose (ed.), *Human Behavior and the Social Processes: An Interactionist Approach*, 86–116, New York: Houghton Mifflin].

Stunkard, Albert J., Sørensen, Thorkild I. A. and Schulsinger, Fini (1983), "Use of the Danish Adoption Register for the study of obesity and thinness," *Association for Research in Nervous and Mental Disease*, 60: 115.

Swami, Viren (2015), "Cultural influences on body size ideals," *European Psychologist*, 20 (1): 1–8.

Sweetman, Paul (2001), "Shop-window dummies? Fashion, the body, and emergent socialities," in J. Entwistle and E. Wilson (eds.), *Body Dressing*, 59–77, Oxford: Berg.

Sykes, Selina (2017), "Six countries taking steps to tackle super-skinny models," *Euronews*, September 6. Available online: https://bit.ly/2pVlq7Y (accessed October 26, 2019).

Synnott, Anthony (1993), *The Body Social*, London: Routledge.

Sypeck, Mia Foley, Gray, James J. and Ahrens, Anthony H. (2004), "No longer just a pretty face: Fashion magazines' depictions of ideal female beauty from 1959 to 1999," *International Journal of Eating Disorders*, 36 (3): 342–7.

Tai, Cordelia (2019), "Report: Racial, size and gender diversity get a boost at New York Fashion Week Spring 2020," *The Fashion Spot*, September 30. Available online: https://bit.ly/2N5r3sk (accessed October 24, 2019).

Tait, Gordon (1993), "Anorexia nervosa: Ascetism, differentiation, government, resistance," *Australian and New Zealand Journal of Sociology*, 29 (2): 194–208.

Taylor, Lou (2002), *The Study of Dress History*, Manchester and New York: Manchester University Press.

Thesander, Marianne (1997), *The Feminine Ideal*, London: Reaktion Books.

Thomsen, Steven R., McCoy, J. Kelly, and Williams, Marlene (2001), "The influence of the thin ideal in fashion magazines on women at risk for anorexia," *Eating Disorders*, 9: 49–64.

Thompson, J. Kevin (1986), "Many women see themselves as roundfaced and pudgy, even when no one else does," *Psychology Today*, 4: 39–44.

Thompson, J. Kevin, Heinberg, Leslie J., Altabe, Madeline N. and Tantleff-Dunn, Stacey (1999), *Exacting Beauty: Theory, Assessment and Treatment of Body Image Disturbance*, Washington, DC: American Psychological Association.

Thompson, J. Kevin and Stice, Eric (2001), "Thin-ideal internalization: Mounting evidence for a new risk factor for body-image disturbance and eating pathology," *Current Directions in Psychological Science*, 10: 181–3.

Thompson, John B. (1995), *The Media and Modernity: A Social Theory of the Media*, Cambridge, UK: Polity Press.

Thompson, Marjorie and Gray, James J. (1995), "Development and validation of a new body-image assessment tool," *Journal of Personality Assessment*, 64 (2): 258–69.

Tseëlon, Efrat (1995), *The Masque of Femininity: The Presentation of Woman in Everyday Life*, London: SAGE.

Turner, Stephen (1994), *The Social Theory of Practices: Tradition, Tacit Knowledge, and Presuppositions*, Chicago, IL: The University of Chicago Press.

Turner, T. ([1980] 1993), "The social skin," in C.B. Burroughs and J. Ehrenreich (eds.), *Reading the Social Body*, 15–39, Iowa City: University of Iowa Press.

Turney, Joanne (2018), "Clothing the criminal or the horror of the 'hoodie,'" in L. Guerrini and P. Volonté (eds.), *Dialogues on Design: Notes on Doctoral Research in Design 2018*, 75–86, Milano: FrancoAngeli.

Twigg, Julia (2013a), *Fashion and Age: Dress, the Body and Later Life*, London: Bloomsbury.

Twigg, Julia (2013b), "Fashion, the body, and age," in S. Black et al. (eds.), *The Handbook of Fashion Studies*, 78–94, London: Bloomsbury.

Veblen, Thorstein (1899), *The Theory of the Leisure Class*, London: McMillan.

Vester, Katharina (2010), "Regime change: Gender, class, and the invention of dieting in post-bellum America," *Journal of Social History*, 44 (1): 39–70.

Voges, Mona M., Giabbiconi, Claire-Marie, Schöne, Benjamin, Waldorf, Manuel, Hartmann, Andrea S. and Vocks, Silja (2019), "Gender differences in body evaluation: Do men show more self-serving double standards than women?," *Frontiers in Psychology*, 10 (544): 1–12.

Volonté, Paolo (2008), *Vita da stilista. Il ruolo sociale del fashion designer*, Milano: Bruno Mondadori.

Volonté, Paolo (2017), "Il contributo dell'Actor-Netwok Theory alla discussione sull'agency degli oggetti, " *Politica e Società*, 6 (1): 31–60.

Volonté, Paolo and Pedroni, Marco (2014), "L'obesità nella società contemporanea," in M. Canina and P. Volonté (eds.), *Overfashion: Nuove prospettive per la moda nella società che ingrassa*, 41–60, Milano: FrancoAngeli.

Von Mises, Ludwig ([1949] 2007), *Human Action: A Treatise on Economics*, Indianapolis, IN: Liberty Fund.

Voracek, Martin and Fisher, Maryanne L. (2002), "Shapely centerfolds? Temporal change in body measures," *British Medical Journal*, 325: 1447–8.

Wacquant, Loïc (2004), *Body and Soul: Notebooks of an Apprentice Boxer*, Oxford and New York: Oxford University Press.

Walden, Keith (1985), "The road to fat city: An interpretation of the development of weight consciousness in Western Society," *Historical Reflections/Reflexions Historiques*, 12: 331–73.

Wang, Meng (2007), "The U.S. plus-size female consumer: Self-perception, clothing involvement, and the importance of store attributes," Master Thesis, The University of North Carolina, Greensboro, NC.

Wann, Marilyn (2009), "Foreword: Fat studies: An invitation to revolution," in E. Rothblum and S. Solvay (eds.), *The Fat Studies Reader*, ix–xxv, New York and London: New York University Press.

Warde, Alan (2005), "Consumption and theories of practice," *Journal of Consumer Culture*, 5 (2): 131–53.

Warde, Alan (2014), "After taste: Culture, consumption and theories of practice," *Journal of Consumer Culture*, 14 (3): 279–303.

Watzlawick, Paul, Beavin, Janet Helmick e Jackson, Don D. (1967), *Pragmatics of Human Communication: A Study of Interactional Patterns, Pathologies, and Paradoxes*, New York: W.W. Norton & Co.

Webb, Jennifer B., Warren-Findlow, Jan, Chou Ying-Yi and Adams, Lauren (2013), "Do you see what I see?: An exploration of inter-ethnic ideal body size comparisons among college women," *Body Image*, 10 (3): 369–79.

Weber, Max ([1921/2] 1978), *Economy and Society: An Outline of Interpretive Sociology*, Berkeley: University of California Press [original edition: *Wirtschaft und Gesellschaft. Grundriss der verstehenden Soziologie*, Tübingen: Mohr].

Weinswig, Deborah (2018), "Opportunity in the US plus-size apparel market," *Coresight Research*, March 29. Available online: https://bit.ly/33uB21p (accessed November 7, 2019).

Westervelt, Amy (2017), "Startups See Lucrative Niche in Plus-Size Clothing," *The Wall Street Journal*, November 26. Available online: https://www.marketwatch.com/st ory/entrepreneurs-move-in-on-a-21-billion-plus-size-fashion-market-2017-12-12 (accessed July 6, 2019).

Wilson, Elizabeth (1992), "Fashion and the postmodern body," in J. Ash and E. Wilson (eds.), *Chic Thrills*, 3–15, Berkeley and Los Angeles: University of California Press.

Wilson, Elizabeth ([1985] 2003), *Adorned in Dreams: Fashion and Modernity*, London and New York: I.B. Tauris.

Wilson, Margaret (2002), "Six views of embodied cognition," *Psychonomic Bulletin & Review*, 9 (4): 625–36.

Wiseman, Claire V., Gray, James J., Mosimann, James E. and Ahrens, Anthony H. (1990), "Cultural expectations of thinness in women: An update," *International Journal of Eating Disorders*, 11: 85–9.

Wissinger, Elizabeth (2007a), "Always on display: Affective production in the fashion modelling industry," in P. Clough and J. Halley (eds.), *The Affective Turn: Theorizing the Social*, 231–60, Durham, NC: Duke University Press.

Wissinger, Elizabeth (2007b), "Modelling a way of life: Immaterial and affective labor in the fashion modelling industry," *Ephemera: Theory and Politics in Organization*, 7 (1): 250–69.

Wissinger, Elizabeth (2013), "Fashion modelling, blink technologies and new imaging regimes," in D. Bartlett, S. Cole and A. Rocamora (eds.), *Fashion Media: Past and Present*, 133–43, London: Bloomsbury.

Wissinger, Elizabeth (2015), *This Year's Model: Fashion, Media, and the Making of Glamour*, New York: New York University Press.

Wittig, Monique ([1980] 1993), "One is not born a woman," in H. Abelove, M. A. Barale and D. M. Halperin (eds.), *The Lesbian and Gay Studies Reader*, 103–9, New York and London: Routledge [original edition: "On ne naît pas femme," *Questions Féministes* 8 (8): 75–84].

Wolf, Naomi (1991), *The Beauty Myth: How Images of Beauty are Used Against Women*, London: Vintage Books.

Women's Wear (1915), "Scientific specialization in stouts," *Women's Wear*, July 9: 4, 9.

Woodward, Sophie (2007), *Why Women Wear What They Wear*, Oxford: Berg.

Wooley, Orland W. and Wooley, Susan C. (1982), "The Beverly Hills eating disorder: The mass marketing of anorexia nervosa," *International Journal of Eating Disorders*, 1 (3): 57–9.

Wray, Sharon and Deery, Ruth (2008), "The medicalization of body size and women's healthcare," *Health Care for Women International*, 29 (3): 227–43.

Wykes, Maggie and Gunter, Barrie (2005), *The Media and Body Image: If Looks Could Kill*, London: Sage.

Young, Iris Marion (2005), *On Female Body Experience: 'Throwing Like a Girl' and Other Essays*, Oxford: Oxford University Press.

Zangrillo, Frances Leto (1990), *Fashion Design for the Plus-Size*, New York: Fairchild Publications.

Zhang, Jing (2019), "Chinese godmother of modelling talks about training supermodels and finally getting on the catwalk," *South China Morning Post*, February 28. Available online: http://bit.ly/2KRNIbx (accessed August 24, 2019).

Index